The Underneath of Things

The Underneath of Things

Violence, History, and the
Everyday in Sierra Leone

Mariane C. Ferme

THE UNIVERSITY OF CALIFORNIA PRESS
Berkeley · Los Angeles · London

University of California Press
Berkeley and Los Angeles, California

University of California Press, Ltd.
London, England

© 2001 by the Regents of the University of California

Library of Congress Cataloging-in-Publication Data

Ferme, Mariane C. (Mariane Conchita).
    The underneath of things: violence, history, and
the everyday in Sierra Leone / Mariane C. Ferme.
        p. cm.
    Includes bibliographical references and index.
    ISBN 0-520-22542-2 (cloth: alk. paper)—
ISBN 0-520-22543-0 (pbk: alk. paper)
        1. Mende (African people)—Material culture.
    2. Mende (African people)—Social life and
    customs. 3. Sex role—Sierra Leone—Kpuawala.
    4. Landscape assessment—Sierra Leone—
    Kpuawala. 5. Kpuawala (Sierra Leone)—Politics
    and government. 6. Kpuawala (Sierra Leone)—
    Social life and customs.
    I. Title.

    DT516.45.M45 F47 2001
    305.896′3480664—dc21   00-048845

Manufactured in the United States of America
10   09   08   07   06   05   04   03   02   01
10   9   8   7   6   5   4   3   2   1

For Luca,
and to the memory of Mama Kema and Jina

Contents

Illustrations

Acknowledgments

At the close of a decade of civil war in Sierra Leone, it is especially painful to remember all those whose help made my work possible during three research trips in 1984–1986, 1990, and 1993. In particular, the memory of "big women" like Mama Kema and Jina Mussa, and the continuing friendship of Mami Norh and Mama Kɔɔ, who once resided in Wunde Chiefdom, Bo District, kept the writing project alive, even when the violence made it unbearable. The children who accompanied me everywhere are also on my mind as I imagine Sierra Leone's future. Some will never live to see it, like the strange, gifted, Moiforay, one of the first victims of rebel cruelties visited upon Kpuawala—the village where I made my home in Sierra Leone. Adored by his grandparents, shunned by others who feared him, he taught me much about the ambiguous, unpredictable place of children in this society. It is a tragedy of this war that he will not be part of the effort to end it, as his peers Momoh, Jussu, and Vandi—now all grown—might still have a hope of doing. To all these women and children, and to Braima, Sylvo, and Mussa, my friends and age mates in Kpuawala, I owe a great debt of gratitude. Some may recognize themselves—if not their names, which I changed whenever it seemed necessary to conceal identities—in the stories I tell. I am also thankful for the support of the elders and authorities in Kpuawala, Wunde Chiefdom, and Bo District.

Friends like the Komes and Feikas in Bo, and especially the family of Veronica and Larry Lumeh in Freetown, Dandabu, Washington, London, and Cairo, have offered hospitality and have shared their experiences with me whenever we met. I thank the Catholic Missions of Blama, Kenema, and Bo (especially sisters Patrick and Mary Immacolata of the Holy Rosary School), along with the staffs at the Kenema Pastoral Center and the Serabu Hospital, for their hospitality, support, and even needed medical attention.

Different phases of my research and writing were supported by the Fulbright-Hays Doctoral Dissertation Program, the Woodrow Wilson Foundation (Women's Studies grants), the Carter Woodson Institute for African and Afro-American Studies at the University of Virginia, the Harvard Academy for International and Area Studies, Harvard University, and the University of California at Berkeley (Committee on Research; Hellman Family Faculty Grants).

I am grateful to Jean Comaroff, John Comaroff, and Nancy Munn, who have been generous interlocutors ever since my graduate school days at the University of Chicago. Among my colleagues in the Berkeley Anthropology Department, Lawrence Cohen, Elizabeth Colson, Stefania Pandolfo, and Nancy Scheper-Hughes have at different stages given valuable advice. Paul Richards and Jane Guyer proved to be especially helpful readers of earlier drafts of this manuscript for the University of California Press. Paul Richards, Bill Murphy, Rosalind Shaw, Clarke Speed, Melissa Leach, Ibrahim Abdullah, Peter Geschiere, Murray Last, and Jimmy Kandeh have been generous and collegial in sharing at critical times their insight into things Sierra Leonean and West African. Writing would not have been possible without the equally critical help of Cécile Pineda and of the one who wrote me about storks in the autumn sky.

I owe much to my parents for their support and intellectual example. I dedicate this book in part to Luca for the many debates in front of the computer screen, without which this book would never have come together. Had I been more open to his suggestions, this would undoubtedly be a better book. Since his arrival, our son Gilo—whose Mende name, "this one remains/stands fast," evokes both stability and the demand for a future—has been my lifeline.

Introduction

The first constraint of discourse consists in prescribing for
beginnings what is in reality a point of arrival, and even what
would be a vanishing point in research. While the latter begins
in the currency of a certain conceptual or institutional
apparatus, the exposition follows a chronological order. It
takes the oldest point as its beginning. . . . While research is
interminable, the text must have an ending, and this structure
of finality bends back upon the introduction, which is already
organized by the need to finish.

Certeau (1988: 86)

In this book I explore the links between a violent historical and political
legacy and a cultural order of dissimulation in the Upper Guinea Coast of
West Africa—a region comprising Mende-speaking southeastern Sierra
Leone, where I carried out fieldwork, as well as Liberia and parts of
Guinea. Since 1990 this region has been intermittently in the international news because of the civil war that has caused population displacements and regional instability. News stories have reported the systematic
mutilation, rape, and murder of civilians in Liberia and Sierra Leone,
thereby raising the specter of new forms of "barbarism" in the African
continent. This book addresses the broader sociocultural and historical
context in which these events have unfolded. It probes not only questions
of origins ("How could this occur?") but also issues of a sociocultural
nature, examining institutions, values, and views of self and sociality that
sometimes are associated with violent practices. What I explore here,
then, are the ordinary conflicts that may erupt in times of peace. In doing
so, I hope not only to paint a portrait of a society on the brink of violence, and to explore some of the factors that may have led it to this
point, but also to show wherein lie the strengths that support hope for a
better future in the Sierra Leonean postcolonial state.

In the chapters to come, I analyze how strategies of concealment permeate multiple levels of discursive and spatial practice, from the realm of
regional politics to the more mundane realms of domesticity and productive

activities. The point is to understand how the visible world (as it appears, for instance, in ritual, political, and domestic appropriations of public space) is activated by forces concealed beneath the surface of discourse, objects, and social relations. Such forces manifest themselves in everyday conflicts through the potential disruption of the deceptive order of ordinary appearances. For example, what appears on the surface as generous action toward friends, family, and strangers may suddenly change into a violent encounter with the enemy, within and without the confines of village space. Friends may turn into enemies in cases where someone is accused of witchcraft. Poor strangers (settlers who regardless of how long they had lived in an area had no kin ties to the original landowning lineages) may become rich and powerful through the strategic, though illicit, exploitation of secret knowledge of the landscape and of its mineral resources, such as diamonds. Material objects themselves may be invested with potent forces, influencing the people who come into contact with them, and thus becoming potential sources of conflict. Hence the necessity of understanding not only how everyday conflicts arise but also how they crystallize and develop unpredictably, and in contestable ways. Specific, potent social and political roles, discursive forms, and objects exist within the cultural and historical repertoire of this region to operate such mediations. These figures and sites of mediation are themselves the legacy of struggles where the effective use of ambiguity has been—and continues to be—more productive than the pursuit of social ideals of transparency.

The focus here is on the production of meaning (semeiosis) as it emerges from the tension between surface phenomena and that which is concealed beneath them. In *African Islam* René Bravmann includes two images that are emblematic of this tension (see book cover). They are photographs of masks presumed to belong to powerful members of the men's Poro society, an esoteric institution common across this region of West Africa. Unlike other pictures of masks in the book, these two show the side not visible to the public—the obverse of the mask's face. On the surface in contact with their wearers' faces, but invisible to others, the masks bear inscribed magic squares with Arabic letters and numbers (Bravmann 1983: 44–45). These characters inscribed in a grid of squares are cryptic, but specific, references to Qur'anic passages and to the practices that must be deployed to make the masks effective in performance. Although the viewing audience sees the mask's face, it is what happens at the point of contact between wood and skin surface—between the inert object and the living human body—that activates a new entity made up of both. The human body animates this transformed entity from the inside but is possessed, in turn, by activating powers transmitted to it by words and substances concealed within the mask. However, the fusion between these elements is limited to the time and space of a performance. Indeed, the identity of Poro performers and their masks must remain concealed outside of the performance context, their invisibility serving to protect them, and to protect others from them, but also perhaps to enhance their powers and reinforce the notion of their essential unity in public arenas.[1]

The ritual language of performance brings about this fusion between social actor and object, through the inscriptions that touch both the inner surface of the mask and the outer surface of its wearer's face. Sacred words are part of the process, multiply concealed through cryptic encoding, through their being foreign and illegible to the majority of those who might see them, and through their being inscribed in places not readily accessible. Indeed, these strategies of concealment are crucial to the efficacy of all Muslim magic squares, regardless of where they are inscribed. They are folded and wrapped into bundles: they are encased within containers made of materials ranging from plastic and cotton to precious metals before being worn on the body or incorporated into houses or into the landscape. The powers manipulated through the production of these objects work best in contained, inaccessible sites—underneath and inside other things.[2] But the process of containment is not always successful, and thus it reminds us that the tensions between concealing and revealing that are embedded in masking are also violent. The mask as an object cannot be isolated from the context of performance, in which multiple provisional transformations may occur. Masked performers may lose control and attack bystanders and steal their property. The mask confers on its wearer the ability, through assuming a new identity, to carry out such acts of violence legitimately and with impunity, because his or her real identity is concealed. This aspect of masking has always been put to use in war, and particularly in this region's civil wars, where cross-dressing, masks, and amulets have played key roles in the material culture of war.

In similar fashion, visible and more easily accessible practices in Sierra Leone are presumed to be activated by forces and meanings "underneath" them.[3] These forces shape the perception of the visible world—the meaning of language and names, the history of places—and social relations ranging from the domestic to interactions with strangers. They infuse appearances with suspicion, and evoke instead a deeper understanding of what lies beneath the surface. The Mende word for meaning, *yembu*, "that which is underneath" things, points explicitly to the primacy of the concealed in understanding the visible. It is a world where the perceptual domain is destabilized by forces that inhabit features of the landscape, that lie beneath the surface of solids and fluids, and that often take concrete form in particular objects to effect auspicious or adverse outcomes in the lives of individuals or entire communities.

Classic anthropological accounts of such forces from E. B. Tylor onward have used such words as *animism*, *fetishism*, and *magic* to refer to these agentive forces and have analyzed them within the context of systems of belief and knowledge in which the material was seen as a mere vehicle for the spiritual (e.g., Tylor 1970: 9–10). The sharp distinction between material and spiritual—as Talal Asad reminds us—is a legacy of the Eurocentric and Christian genealogy of the anthropology of religion (Asad 1993: 27–79), I adopt instead a Mende perspective on the classification of these phenomena—a point of view that is always grounded in the material—while remaining attentive to the politics of their deployment. In Sierra Leone some of these agencies, and their material forms, appear to coincide with those that drew the attention of scholars of comparative religion. Thus masks and ritual objects "pulled" from under the surface of ground and water are said to be gifts of male and female ancestors, and witch spirits are thought to temporarily inhabit features of the landscape or the bodies of animals and humans. But this continuum also includes the transformative powers of incompletely controlled forces and materials whose history in Sierra Leone is linked not so much to religious beliefs as to the material experience of modernity and to the magic associated with it in Africa and elsewhere (Coronil 1997: 3–4; Geschiere 1997; Taussig 1980; Watts 1992: 21–63). Thus the esoteric knowledge and gestures that transform ordinary objects like mortars and rice fanners into powerful ritual objects is of the same order as that which discerns a diamond from among many worthless stones with similar dull surfaces (not to mention, at a different level, the arbitrary workings of consumption and desire that transform these common stones into precious, rare gems). The skill to see beyond the visible phenomenon and to interpret deeper meanings is, then, a culturally valued and highly contested activity, because on it are predicated all social and political actions and different forms of wealth. It is a skill that bridges the gap between history and the present, between old and new technologies of communication and interpretation.

New elements map onto older forces grounded in regional history and culture, and do so on the same terrain, so that modernity reinforces their magic and potentiality. Thus diamonds, gold, and other precious minerals found in Sierra Leonean soil and waters, and exploited by foreigners during the twentieth century, emerge from the same concealed domains that have long been haunted by powerful agencies, which ordinary rural people only imperfectly controlled. The magic of Sierra Leonean modernity magnifies that of older tricksters and transmogrifying figures that once accounted for the dangers of the forest, the evils of enslavement, and the historical betrayals that made kin and friends into enemies. Here the figure of the hunter-warrior has an important role in blending crucial hunting skills (the skills required to see beyond surface appearances and interpret concrete traces in the landscape) with modern technologies of warfare. The random wealth conferred on people almost instantaneously by diamonds and gold—once their dull surfaces are worked to reveal the reflective brilliance underneath—resonates with the good fortune of the hunter who finds and kills his prey after following its traces in the forest.[4] At the same time, both the search for precious minerals and the pursuit of animal prey are dangerous, violent activities carried out over difficult terrain.

The links between violence and the extraction of natural resources are not limited to the local terrain but cut across multiple scales of sociopolitical and economic organization, often in a covert manner. Much has been written about the interests in diamond extraction by all parties in the Sierra Leone civil war (e.g., Reno 1997; Richards 1996b; Smillie, Gberie, and Hazleton 2000). These interests cut across local and national domains, for the organized (though often covert) linkage between the extraction of precious resources and violence is a global business. Consider the institutionalization of these linkages in firms like the South African Executive Outcomes (dissolved in 1998) and the British Sandline International, which since 1993 have been engaged in *both* the provision of security (in lieu of government military troops) *and* diamond mining. Diamonds paid for security and weapons, and in turn, the protection of mineral resources governed where security forces and weapons were deployed (Reno 1997). Thus the war's local resonances with a traditional hunting lore must not blind us to the new global alliances between covert business interests and the organization of terror.

In this book, I explore a range of modalities through which material objects, language, and social relations become sites where a sometimes violent historical memory is sedimented and critically reappropriated.

Occasionally, traces of this violence also generate partial genealogies or historical narratives. Most of these historical accounts are occasioned by contingent events—a walk through ancestral farmlands, a dispute, an encounter with an unfamiliar object or word—and are told in isolated fragments spilling over from everyday practices. Thus local histories are bound up with matter, which carries sometimes eloquent and explicit, sometimes concealed clues to this region's entanglements with slavery and institutionalized inequality, with warfare, and with the precarious balance between economies characterized by the mobile exploitation of natural resources (hunting, alluvial diamond mining) and economies based on the more stationary cultivation of those resources (farming of staple and cash crops).[5]

The point of analyzing "the underneath of things" is not to develop an ontology of Mende secrecy, that is, an elaboration of the structures that undergird surface phenomena and events. Any such pursuit would be frustrated by the fact that meanings are perceived always as unstable and different from prior manifestations. However, the notion that "real" meanings, events, and entities are deferred to other domains may lead to the reification of those other, unavailable sites. This facilitates all sorts of mystifications—a process that has its own political and truth effects, but also creates the conditions for contesting claims to power that are based on concealed knowledge. Thus my premise is that the domain of secrecy is essentially political at multiple levels. In a setting where speaking truth to power can lead to arbitrary danger and death, secret domains are also where popular cultural creativity produces alternative discourses that limit the exercise of political power, through the systematic intrusion of unpredictability. The notion that some people and agencies may arbitrarily control others is always tempered by the countervailing one that power stands on fragile, and temporary, foundations. And at the existential level, the importance of anticipating where power is produced in this highly unstable setting undermines cynicism: people do have strong beliefs about the dynamics of political events and mobilize accordingly. What does it mean, then, to situate meaning (of Mende discourse, culture, and practice) underneath its visible referents and signs—inscribed into the landscape? The Mende hermeneutic of concealment is not unique; on the contrary, ambiguous practices and discourses are common in situations of political danger. But among the Mende and other people of the Upper Guinea Coast of West Africa these common strategies unfold in the absence of ideals of transparency in the exercise of political and social agency in "normal" times. Here a person who communicates directly what she or he desires or thinks, or who draws unmediated inferences from sensory data and texts, is considered an idiot or no better than a child. Instead, ambivalence is prized. Great value is attached to verbal artistry that couches meaning in puns, riddles, and cautionary tales and to unusual powers of understanding that enable people to both produce and unmask highly ambiguous meanings.[6]

My argument is that a hermeneutic of suspicion—valuing a whole range of cultural skills aimed at producing and interpreting deferred meanings—is partly the product of a violent history. This history has intruded in the present at critical moments, when it has shaped local idioms of violence and factional alliances in conflicts precipitated by contingent events on the regional and global scene. These regional and global forces are still at work in different forms, and we must keep them in mind when looking at the local articulations of specific struggles. It is this history, embedded in the landscape, in material objects, and in socioeconomic and political relations, that makes available the symbols that mobilize political projects in the present.

The potential for conflict already exists in Mende ideas about truth as a site for contestation and public debate, in which rhetorical skills are critical. The realm of the truth is never immediately apprehended on the surface of a verbal or facial expression, of the visible landscape, or of human and animal appearances. Rather, truth is what lies under multiple layers of often conflicting meanings. In this hermeneutic encoding of the real, the shifting order of visibility works less as a transparent surface, through which deep intentions and knowledge become accessible, than as a mirror, which mimetically doubles what is in front without giving away what is beyond the reflection. This impossibility of appealing to the truth behind the surface makes contestation an integral aspect of arriving at the truth, despite apparent declarations to the contrary on the part of social actors.

Indeed, the mirror and its shiny, precious referents—diamonds and gold—have important places in the Mende everyday and ritual imaginary. They figure in ritual settings and even in the protective magic of hunting militias in the civil war. According to one particular account, a group of fighters in the civil war was said to be led in battle by a naked woman walking backwards, who found her way by looking over her shoulder via a mirror (Tostevin 1993: 26). The process was supposed to render both her and the warriors following her invisible. Thus the enemy was made blind to the advance of warriors behind the mirror's reflective face and the woman's naked back through the double operation whereby their own advance was reflected in the hands of an elusive (turned away) object of sexual desire. While the naked woman might be invisible (unattainable) to the enemy to whom she turned her back, her ambiguous availability to the troops with whom she sided must also have acted as a powerful incitement to battle. Her naked body faced her followers, but her backward-looking gaze focused on what was behind her and ahead of them, thus making her tantalizingly unavailable, at least until the resolution of combat.

To interpret in this way the image of a naked woman leading men into battle while walking backwards and looking over her shoulder via a mirror, we must juxtapose the practices that link warfare and heterosexuality both before and after battle. On the one hand, the hunters and warriors of tradition and of the present are said to avoid sexual contact with women before an especially difficult mission; in some accounts, they even avoid accidental physical contact (McKenzie 1998). Such practices are usually interpreted as having to do with cleansing and sources of pollution, conserving strength, and so on. But one might also read such avoidances as strategies to increase sexual desire and channel it into another kind of "work of darkness" (*kpindi yenge*), as sexual intercourse is called in Mende. On the other hand, the removal of the protection of clothes should not blind us to how the special treatment of the body surface can bestow upon it superior coverage of a different kind. Thus during both the Liberian and the Sierra Leonean civil wars of the 1990s, there were reports of rebel brigades fighting naked in the belief that in so doing, they were protected against bullets (Ellis 1999: 267). The individual's body, then, becomes the site for locating hidden, potent forces of the underworld, as well as for contesting and reorganizing the sociopolitical order.

METONYMY AND THE POLITICS OF MEANING

Central to this book, therefore, is the politics of cultural meanings contested between different orders of knowledge and communication, as they are negotiated between different individuals, social categories, and the sexes. This contestation shifts from the rhetorical register to that of practice in the arenas of aesthetics, politics, and technologies of production. The cultural idiom of ambiguity in this region's societies shifts our attention to material locations of meaning that have not been linked, so far, to practices of concealment. These have generally been analyzed in connection with discursive and masking practices linked to formal structures of secrecy, such as the region's ubiquitous esoteric associations. By contrast, scholars who *have* analyzed everyday productive practices and material culture have done so without linking them to the politics of ambiguity. They stressed, for example, technical experimentation in the production of rice, the region's staple crop (Johnny, Karimu, and Richards 1981; Richards 1986), the allocation of gendered forest resources (Leach 1994), and continuity and change in cloth production (Edwards 1988; Lamb and Lamb 1984), but they did not address how the experience of the material world and practices were shaped by an aesthetics of ambiguity.

This book's original contribution is in linking (1) a historically grounded analysis of everyday material culture, language, and social practices and (2) an account of the aesthetics of ambiguity that is widespread in this West African region. Such an analysis has implications beyond this ethnographic case and the regional literature—for any social setting characterized by the elaboration of a cultural idiom of indirectness. Thus it is precisely in the historical development of Melanesian "cultures of secrecy" that Andrew Lattas identifies the legacy of colonialism, missionary work, and the dynamics of the postcolonial political economy in the present (Lattas 1998). Despite the fact that anthropologists have begun to pay attention again to questions of secrecy, their focus is still primarily on discursive domains, on historical memory, and generally at the level of consciousness. Instead, my focus here moves beyond the paradigm of consciousness toward an analysis of the material bearers of collective memory and an examination of these contested meanings. For example, although the symbolism, aesthetics, and political economy of Mende and Sierra Leonean cloth production and exchange are well documented in the literature (Abraham 1976; Alldridge 1894), I explore here the semiotic and gendered implications of the link among cloth production, net making, and hair plaiting in Mende, all of which fall in the category of "weaving" (*fɛɛ*). These are links that go well beyond dictionary definitions associating weaving or plaiting (Innes 1969) with the technologies of warfare, where historically the idiom of sewing and cloth making was central to the distinctions among warriors, and the exchange of cloth to the peacemaking process. Hence I examine contested meanings as they shift between the order of language and that of practice, which are never isolated from each other.

In Mende everyday life, material bearers of meaning are often inscribed within a dialectic of large and small and of the processes of magnification and miniaturization. Much of what matters in Mende sociality and personhood that connects these states is presented as an *enlargement* of the norm. The language of bigness characterizes power-ful, respected patrons (*nu wai*, "big person"), the upland rice farm collec-tively tended by extended households (*kpaa wai*), the latter's main resi-dence (*pɛ wai*), and some of the shared objects in this space. My desire to examine the miniaturization of these magnified concepts is driven not by the dialectical spirit but rather by the ambiguity and contradiction that beset the "hyper-" representation the Mende make of themselves and of their social institutions. These representations are often contradicted by practices that underscore instead the contingency, impermanence, and historical limitations of bigness in all the domains in which it is marked. Big houses are sometimes such only in the imagination; farming depends on the yearly vagaries of weather and can be accomplished only through a careful management of relations with people whose labor is essential to its success; personal power is never a permanent achievement; and the control of adults over children is often illusory. Ultimately, the key to many of these processes of enlargement is embedded in details—in clues that are secreted away from direct apperception.

This dialectic of small and large coincides with the metonymical process. In his analysis of language, Roman Jakobson suggested that speak-ing is like knitting: Just as one needs two needles to make a sweater—the axis of selection and that of combination—language requires both metaphor and metonymy (Jakobson and Halle 1956). In Jakobson's world, knitting was itself a gendered practice whose subtleties may have escaped him. Otherwise, he might have noted that an alternative to the two intersecting axes (the single circular knitting needle) produces seam-less garments. But even circular knitting needles have two intersecting knitting ends. This differentiates the technique of knitting from crochet-ing, for example, where a single hooked needle pulls a loop of yarn in and out of one or more stitches, depending on a pattern's complexity. Inspired by the technical difference between knitting and crocheting—and by the imaginary and analytical implications of that difference—fem-inist philosopher Luisa Muraro argued that the interdependence of metaphor and metonymy in Jakobson's model has over time given way to a regime of "hypermetaphoricity" in social analysis and science. That is, analyses of symbolic production have come to privilege the metaphorical pole (Muraro 1980: 71).[7] By contrast, in metonymy, there is a *material* link between two elements: One is made more concrete by a sometimes reductive or ironic *detail* being substituted for it (Muraro, 61–63). Metonymy moves toward the prosaic and concrete by homing in on the related (contiguous) detail (Jakobson and Halle 1956: 96) in ways that metaphorical operations, with their unexpected similarities, cannot.[8] Instead of challenging material continuities, as metaphors do, by producing unexpected resemblance between unrelated things, the consubstantiality of metonymy as a form of meaning production makes it more congenial to a project, such as this one, that aims at contextualizing cultural values within the domain of objects and material life. For a feminist rhetoric, Muraro implies, the complexities and material contiguities of crochet's meandering hook are a much more concrete and compelling trope.

GENEALOGIES OF SECRECY

Following my fieldwork in Sierra Leone in 1984–1986, 1990, and 1993, I formulated my analysis of the Mende material world and of gendered perspectives on personhood, sociality, and politics in response to a regional literature in which discussions of gender had focused on narrowly defined institutional or political domains.[9] Much of this literature did not link questions of gender and secret institutions to the materiality of language, productive technologies, and social practices. Despite its goodwill in challenging obsolete perspectives on male and female domains and institutions, this feminist anthropological literature did not let a radically different scale of analysis shape its projects. The aspects overlooked in this literature as being perhaps too insignificant are the focus of my critical analysis of Mende material culture. My intention is not to debunk prior scholarship on this region, which has shaped my own initial project, but to insert a disruptive anthropological voice and a radically new scale of analysis. In the spirit of a feminist practice of theoretical engagement, my approach allows for the creative retrieval of overlooked aspects of Mende material culture and for the recognition of my debt to the regional scholarship, but in terms of my own making. In taking this critical approach, I heed Marilyn Strathern's warning that a feminist anthropology should exploit the radical potential of destabilizing theoretical models and approaches in the discipline as a whole, rather than replacing the straw men of an earlier male-dominated anthropology with the rustling of women's skirts and adding women to the picture without fundamentally challenging the prevailing consensus (Strathern 1981, 1988; see also Weiner 1974).

Beyond feminist anthropology, novel theoretical contributions have been made by scholars whose dialogic engagement with African epistemic configurations from this region have resulted in eccentric shifts within the discipline as a whole—indeed, in its displacement along the lines advocated by Strathern. Michael Jackson's work among the Kuranko of northern Sierra Leone and his reflection on earlier fieldwork problems and interpretations have been a key contribution to his manifesto for a "radical empiricism" in ethnographic inquiry (Jackson 1989; 1997). A more specific focus on power and its aesthetics—and on the implications of secrecy and ambiguity for particular forms of cultural life—appears in the work of Murphy (1998) and Speed (1991). In particular, Murphy's writings on the implications for political discourse (1990) of a dialectic of concealment and manifestation in Mende aesthetics of secrecy has had a major impact on art historical studies of African masking (e.g., Nooter 1993). Kris Hardin's work on Kono aesthetics has also attempted to locate in material culture the elements of a relationship between structure and action, where gender is a critical orienting feature, but it did not go far enough to free itself of the static model of British structuration theory (e.g., Giddens 1984; Hardin 1993, 1996: 32).

Questions of gender are also addressed in Melissa Leach's work on the management of forest resources (1994). Indeed, her understanding of the micropractices surrounding the integration of farming and forest-harvesting practices in the ecological border areas between savanna and forest zones of West Africa has broken new ground in the budding field of political ecology, as well as methodologically situating itself at the interface between anthropological scholarship and policy making (e.g., Fairhead and Leach 1996a; 1996b). Leach's analysis of how farming practices led to forest regrowth in parts of West Africa, an insight acquired by paying attention to local histories in addition to colonial archives, has shown the potential value of joining Foucault's critique of the truth effects of certain discourses (such as the doomsday discourse of progressive deforestation in Africa) to ethnographic and historical inquiry (Leach 1994: 45).

Modern work on the phenomenology of secrecy has been shaped by Georg Simmel (Simmel 1950: 330–376). In particular, Simmel's attention to how secrecy is related to the nonsecret—to the mundane in everyday life—has been a central concern in the work of Bellman among the Kpelle of Liberia, a group linguistically and culturally related to the Mende. Inspired primarily by phenomenology and ethnomethodology, Bellman's first book addressed the cosmological dimensions of Kpelle *ifa mo*, the injunction not to speak about something, in both discursive practices—

where the formula *ifa mo* signals the presence of secrecy in everyday life—and material manifestations that range from medicines to spirits and other agents with special powers (Bellman 1975). Here, though, Bellman's aim is to understand Kpelle notions of intentionality in a setting where all major life events are caused by specific actions—where everyone is, as the book's title declares, either a curer or an assassin. This thread runs through Bellman's later work, where it is also related to the hermeneutic, symbols, and metaphors in men's Poro and other secret institutions (Bellman 1984). Bellman's cumulative work has laid the foundations for the work on the aesthetics and hermeneutic of indirect speech in this region and for understanding the role of linguistic and material clues in a world where ambiguity is pervasive.[10] However, he has not linked the aesthetics of ambiguity to an analysis of encompassing biographical and historical scripts embedded within the material world beyond the intentional practices of social actors. Furthermore, in Bellman's work secrecy is analyzed as an autonomous cultural system, without any indication that a larger historical context of slavery, American hegemony, and the like may have played a part in the formation of modern Liberia. By contrast, these are precisely the questions that inform my own analysis of the politics of ambiguity in a rural Sierra Leonean setting.

The potential for a historically informed analysis located within the bounds of a material world that includes unpredictability is set forth in Certeau's reading of the mystic tradition in relation to questions of power and secrecy. Certeau's work addresses directly the political stakes in the relationship between esoteric knowledge and practices, and between the registers of belief and making believe—in the sense of the power both to create a reality and to shape social practices that conform to it. Language and narration are crucial in mediating this relationship via

[t]wo mechanisms through which a body of dogma has always made itself believed: on the one hand, the claim to be *speaking in the name of a reality* which, assumed to be inaccessible, is the principle of both what is believed (a totalization) and the act of believing (something that is always unavailable, unverifiable, lacking); and on the other, the ability of a discourse authorized by a "reality" to distribute itself in the form of *elements that organize practices*, that is, of "articles of faith." These two traditional resources are found again today in the system that combines the narrativity of the media—an establishment of the real—with the discourse of products to be consumed—a distribution of this reality in the form of "articles" that are to be believed and bought. It is the first that needs to be stressed.

(Certeau 1984: 185)

Thus it is now possible for me to look at the aesthetics of secrecy without reifying a series of ineffable practices or locating it as an appeal to unavailable and unverifiable practices beyond history. The question then becomes how the linked operations of believing and making people believe operate at the level of political, cultural, and historical formations in which the very tactics deployed by social actors are those that are made possible by the exigencies of their position and the constraints of their history. For example, in modern Sierra Leonean politics, existing idioms of the political, in which secrecy plays a central role, have been appropriated both by a state bent on the autocratic transformation of the order of power under the guise of continuity and by those resisting these projects (Ferme 1999: 160–162). Far from being a manifestation of a putatively static, esoteric tradition, the idiom itself becomes a dynamic site that captures the significations played out in political and historical conflicts.

THEMATIC THREADS

My analysis of "the underneath of things" focuses on the material bearers of meaning inscribed onto the rural Sierra Leonean landscape. The ethnography centers on Kpuawala, a community whose boundaries I establish as flexibly as they are drawn by the practices and categories of its members, rather than in accordance with fixed spatial criteria.[11] For its inhabitants, the landscape encompassing Kpuawala has been in key historical and cultural ways more salient than the settlement itself, in which, depending on the season, they spent a fraction of their time. The historical and physical landscape surrounding Kpuawala encompasses the settlement and is thus the point of departure of my analysis. I suggest that a focus on multiple levels of experience captures the relationship between material and imaginary practices in a way that challenges the primacy of settlements in anthropological descriptions of place. Instead, the nomadic displacements over time and space of settlements and of their names point to an alternative topology, in which the appearance of stability is fragile at best. The inscription of social and village features in the farm's landscape implies that even when it is physically remote, Kpuawala productively shapes its inhabitants' collective imaginary. But history has shown that these cultural practices are part and parcel of actual migrations in the location of communities like Kpuawala. In wars and internal conflicts past and present, farms and work spaces hidden in the forest are the first temporary shelters for refugees from villages, and hence they are the potential beginnings of new permanent settlements.

Thus the cultural practice of transforming space—bush into village and vice versa—and of recognizing the traces of past human occupation in the natural world cannot be divorced from the region's political history.

Anthropological studies of space (even some with a practice focus that aim to move beyond the fixity of structural analyses) often begin with a description of settlements and only later move to analyze how people's lives unfold in place and time (e.g., Moore 1986; Weiss 1996). This approach privileges the organization of space that is most intelligible and accessible to the anthropologist outsider, but it does not tell us much about where a settlement might be located in a different organization of inhabited spaces, one less anchored to ideals of permanence. The exceptions to this practice are peoples whose livelihoods and cultural worlds are so obviously centered on broader landscapes that anthropologists have been forced to acknowledge their mobility as a critical theme; this is the case, for example, with Australian Aborigines (e.g., Morphy 1993: 206; Munn 1973; Myers 1991) and some pastoral peoples (e.g., Prussin 1996).[12]

Kpuawala's name, which (as we shall see in Chapter 1) is derived from a phrase that means "the place of the big farm hut," and the origin narratives that bespeak this settlement's gradual development out of a temporary rice farm, destabilize the tendency to link the community to a permanently settled place. Instead, the discursive and material practices of Kpuawala's inhabitants underscore the settlement's nomadic relationship to the landscape. Gendered dimensions of this landscape are related to the history both of how particular portions of the bush have become settlements or farms and, conversely, of how they have returned to bush. Violence is also inscribed in the Kpuawala landscape; a history of warfare and conflict is embedded in the presumed precariousness of the settlement and in the dangers of the forest. At the same time, I show how political contestations account for the relative remoteness of certain sites. This remoteness is contingent upon modern features of Sierra Leonean history, such as the encroachment of slave-raiding Muslim neighbors to the north and that of colonial and postcolonial states from newer urban centers. All this is intelligible from clues embedded in the landscape, and understanding them falls within the parameters of a venatic (hunting) lore. Thus I examine how the meaning compressed in the cryptic remark, in the nickname, and in the marginal clue provides insights into encompassing social forms. This turning to the detail and the clue is characterized by historian Carlo Ginzburg as a critical transformation in the approach of modern human sciences and other endeavors, particularly clinical medicine, psychoanalysis, art history, and the detective novel (Ginzburg 1989:

96–102).[13] Ginzburg traces a longer genealogy for the "conjectural paradigm" shared by these diverse disciplines to tackle the fragmentary nature of their evidence, in the modes of knowledge of the Babylonian augur. Thus is the hunter's "venatic lore" linked to the domain of belief and making believe, in that it is

> characterized by the ability to construct from apparently insignificant experimental data a complex reality that could not be experienced directly. Also, the data is always arranged by the observer in such a way as to produce a narrative sequence, which could be expressed most simply as "someone has passed this way." . . . the rhetorical figures on which the language of venatic deduction still rests today—the part in relation to the whole, the effect in relation to the cause—are traceable to the narrative axis of metonymy, with the rigorous exclusion of metaphor. The hunter would have been the first "to tell a story" because he alone was able to read, in the silent, nearly imperceptible tracks left by his prey, a coherent sequence of events.
>
> (*Ginzburg* 1989: 103)

Furthermore, I examine how the natural landscape evokes the settlement, and vice versa, through the paired naming of features and agencies in each setting, as "stand-ins" for each other. Wild and domestic varieties of animals and plants, identical names given to town buildings and natural features on the farm, and proper names themselves, given to farms and forest processing clearings, reconstruct village sociality and turn it on its head beyond the settlement's physical margins. I explore the play of scale that accompanies the metonymical operations I have mentioned. How does a hermeneutic of secrecy articulate the tension between larger, often concealed processes and the smaller clues in the landscape that trigger the historical memory? I explore, for example, the demise of the railway in Sierra Leone and its effect on technologies of travel—but also on the social imagination—as a context for the disjunctures in the experience of movement through time and space in the modern history of Sierra Leone.

Three interludes appear at intervals in the book. They focus on the materiality of gestures and objects that play crucial roles in the regional history. These are objects and activities in which gender complementarity, politics, and roles have been pivotal and whose centrality to Mende definitions of cultural authenticity belies the fact that all have been crucial currencies in the regional political economy. Thus the objects around which these interludes are built—kola nuts, locally woven cotton cloth, and palm oil—have been important regional currencies and trade items in a larger world and have at different times been the tokens of a violent incorporation into those domains. The activities with which these objects are associated—splitting, weaving, and smearing substances on the body—maintain the ambivalent status derived from their historical association with the past. They mark domains of distinctiveness and inclusiveness through principles of complementarity or of hierarchical encompassment. Central to these processes is the biographical and historical inscription of social memory. For example, clay and oil are biographical substances that inscribe temporality on the body (seasonal cycle, youth and old age, and so on). The use of these substances on the bodies of children and adults, to produce heat or coolness, in situations of health or disease, and their evocation of different stages of the life cycle make them key elements in the gendering of persons. Thus on a larger scale, these processes shape social transitions in individual life cycles, as well as bodily memories about them.[14]

Nomadic movements across the landscape are linked to the practices of hunting and fishing. My contribution here is in connecting questions surrounding the cultural construction of space to the organization of practices, through a sustained analysis of objects in motion. Following the production of the object and tracing its movements, one can move across space and grasp the elements of practice. For example, hunting and fishing nets are linked both semantically and materially, through their production in the village, with fibers and woody parts culled from the bush. By observing the social deployment of these objects—prescriptions that situate them at different times inside or outside the settlement, in collective meeting spaces or in particular domestic spaces—I outline the engendering of moral and economic spheres. These are not fixed spheres but, rather, are deployed in the order of specific practices. Limitations in the circulation of women's objects and in the scope of their everyday domestic life contrast with the broader social and political reach of processes associated with male productive roles. Men's hunting nets are stored in public meeting places where they can be used by anyone at any time. Furthermore, collective hunting parties point to the village's embeddedness in a nesting order of hierarchical relations. Unlike other techniques for killing game that are also practiced in this area, net-hunting parties are organized primarily at the behest of chiefdom authorities and, more rarely, to rid the farms of prominent community members of crop pests. By contrast, women's fishing nets are personal objects for individual or paired use, and women's catch is destined for their own domestic consumption; furthermore, these fishing nets are used in ways that tend to reinforce their exclusion from inhabited parts of the settlement. Such practices have implications for gendered modes of sociality, whose meanings are both shaped by, and constitutive of, the properties of objects in which they are embedded. I also examine how different nets and hammocks, whose nature as objects of entrapment makes them particularly rich carriers of the ambiguous dialectic of concealment and manifestation, can become traps at other levels.

By focusing on how particular social actors use objects in specific contexts, I explore the contingency of meaning configurations. Thus all meanings, including gendered ones, cannot be fixed but depend on the historical and political circumstances in which they are activated. The prevailing significance of context accounts for the complementary distinction made in Mende cultural aesthetics between male and female objects, sitting places, postures, and practices such as hunting and fishing, and for the gender ambiguity of the *mabɔle*, a female member of the men's Poro society. Ritual roles such as that of the *mabɔle* do not present straightforward evidence about everyday gender boundaries. On the contrary, anthropological studies of ritual have long illustrated how, in this domain, cultural norms that govern everyday life are reversed or suspended. However, instead of focusing exclusively on the significance of their ritual roles, I analyze how Kpuawala's *mabɔlesia* are confronted with their gender ambiguity in myriad ways in their *ordinary* lives, and hence how they also confront those around them with this issue, on a daily basis.

Gender relations bear a history of violence that is embedded in the very language of intimacy and domestic relations. I argue that Mende marriage must be understood in the context of slavery and in terms of how this institution shaped forms of dependence in the region. This perspective highlights the tensions and inequalities embedded in the idiom of marriage and kinship. I examine several cases involving people at different stages in their lives and from the perspectives of wives and husbands. The connotation of stability implied by the terminology of marriage (*hei*, which also means "sitting") is deceptive: the conflicting demands placed on wives by their kin bring tensions to relations with husbands and in-laws. But in addition to these structural tensions, historical changes ranging from the demise of pre-colonial domestic slavery to the economic pressures of structural adjustment programs in the 1980s are key to understanding the increased fragility of marriages in modern rural Sierra Leone. Here, too, relations of inequality, and the potential role of marriage in shaping or erasing them, are evoked in titles, forms of address, and prescriptive behaviors that point to the emergent violence in the Mende historical and social landscape, as well as to the means through which it is overcome.

In examining Mende ways of inhabiting places like the "big house" in village compounds, my central concern is with space as the site for imagining key social and political practices. The "big house" is both social institution and lived space of the extended farming household. The semantic slippage among the house as a place, as a social concept, and as a labor unit offers a context for reexamining the literature on the house and domesticity, within which important discussions of gender have occurred in anthropology. The slippage, I argue, is also due to the historical transformation of this unit, which was once a key element in the organization of captive farm labor. In examining the everyday life of a big house and its shifting population over time, I present a picture of the mobility of female and junior male dependents. I also explore the metonymic relationship between women's individual and collective property and the big house as a whole, and I discuss related "big" institutions, sites, and objects—the big farm, the big pot, and so on.

This leads to a more sustained analysis of the extraordinary status of "big persons" and of the gendered practices through which this status can be achieved. The different connotations of "big person" are linked to Mende bodily cosmology and to an aesthetic of secrecy. Once again, the emphasis is less on the status of big persons, social relations, or constituted space *per se* than on the mediating role of objects as the bearers of social meaning in making and unmaking them. The ability to contain secrets and powerful substances is a key attribute of the big person. However, the analysis of particular cases reveals ambiguities in Mende notions of the big person and of power relations. The question addressed here concerns strategic shifts in the scale, the substitution of parts for wholes, and how these changes can create spaces for unexpected reversals of fortune. That is to say, unpredictability is the principle of practice and is the cultural logic—bolstered by many remembered cases in local history— through which poor strangers became wealthy rulers, or children and other apparently weak beings concealed unsuspected powers.

I then explore the ambiguous status of children, their linkages through twinship to the social figuration of the stranger, and other forms of doubles. In particular, I address the circumstances through which people are paired in relationships that display a broader set of characteristics than the tense complementarity of social relations. Upon closer scrutiny, one

sees that the binary logic of twins, namesakes, and other similarly structured, interdependent relationships (between men and women, patrons
and clients, and hosts and strangers) is disrupted by a third element. For
example, Mende notions of twinship encompass the child born *after* a set
of twins or the third-born of triplets. Similarly to the *mabɔle*, who complicates gender dichotomies, Gbesse (the name given to a child born after
twins) transcends the paired relationship in being a required component
in the completion of a twin birth. Indeed, three is a female number in
Mende, but it is also the quantity of mediation and ambiguity. The
"twinness" of the child born *after* a set of twins points to the deferral of
closure to a later event—to the fact that in a life of messiness and unpredictability, what appear to be paired relations inevitably lead to multi-
plicities of relations. Gbesse points to a Mende valuation of history,
where only the vantage point of hindsight offers an understanding of
experience—an understanding that can only be suspended in the present.
Thus the multiplicity of three undermines its surface identification with
only one (female) gender, to explode at a higher level the apparent oppositions in Mende daily life. Here too, Simmel's concern with sociocultural
forms provides theoretical insights, for he saw in the number three not so
much an intrinsic value but the very principle of multiplicity—of social as
opposed to individual interactions. The third is the witness, and "the sensitive union of two is always irritated by the spectator" (Simmel 1950:
136). However, the third is not merely an irritant: it can transcend the
oppositional form of dyadic relationships when the instant reciprocity
and intimacy of the pair leads to jealousy. The two who are bound in a
dyadic relationship also encounter "many disturbances and dangers
into which confidence in a third party in the triad itself might lead the
two" (ibid.).

Finally, I argue that the relationship between social practices and the
materially experienced world is shaped by a dialectical—dialogical—
logic. This is a historical logic, which has left more or less intelligible
clues. The ability to recognize these clues, and to make one's own interpretation of them gain acceptance among many, forms the basis of the
achievement of power in Mende society. However, this process is characterized by struggles, whose outcome is rendered all the more uncertain by the shifting grounds of a hermeneutic of ambiguity, which has
been activated by a violent history. This history has permeated social
relations at all levels, from the politics of chief–subjects relations to
marriage and kinship. Thus the latter, and the gender relations they

mediated, have become the very sites for shaping and contesting historical events. The contingency of social practices that shape understanding must be linked to the materiality of everyday life. In the end, this book claims that the material world matters, but that the life that objects and substances take on, from circumstances not of their own making but of their made-ness, produces unstable meanings and unpredictable events.

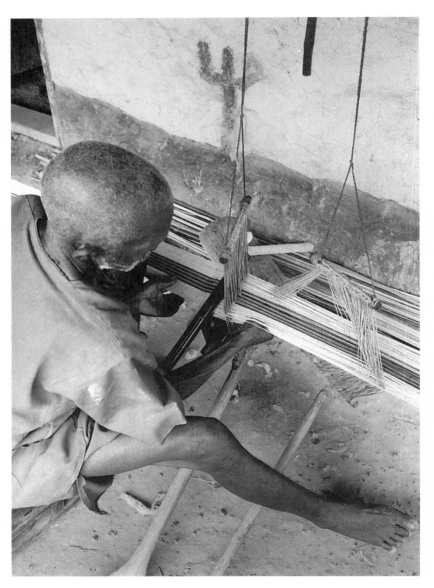

"Janguema" (1985)

CHAPTER I

Immaterial Practices

Clues in a Modern
Sierra Leonean Landscape

Hotɛi a kamba ninɛi gɔlo, kɛ ii kɔɔ yɔ la hu.
A stranger recognizes a new grave, but does not know who
lies in it.

                      Mende proverb

Places are fragmentary and inward-turning histories, pasts that
others are not allowed to read, accumulated times that can be
unfolded but like stories held in reserve, remaining in an
enigmatic state, symbolizations encysted in the pain or pleasure
of the body. "I feel good here": the well-being under-expressed
in the language it appears in like a fleeting glimmer is a spatial
practice.

                Certeau (1984: 108)

Like other parts of postcolonial Africa, the natural landscape of Sierra
Leone was littered in the 1980s with relics—traces left behind by the
colonial state and its modernizing project. These relics were being swal-
lowed up by vegetation, which was reclaiming these sites at a time when
the postcolonial state no longer provided services, or constituted much of
a presence, in rural areas lacking significant mineral resources. Paved
roads reverted to dirt tracks, each rainy season leaving behind fewer bits
of tarmac. Along these rural roads, rusty commercial signs advertising
gas stations were abandoned sites with no apparent signs of human activity. These were among the material reminders to most Sierra Leoneans
that their experience of modernity was not one of increasing integration
within a developing country—as the progressive narrative of modernization would have it. Instead, this experience was about the clash between
a past remembered as progress-oriented, and a present made captive by
that past through nostalgic memories of better days.

In this experience, modern relics were made up as much of particular
configurations of the natural landscape—trees and other kinds of vegetation—as by objects of human making (e.g., buildings and roads). In other
words, nature itself had stories to tell about the human occupation of the
landscape, and about the failure of state-driven modernization projects.
During the civil war that broke out in 1991, pockets of rebellion formed
within the same regions abandoned by the postcolonial state. These were
linked in local folklore to events on the global popular cultural scene
(Richards 1996b), but also to memories of the 1898 insurrection in this
region against the establishment in Mendeland of the colonial state.

In colonial accounts of West Africa, human violence, particularly
when perpetrated by Africans, was often set against the backdrop of a
luxuriant natural landscape. The narrative interpretation of this landscape as peaceful made the contrast with the violent events that unfolded
there all the more shocking. Several British colonial officers published
accounts of the 1898 insurgency that broke out in the Sierra Leone Protectorate, after authorities decided to impose annual taxes (e.g., Alldridge
1901: 305–333; Wallis 1903). Captain Wallis, a British military officer
who had himself narrowly escaped with his life during the insurrection,
had this to say about his arrival at a forest site where a few days earlier an
American missionary woman had been raped, mutilated, and killed:

> And this foul deed, too awful to be described in full, was perpetrated in the
> beauty and grand solitude of an African forest. The leaves all round the spot
> were splashed with blood, and the ground was tramped down with the prints
> of many naked feet. Yet after the foul deed had been committed, the sun con-
> tinued shining in the heavens, and the birds sang close by as they flew from
> tree to tree! Nature seemed all unmoved at this grim tragedy. One would
> almost have expected the very earth to shake, and the sun to put out his light,
> after witnessing such dreadful scenes.
>
> *(Wallis 1903: 142)*

In every sentence Wallis's narrative contrasted the awe inspired by the
African forest's quiet and beauty with the revulsion produced by the violent "foul deed" it witnessed. Wallis saw nature as indifferent to, and
"unmoved" by, human tragedy unfolding in its midst. Presumably the
signs left on the landscape—the blood-splattered leaves and trampled
grass—would be erased in a matter of days by rain and natural regrowth.
Wallis's regret at the fact that the earth did not tremble or the sun go dark
in response to the massacre seemed to be in part about the fear that without natural disasters, which produce more lasting ruins and memories,

human witnesses at the scene might find it difficult to summon the suitable emotional outrage.

In Wallis's account—and in other similar ones—nature was assumed to be benign. By contrast with the loss of human life, the trees covered in foliage, singing birds, and sunshine were part of healthy, vital processes devoid of violence and pain. Nature, for Wallis, should respond to human events just as did the humans who inscribed their passage on it. This was not always the case in accounts of violence. In contrasting accounts of colonial notions of the equation between "jungle" and savagery—and hence of the equation between human others and nature itself—Michael Taussig has given an account of the Amazonian setting as "the colonially intensified metaphor for the great space of terror and cruelty, . . . [where] the brutal destructiveness imputed to the natural world serves to embody even more destructive relations in human society" (Taussig 1987: 75). In the accounts of Colombian rubber tappers during the colonial period, whose hands "inflict on the trees [what] they can also inflict on men" (Rivera cited in Taussig, ibid.), a violent nature, and violence perpetrated *against* nature, participated in the death and terror visited upon humans.[1]

Thus for those who can read the forest landscape, some natural features are as tragic as any scene of violent destruction. Certain trees are, and were, planted for food, defense, and shade only at sites of human settlement or farming. And when such rural settlements disappear, with their constructions of mud, sticks, and thatch, clusters of kola and fruit trees planted in village gardens quickly become the only visible traces. By contrast, the presence of gigantic "cotton trees" (*Ceiba pentandra*) among second-growth forest points to ritual spaces belonging to esoteric associations or to older settlements—where such trees initially provided material for fortification purposes and eventually took root.[2] In most cases, only those who recognize the human plan that shaped the clustering together of certain trees know that these features of the natural landscape are ruins. And only those who know the story of how they became ruins know whether a violent event is at their origin.

Trees and other natural landmarks can be read as ruins—inscriptions of violent encounters or at least of abandonment of a once-inhabited site—as much as decaying, destroyed buildings. In rural Sierra Leone, growing vegetation is often the only recognizable trace of human intervention in the landscape. It is both a memorial to the past and a sign that the past is yielding to new forms of life.

In addition to particular configurations of vegetation, past settlements are also marked by the slightly elevated spots in the forest floor where houses once stood and by the sunken hollows where graves repose. Graves and the dead they conceal remain one of the lasting ruins of past live settlements. A casual walk on forest paths can take one by several such sites, and if someone in the company has specific knowledge of them, the conversation often turns to the ruin's history. This story is always told backwards in time, from the events that triggered abandonment and decay. It defies straightforward teleologies and hence offers myriad opportunities for alternative narratives of the past. But others walking by ruins in the forest may recognize from surface signs the traces of earlier settlements without there being a meaningful connection that might create an opportunity for the dead to return to life in the remembrance of the living. As the Mende proverb puts it, "A stranger recognizes a new grave, but does not know who lies in it." The crucial knowledge of the underneath of things is not limited to the surface recognition of a grave site but, rather, reaches down into the deeper history of those who are under the surface and into how they got there. Thus the ruin is a site of the departed, but one whose recognition as such depends on the response it triggers in the living who encounter it. This response, in turn, depends on a prior knowledge that makes possible the interpretation of material remains.

DISSIMULATION AND THE ARTS OF INTERPRETATION

The ability to read clues from surface signs in the landscape and to construct a deeper interpretation is part and parcel of the hunter's skills. In hunting lore shared across a wide spectrum of West African societies, but especially in the Mande world whose history dominates this region, hunter-warriors have special powers of dissimulation and interpretation (cf. Cosentino 1989; McNaughton 1982; Van Beek and Banga 1992). At night, Mande hunters go out in the forest to search for prey that remains in hiding during the day. But this is an especially dangerous time for hunters, too, because witches and other transmogrifying creatures also frequent the night. For hunters as well as warriors, survival depends on their own powers of dissimulation (the need to make themselves invisible in the surrounding landscape), as well as on their ability to identify the traces left behind by prey or enemy and to recognize the guises in which they conceal themselves. The circumstances under which some shape-shifters change in and out of animal form are linked to local history, which in turn is embedded in the landscape and its ruins. Accordingly, hunter–warriors are great knowers and tellers of histories (Cashion 1982; Cisse 1964). They also acquire protective powers against harmful attacks on their own lives through medicines and amulets. The two figures often overlap in West African history and myth—and again, particularly, during the civil war that began in 1991 in Sierra Leone. Beginning in 1993, a year after a coup brought the military NPRC regime to power, both town- and rural-based political leaders began to call on hunters and organized hunting societies to form civilian militias for protecting the population against abuses at the hands of both rebel and government military forces (Muana 1997).

However, these latter-day hunter–warriors were more than a grassroots resistance movement inspired by local history. Quite to the contrary, the Sierra Leone case suggests that notwithstanding the legitimizing narratives and rituals from hunting lore circulating among fighters, they are by and large a modern guerilla force trained and armed for modern warfare. Following the 1997 reestablishment of civilian rule in Sierra Leone, this modern identity was signaled in name too, with the transmogrification of the *kamajɔ* militia (*kamajɔ* is Mende for "hunter") into a "Civil Defence Force" (CDF) made up of paramilitary units aligned with the Sierra Leonean Army. The label *hunters* continues to be used, and deliberately so, for its rich historical and cultural resonance, in the popular imagination, with all that this term conjures up. In particular, hunters in the war have visibly claimed, through ritual objects like magical amulets covering their bodies, the powers of dissimulation associated with their craft, including the ability to make themselves invisible and impermeable to bullets. However, the very visibility of these magic objects, clothes, and rituals points to their superficiality, in a context where the combatants' youthfulness argues against their having deep interpretive powers. To be sure, the young members of the hunting militias are taught to kill, but in a gross manner, and in combat against visible enemies. They lack the historical knowledge that, by guiding interpretation of traces in the landscape, generates a narrative about the enemy's behavior that can identify him or her even in disguised form and in hiding.[3] Hence the ambiguity of traces in the landscape is lost on the youthful warriors in the present conflict in Sierra Leone—though not on the older, rural members of the militia, whose activities have been largely restricted to the areas they inhabited before the war and have occurred under the leadership of local Paramount Chiefs.[4]

Discourse about hunting is one domain in which experienced hunters confront neophytes with their superior knowledge. Vandi, a Kpuawala elder, once had all younger men in the community guessing for several days what a "*gɛgbɛwuli*" was. Some thought it was another name for a tree in the forest (from the word's ending, *ng/wuli*, "tree, wood, stick"). Others thought it an animated object. Finally, Vandi explained that it was the stick (*wuli*) from the recent (*gɛ*) hunt (*gbɛ*). Still many had no idea what a stick from a recent hunt might be, given that hunting is done with guns or nets and with cutlasses. Then Vandi began to take his rapt audience for a narrative walk in the woods.

> A stranger walking a bush path in an area he does not know can tell how ripe the trees are—how long they have been left fallow since the last farming—by the mushrooms and combinations of woods, their size and so on, right? And say he were to walk upon sticks left there from a recent hunting expedition, you know, the sticks you quickly and silently cut from trees surrounding your assigned position, to plant into the ground so you can prop your nets on them? *Gɛgbɛwulilɔ*, that stranger will say, it's a stick from a recent hunt. For once they roll up their nets and leave the forest, hunters never bother to pull up those sticks from the ground, do they?

The elderly Vandi's game obviously delighted his audience. Everyone was spellbound by his skill in unraveling an apparently meaningless word to reveal its fragments of sense, but also by the narrative of customary hunting practices he told in this decoding process. He cracked the story buried in a meaningless word and thus provided the equivalent to the identity of the recently buried deceased in the proverb about the ignorance of strangers. Vandi rehearsed every move and sound—all the strategic details about his location that cross a hunter's mind as he quietly listens by his propped-up net for the sound of approaching dogs, which tells him the prey is heading his way. He modulated his voice, shifting from barely perceptible murmurs while describing the preparations, to loud, excited shouts once he got to the hunters' chase. The audience's response mimicked his tone: Whispered comments were followed by loud verbal virtuosity and laughter, as people added details based on their own reminiscences of similar events. The elder's story was about decoding the landscape for signs one could recognize only from one's own participation in similar events. Some of the young men from town had never been on a net-hunting expedition. For them, these signs of social activity would have remained concealed in the forest landscape, just as the word *gɛgbɛwuli* had been unintelligible before they heard the story.

But this was not just a statement of the primacy of direct experience in the acquisition of knowledge: Vandi's audience included men who had been on hunting expeditions without ever having learned about *gɛgbɛwuli*. Vandi's verbal dexterity implied that there was an esoteric dimension required to make meaningful use of experience, or to "do things with words" (Austin 1962: 12–13). Special guidance was needed to learn to read the light, scattered traces left on the landscape by animals and hunters and to plot them into a coherent narrative, which was then masked and presented as an inscrutable riddle. This achieved the dual purpose of unmasking those who already knew "deep Mende" and of selectively revealing it to others. This technique of secrecy, in which words are masked to conceal for most what they communicate to the few, and to convey to all the presence of secret knowledge, has political dimensions as well.[5] Vandi's explanation had the effect of reminding most of his audience how little they knew not only about hunting, but also about an elusive set of "Mende" traditions. Such reminders supported his position as respected elder, reinforcing the notion that he was one of the gatekeepers, or "brokers" (Murphy 1981), to whom others had to appeal to acquire culturally valued knowledge. However, individuals using stories like Vandi's to claim knowledge of "deep Mende" could also see them dismissed as wholesale inventions. Thus political dimensions are seldom extraneous to most claims or challenges to secret knowledge.[6]

In his *gɛgbɛwuli* story, Vandi was referring to collective hunting parties that used nets to capture their prey. This was not how the hunter–warriors of the region's heroic past, or of its present, practiced their craft. Instead, they went out at night, often alone, with guns. Their craft was closely allied with that of gun makers, who were usually hunters themselves. Kpuawala's blacksmith was among the handful of skilled gun makers in the region, and he attracted hunters from great distances, who commissioned weapons from him or brought them for repairs. Though he spoke of ancestral knowledge about iron extraction and smelting, his preferred method for fabricating guns (and one that he implied had long been in use among ancestors as well) was to recycle old metal bought from scavengers of car wrecks along the chiefdom roads. His technology was experimental, and he made do with what was at hand, sometimes begging European visitors of mine to procure him soldering chemicals available only at great expense in Freetown, other times employing locally available substitutes. He was hardly a figure from the past, nor was his hunting, dependent as it was on the availability of imported cartridges that had to be procured in large market towns or through mobile intermediaries like lorry drivers or wealthier travelers.

If hunting can be seen as a sign of modernity's presence in this forest region, so can the process of history making and interpreting embedded in the venatic lore of its practitioners. The assumptions embedded at first sight are that the forest is a place with stable configurations, intelligible to those in the know, where action is made "legible" by being frozen in time. It has a location, defined by the synchronic contiguity of elements that make the landscape intelligible as bush, farm, road, village, house, and so on. By contrast, as we shall see, space is produced by (imaginary) gestures, movements, and variations in speed and duration. It lacks a stable location and is by definition made of temporary sets of serial proximities, contractions, and expansions. Space is *practiced*, inhabited in real time (see Certeau 1984: 115–130). What these practices have in common is that at different levels they make, or invent, the landscape in which they move. As one moves across the landscape, one does not merely find clues of an objectively present world, as might be implied by Ginzburg's conjectural paradigm. Rather, one also refashions that very world for particular purposes and to give legitimacy to emergent political strategies in the present.

UNDERGROUND TRAPS

The Mende word for "underground, that which is in the earth," *ndɔ(l)ɔwu*, is also the Mende word for "hidden," or "secret." Like the word for "meaning" or "that which is underneath" (*yɛmbu*), *ndɔ(l)ɔwu* points to the underneath of the visible world. Both concepts have spatial and relational connotations, and both encompass tensions between a *fixed* location (underneath something else) and a *relational* site that is both changing and contextual (there can be multiple layers of "underneath," with some meanings more accessible than others). Thus the insistence on concealing important knowledge, separate from the realm of appearances, belies the fact that in practice, people constantly challenge the boundaries set between visible and invisible worlds.

The question of the underground has to do with the possibility of unearthing a forgotten history. As Edouard Glissant once pointed out in relation to the embeddedness of a tortured Caribbean history of rootlessness, slavery, and death in the islands' muted landscape, there can be different degrees of foreignness in relation to a place (Glissant 1996: 11). The emergent awareness of a forgotten history can make strangers "come to a halt, not certain what slows us down at that particular spot with a strange uneasiness. These beaches . . . are the ultimate frontier, visible evidence of our past wanderings and our present distress" (Ibid.). By the same token, some familiarity with the Sierra Leonean landscape is necessary to make intelligible as graves the sunken spots dotting the ground surrounding rural settlements, long after animals and elements have erased mounds and scattered stone and plant markers.

These inscriptions on the landscape are monumental in the sense that they are intelligible historical markers, even if they are not made of durable, large-scale materials. They consist of transmitted narratives about rock formations and trees, as opposed to monuments that have made history intelligible to outsiders. This is particularly true in the Caribbean and the Upper Guinea Coast, where historical traces on the underside of beaches, abandoned graves, and settlement sites are reminders of the long history of violent wars, capture, and enslavement.

Ancient forest sites are also the shifting grounds where the visible and the invisible world may intersect. Walking by a grave or by an old settlement's ruin might entail the possibility of encountering shape-shifters or trickster figures. Ndɔgbɔsui is one of the key transmogrifying tricksters roaming the Mende landscape. In the scholarly literature, he is described variously as "of unusual shape and large size" (Hofstra 1942: 176), as "a spirit which . . . sometimes assumes the form of a hairy man and is often encountered by hunters" (Harris and Sawyerr 1968: 45), and as a man "with a white skin and a long white beard . . . [who tricks lonely travelers] into following him deep into the forest" (Little 1951: 223). In Kpuawala he appeared as a familiar acquaintance who could draw unsuspecting followers deep into the forest to entrap them there forever (see Harris and Sawyerr 1968: 45; Hofstra 1942: 176). Despite this range of appearances, all versions of Ndɔgbɔsui shared the fact that their victims, in order to extricate themselves from his control, had to answer his questions about aspects of daily life and landscape in a manner that was contrary to experience and concealed their real knowledge on the subject. Thus, to a question about how one carries water, one must answer "with a fishing net," and so on (see Little 1951: 223). The point is that the order of dissimulation that makes Vandi encode in riddles his knowledge of hunting also shapes encounters with Ndɔgbɔsui. On the one hand, the trickster himself takes on different appearances, and (in the Wunde version at least) his deception is all the more insidious for its familiarity. On the other hand, potential victims can find safety in hiding their real intentions and knowledge behind absurd answers. The absurd, as others have noted, is an effective weapon for unmaking the world as we know it—for destroying predictable meanings—but also for surviving this act of destruction (Nordstrom 1995: 142–148).

Like witch spirits, Ndɔgbɔsui is concealed by deceptive appearances, although he is unlike them in that he does not possess his victims. These shape-shifting beings are encountered in the same sites at the boundaries between different worlds: animals and humans, village and bush, sleep and waking. For it is on the boundaries that dangerous, albeit empowering, transformations can occur. For many rural Mende such as the Wunde residents, encounters with the modern postcolonial state and its historical antecedents have had similar connotations of deception, unpredictable identity shifts, and ultimate entrapment. Thus during the 1982 elections, campaigns by disguised thugs who attacked and destroyed villages in the neighboring chiefdom came to be known as the "Ndɔgbɔsui troubles." Despite their disguises, these attackers were sometimes recognized, although people were so used to the notion of the familiar transmogrifying into the alien that they seldom acknowledged the assailants' identities.

As with the proverb about the stranger who might be able to recognize a grave but not know who occupies it, a familiar reality masks different layers of meanings. Only an eye for telltale clues can identify trickster figures such as Ndɔgbɔsui, who is said to be recognizable only by an ant lodged between his toes. Furthermore, only an absurd, deceptive dialogue with him can save a potential victim from certain death. Hence the political and historical salience of those, like hunters, who were experts in putting together events and narratives to make sense of disparate clues in the landscape and who could tell the stories of ruins. At the same time, these figures were guardians of this knowledge, which was not revealed to all because of its real political import.

PRODUCING REMOTENESS

JOADI: When suddenly, the white government[7] wrote me a letter saying, "Joadi Modima."

"Yessir" (standing to attention, military style), they said, "We finished building your railroad. So now it will be arriving. . . ."

That train would pick up one foot and move it forward, then pick this one up and move it forward. People used to hang off it in the air. This was somewhere else, not in this land. One would travel there, out in the air, *juku-jeke, juku-jeke, juku-jeke.*

Oh, my friend, I tell you. Once a person took that trip, when suddenly a snake bit his foot, and he lay there, foam coming out of his mouth.

So I immediately wrote a letter to mammy Queen,[8] saying, "The train is broken. Enough of that. Send me an airplane."

CHORUS: This is why I say, "Personal enmity came to this world long
          ago: while I was still in my mother's belly, they assigned me
          to mandatory chiefdom labor."
JOADI: Suddenly, they started building a fence in the sky, and made a
          trap in it. When that airplane arrived, it was caught in the
          trap, and a fight began, you know. They fought for a long
          time. . . ."

> *Joadi Modima, storyteller*[9]
> *Kpuawala, performance on February 28, 1986*

In this snatch of storytelling, Joadi, a local performer, narrated the arrival
of the railroad in rural Mendeland as an event announced by the colonial
government ("They wrote me a letter"), but the decision to dismantle it
was presented as his own. Joadi wrote to the Queen to get rid of the inefficient railroad system and requested airplanes instead. His sarcasm was
not lost on his audience, which erupted in laughter and ironic commentary. At the time of this performance, airplanes were usually seen flying
only on the rare private flights to the Kono diamond fields to the north.
The improved road network that was to replace the railroad (dismantled some 16 years earlier) had not materialized, and transportation
had become increasingly unreliable and expensive. Far from traveling
by air, many Kpuawala people now walked the 18 or so miles to the
market in Blama.

The railroad had served as a key element in integrating rural Mendeland into the Sierra Leonean colonial state.[10] Initially, the railway had
been planned to link Freetown to its northern hinterland, the Guinean
highlands, and the trans-Saharan trade, and a northern tract was indeed
built (Clarke 1969: 104).[11] But most of the track was eventually oriented
in the southeastern direction, through Mende territory, almost to the
Liberian border. This area, which was rich in oil palms, was judged to be
the only one with enough trading goods to make construction of the railroad pay (Riddell 1970: 23), given the absence of large-scale mineral
operations that elsewhere in the empire made such projects more prof-
itable (Clarke, ibid.). Ironically, by the time such large-scale mineral
operations were set up in Sierra Leone, the railway system had deterio-
rated beyond repair. In any case, the most precious Sierra Leonean minerals—diamonds—are small and light enough not to require railroad
transport. Though the language of colonial administrators at the time
emphasized the economic and civilizing benefits of opening the Sierra
Leone interior to transport by rail, many contemporary observers of the

imperialist venture had no doubts about the primacy of political factors instead (see Weber 1978, II: 915).

In Sierra Leone, where almost from the beginning the railroad proved to be an inefficient, slow financial drain, the politics of its location was always clear in the minds of the Africans whose lives it affected, if not of the British administrators who helped plan it. The project was begun in 1895, a year before the formal annexation of this territory to Sierra Leone as a protectorate, and it was first opened to traffic in 1899 (Alldridge 1910: 110), only months after the British repressed a bloody anticolonial insurrection in the region. The insurrection followed the introduction of taxation by the protectorate administration. Mende warlords and their fighters played a prominent role and were severely punished by the British with public executions. Thus the coming of the railroad was tied in Mende historical consciousness to the arrival of taxes, the colonial government, and its violent strategies for annexing the rural hinterland.[12]

By 1907 the railroad had become the backbone for urban development in the interior of Sierra Leone, and several major towns grew up around its main stops, attracting administrative, educational, and trading institutions. Feeder roads were built to link rural areas to the new railway towns of Bo, Blama, Kenema, and so on, further reorienting rural social, political, and economic networks toward these urban centers. The centrality of the railroad to this project in Mendeland was underscored by the fact that the British administration labeled the new administrative unit encompassing this area the Railway district (Riddell 1970: 16). The railroad became "the main axis of up-line development and 'cultural creolization' in Sierra Leone" (Richards 1996b: 38), putting Mendeland at the forefront of the process.

Just as the rise of the railroad helped shape the Sierra Leonean state in its twentieth-century form, so too was its demise seen as symptomatic of the state's progressive weakening. After the railroad was dismantled and sold for scrap in 1974 (Kaindaneh 1993: 35), paved roads replaced it in some areas but not in the easternmost region of the country.[13] This corner on the border with Liberia and Guinea produced over half of the country's export agricultural crops and was the site of a major regional market. Therefore, many read its neglect as a deliberate political act meant to weaken links between Freetown and a stronghold of (Mende-based) opposition politics in the age of the single-party rule of the All People's Congress (see Abraham and Sesay 1993: 119–120; Richards 1996b: 42). Richards (1996b) has argued that this politically motivated "rustication" of border regions once linked by communication networks to the state's capital and other urban centers goes a long way toward explaining the civil war that broke out in 1991 in these areas.

Joadi's song was also a reminder of how the railroad and the very project of modernization came about at the cost of exploitative relations of production: It was usually the forced labor of rural people that, through the mediation of chiefs, built them for the government (see Reno 1995: 37). Indeed, during my own stay in rural Mendeland, periodic demands by the Wunde Paramount Chief for labor parties for road and bridge maintenance were met with responses ranging from surface compliance to outright resentment and absenteeism. Fines, and court cases brought against those who had failed to show up, invariably followed these required projects. Labor on roads and the railway tended to be a site of political contestation, thus situating communications and mobility at the very center of local struggles and as a focal point in the search for autonomy from central authorities by rural peripheries. In 1920 the organization of railway workers into a union (and their pioneering use of the strike as a means for advancing their demands) began the process of unionization in Sierra Leone. Here, as elsewhere in the colonial world, this process led to the political radicalization and anticolonial struggles of the post–World War II period (Kilson 1966: 105 ff.). Thus on several different levels, the railway marked political turning points in postcolonial Sierra Leone.

The strategies evoked in Joadi's song, as well as the foot dragging and strikes that shaped railway labor history, point to the fact that the construction and dismantling of tracks and other infrastructures are not merely top-down processes controlled by the government. People in Kpuawala were keenly aware of the political implications of bestowing and withdrawing development aid for the sake of progress and themselves participated in this process (see Ferme 1998). There may have been efforts to coerce people into building and maintaining avenues for communication, but these projects were not successful unless rural people perceived them to be in their interest. The trap Joadi and his friends built in the sky, into which the airplane fell, suggests one way in which "traditional" knowledge could serve to undermine even the most sophisticated technology. I was reminded of the entrapped airplane story when I saw recycled copper and wood from telephone poles making their way into jewelry, firewood, and other useful things in the everyday life of rural Wunde people. For people who had never benefited from the access to national and international phone communication, such infrastructures might as well serve for cooking food and decorating the body, rather than keeping urban dwellers "wired" to the wider world.[14]

The tactics evinced in Joadi's story were not new. Historically, rural Sierra Leoneans like the residents of Wunde chiefdom have controlled their relations to the outside world by means of strategic interventions on the landscape. In 1889 a British expedition had come to Wunde in search of the famous warrior Ndawa, to stop him from blockading the trade routes linking the interior oil-producing regions with the southern rivers where European factories bought palm products for export (Abraham 1978: 88–89; Fyfe 1962: 481–483). A typical strategy for such blockades was for the men's Poro society to declare a moratorium on the harvesting of palm fruits and on the maintenance of bush paths, which could make travel more difficult. In more recent times, too, the strength or weakness of political ties among leaders associated with particular settlements was reflected in the state of the paths connecting them.

During the political election of 1986, which pitted the Wunde Paramount Chief's brother against the brother of one of the four section chiefs in the chiefdom, Kpuawala people associated the villages in which the two chiefdom officials lived with the opposing factions. The challenger, a civil servant, won an upset victory in the election, confirming that the majority of Kpuawala voters had favored this relative newcomer to electoral politics. Consequently, they also sided with the challenger's brother, who lived in the section headquarters town in Wunde "Kambawama."[15] Given the danger of publicly supporting the challenger in a situation where the Paramount Chief had considerable resources at his disposal to threaten factional opponents, political opposition was expressed via minor, daily acts of dissent, which were often inscribed through anonymous marks in the landscape (cf. Scott 1985: 25–33).

In the months leading up to the May 1986 ballot, such gestures marked a change in Kpuawala people's spatial orientation toward alternative sites of power. When supporters of the opposing faction received the request to appear before the Paramount Chief in Gboyama, they just replied, "We don't go there anymore." This meant that they avoided the town by not being found at home or on their farms when court summonses or requests for appearances in administrative matters were delivered. Many also took longer detours through bush paths when they needed to travel to Gboyama. It also became increasingly difficult in Kpuawala to mobilize the work force necessary to maintain the road to the chiefdom headquarters there. Within the span of a few months in the rainy season, a secondary road that could usually be traveled by dirt-road vehicles became overgrown with vegetation. Its rotting palm log bridges were not replaced, so only people on foot could get through by wading waist-deep into the rice paddies or balancing on a single good log over the water. By contrast, Kpuawala and Wunde Kambawama people regularly brushed the bush footpaths connecting their two settlements, and they replaced the light bridge on the creek along the way when particularly heavy rains swept it away. A few days before the elections, when the community gathered to organize a road maintenance party to make Kpuawala accessible to the electoral commission's vehicle, some dissenters said explicitly that they preferred the road to be impassable to motor traffic. This would, they argued, prevent the arrival of large numbers of young thugs from the opposing parties, who were likely to pick fights and "bring noise"—causing verbal altercations and insulting people.[16]

Thus the vegetation overtaking the road connecting Kpuawala to Wunde was hardly a sign of nature's reclaiming what humans had abandoned. It was also not a sign of a failure to progress along the road toward modern forms of development. Both the Sierra Leonean government and the local population appreciated the long-term benefits of better roads and communication systems. But the degradation of the road to Gboyama suggested that they understood the risks as well; it resulted from people's deliberate efforts to *make their site remote*, to isolate themselves from unwanted intrusion. In the previous year, before the elections highlighted profound political fissures, Kpuawala people had enthusiastically provided labor and materials for replacing a palm log bridge with a cement one on that same Gboyama road. At that time, they expressed fervent hopes that someday an improved road might bring regular transportation to the village. The road at the center of these contrasting visions was the only motorable one out of Kpuawala, and it linked the village to the administrative center of the chiefdom. Its maintenance or neglect was one of the ways in which the community negotiated its relations with an encompassing political order.

This pattern of deliberate retrenchment from modernity, and from the administrative forms associated with it, has many precedents in regional history. The exploitative terms on which the encounters of this region with the Atlantic world took place were shaped by the slave trade beginning in the sixteenth century. The "social creativity" required to respond to the dislocations brought about by these encounters often involved a retreat from trade and contact with outsiders into the forest (and institutions linked to it, such as "secret" and hunting societies) (Richards 1996b: 81–84). Today, the forests on the Sierra Leone–Liberian border continue to be sites where people marginalized by a weak state survive in deliberate isolation, practicing illegal diamond mining and cross-border smuggling.

Since the 1950s diamond mining has shaped the Sierra Leonean collective imaginary about the possibility of acquiring sudden wealth. The temporary alluvial diamond-mining settlement is a short-lived and elusive site of potential reversals of fortunes. In 1993 there were rumors in Kpuawala that a man walking on a path in the nearby Pujehun district had found a relatively large diamond and that wealthy Mende and Lebanese businessmen had already come in from the cities with generator-powered pumps and heavy digging equipment. Young men went off to Pujehun to search for diamonds under contract to wealthy patrons. Thus within a few days, hundreds of people could congregate in even the most remote rural areas, transforming them into bustling temporary settlements. After a time, if the rumors were not supported by news of further finds—often without evidence—the sites were deserted as rapidly as they were settled. But in the meantime, the settlers had experienced a life of relative security, during which they could count on a steady supply of food and some cash and gifts with which to purchase some of the imported commodities that were always abundant at such sites. Abandonment of these sites, however, generally brought people back into poverty, sometimes even greater than what had preceded the brief dream of instant riches. When a mine closed or yielded only small, low-quality diamonds, young men found themselves back in the rural villages they had come from, with only a handful of imported goods to remind them of their brief encounters with an elusive wealth.

Furthermore, there were more permanent enclaves, linked to specific geographical places, to which the collective imaginary of many Mende rural people anchored dreams of wealth. Such enclaves were built by multinational companies, often in remote parts of the country, but became ghost settlements after the work of extraction had ended. For the duration of their existence, these sites were similar to single-commodity entrepots[17] anywhere in the world: They were points of encounter between local and global interests, subject to boom-and-bust cycles shaped by the global economy. During the 1980s, Wunde people began to seek employment in a neighboring region's recently established mine for extracting rutile, a titanium ore. Sierra Rutile, the company that owned the mine, was a subsidiary of an American multinational, Pittsburgh Paints and Glass (Reno 1995: 157). To avoid the risks involved in depending on a failing state, the company had its own security. It even constructed, on a nearby river, a deep water dock that could accommodate sea-faring container ships, to bypass the Freetown port. The Sierra Rutile compound, inhabited largely by the mine's foreign employees, looked like a hyper-modern enclave of prefabricated Florida ranch houses with a swimming pool and golf course. It offered the allure of comforts and commodities increasingly unavailable in state-regulated areas. The comforts available here were visible but unattainable to most of those who saw them from the surrounding villages, given the tight policing of this fence-enclosed space.

The atmosphere of combined visibility and inaccessibility enhanced the magical appeal of this island of prosperity on the collective imaginary of the surrounding population. This population was also keenly aware that the existence of such enclaves depended on the value of natural resources concealed in the ground, a value of which they had been unaware when they inhabited the land that was now being mined. This aspect strengthened their belief that secret knowledge of substances, places, events, and persons was crucial for reversing personal and collective destinies. The real basis of economic prosperity for them was founded on the interpretation of occult phenomena[18] and on finding mineral substances that were linked cosmologically to the concealed domains of ancestors and spirits located under the surface of local soils and waters. Indeed, a harbinger of potential fortune (or misfortune), especially for Mende men, was the appearance in dreams of *Tingɔ*, a female water spirit with fair skin and long hair.[19] In erotic dreams, *Tingɔ* could bestow on the dreamer the gift of a magic, invisible ring that brought wealth to its wearer. First, though, the dreamer had to exercise great cunning and control in the face of *Tingɔ*'s erotic advances. He had to steal something of great value to her, like her hair comb, in exchange for which she might be willing to part with her magic ring (see Harris and Sawyerr, 1968; Little, 1951: 222). If this was not done, the outcome of the oneiric encounter with *Tingɔ* could be disaster, rather than fortune, for the dreamer. Here again, the control of ambiguity is essential to a positive outcome, for it is an initial act of deception, the theft of *Tingɔ*'s comb, that forces her to promise prosperity in exchange for the return of the object of value to her (see Hofstra 1942).

KPUAWALA ORIGINS: HISTORY OF A LANDSCAPE

[M]ovements form one of these "real systems whose
existence in fact makes up the city." They are not
localized; it is rather they that spatialize. They are no
more inserted within a container than those Chinese
characters speakers sketch out on their hands with their
fingertips. . . .
   The trace left behind is substituted for the practice. It
exhibits the (voracious) property that the geographical
system has of being able to transform action into
legibility, but in doing so it causes a way of being in the
world to be forgotten.

                                                    Certeau (1984: 97)

Reading, Certeau reminds us, means moving, visiting. Thus reading the
landscape for relics of old villages calls for the ability of the wanderer
who is experienced with motions, gestures, and sounds. The rice farms
and bush clearings surrounding rural Mende settlements are an ideal
place for looking at how practices "spatialize"—that is, how they make
places and customs anew, out of space, while losing themselves into
something else by leaving traces behind. Indeed, it is precisely by losing
themselves that practices become localized and intelligible. If practices
are temporary and fluid, then any effort to evoke in writing such fleeting
phenomena is doomed to be paradoxical. Writing lends itself to the
absence of the other (Certeau 1973: 116). And yet writing is necessary
not just to make Mende ways of being in the world intelligible to readers,
but also because being involves a certain degree of objectification. All history, according to Certeau, is made of traces left behind. And though one
knows that history is as much about forgetting as about remembering, it
can be recovered only by reading traces left by others.[20] Thus it is in the
relation between the fleeting and the stable, spatializing motion and localized signs inscribed on inhabited landscape that practices come to have
meaning and, conversely, places and material objects begin to make sense
through their uses.
   Along Mende paths, traces of past rice farming are visible, to the
trained eye, in the different maturity levels, clustering, and growth of forest trees. These are also telling signs that one is approaching a living settlement. Upland rice farms are cleared and worked one year every seven or so,
and remain fallow the rest of the time. The rice farm has an intermediate

place between the settled village, with its intelligible though changing forms, and the more dynamic realm of temporary practices that brings farms and settlements into being. A farm's life is shorter than that of a settlement, but since it is by definition intelligible as a particular kind of place, it shares some of the same attributes in relationship to more temporary places of human occupation, such as the uncultivated bush.

To my eye a Mende farm seemed unintelligible at first. My urban upbringing and sporadic summer contacts with farms had not prepared me to recognize the heterogeneous appearance and seasonal changes of Mende hillside rice farms. On my first tour upcountry, during the January–April period when forest sites for farm plots were assigned, cleared, and burned, I assumed that before rice farming began, the blackened, charred terrain surrounding rural villages would be cleared of the clutter of burnt branches and tree stumps sprouting new green leaves and propping up bean vines, termite hills, and rocks. It took me a long time to understand all the principles that underlay the apparent disorder on Mende rice farms: the microgeography of soils and drainage patterns, the fertile properties of termite hills, and the usefulness of fallen branches as boundaries between different terrains and as sources of firewood. Careful planning went into the locating of crops on these farms, and into the methodical timing of brush burns that reduced cut and dried vegetation to ashes, while leaving palm trees standing to be harvested for their oil-bearing fruits. These ashes, and a good burn of the cleared vegetation on the future farm's site, had fertilizing and weed-killing properties that were crucial to the health of rice and other crops.[21]

The relationship between town and rice farm must be viewed in the context of a history in which one often *became* the other. Kpuawala was a case in point, as the etymology of its name records. "The place of the big farm hut" (*kpowa wai la*), its inhabitants claimed, was once a "big farm" where people sometimes took up residence to avoid the long walk to their village during times of intensive farming or to protect their crops (which in the past were stored in the farm hut) from theft.[22] Eventually, a dispute between Baion and Kpevai (two Wunde Kambawama warriors) led to a split, and Kpuawala, which was Baion's main farm, became its permanent settlement. The notion of Kpuawala having been the farming hamlet of a warrior fits the history of precolonial settlement patterns in this region, where fortified warrior towns (in this case, Wunde Kambawama) were surrounded by farming hamlets.[23] The pattern of taking up residence on farms in times of crisis, of finding the temporary shelter more secure than the relatively permanent village, has continued. When I returned to Kpuawala in 1993, after the village had suffered several rebel and soldier incursions, I was told that during those events, the entire community had scattered and hidden on rice farms and in bush shelters.

Kpuawala's name may have been descriptive of the place where the settlement originated, but it no longer described the site it occupied when I inhabited it. The settlement had moved from its original site on a big farm. This was indicated by the presence, along one of the bush paths leaving Kpuawala, of a *tumbui*, the remnants of a previous village among some kola trees and old forest growth, where sunken spots indicated graves and mounds house sites. The village moved sometime after World War II, probably to take advantage of a location closer to the roads that were being built under the auspices of the colonial government. This points in yet another way to the dangers to which Certeau alerted us, the hazards of trying to decipher a place without being able to imagine the fleeting gestures that leave behind fainter traces. In this case, "reading into" Kpuawala's etymology in an effort to understand how it came to exist at the particular site it occupied in the 1980s would miss the fact that this Kpuawala (II) was a second, reconstructed settlement built a few miles away by the inhabitants of the earlier Kpuawala (I), which *may* have been the site of "a big farm hut."

The pattern of memorializing in a new site a previous settlement of the same name has historically been reproduced over a much larger scale in Sierra Leone. Several villages named Mendekelema, which means "the last (the border) of Mende," are today in the heart of Mende territory, both because this territory has expanded over time and because settlers from a border site who moved elsewhere were likely to name their new village after the place they had left. Thus despite their descriptive appearance, names of rural settlements offer clues of a genealogical nature, pointing more to a contested history of settlement and displacement than to the characteristics of a place. The proliferation of identical names across the inhabited rural landscape often leaves uncertain the exact referent in a particular context (to which of the several "Nayagolehu" is somebody referring?). This ambiguity is reproduced on a smaller scale in the names rural people give to their permanent workplaces in forest clearings (*walii*). These places are carved out of the bush near a source of water. They are marked by planted fruit-bearing or palm trees and by large earthen vats built in the ground for processing palm oil. They are often referred to as hamlets (*fulɛi*), as though to signal their potential as alternative residences to the village. These clearings were often named after faraway places. Kpuawala farmers had clearings named Sefadu, after an important diamond-mining center to the north of the country; Nayagolehu, the place in the white sand; Waterloo, a town near Freetown on the Sierra Leonean coast; and even Italy, to mark the occasion of my mother's visit from that country. Thus they marked places with which people had direct experience (in the case of Sefadu, its owner had spent time there in his youth mining for alluvial diamonds), whimsical connections (Waterloo the clearing was by a swamp that flooded during the rainy season: its owner intended the name as a play on "water" rather than as a reference to the Napoleonic era battleground), or an imaginary link through others, as in the case of Italy. This whimsical, and utterly modern, practice of naming reinscribed a larger, cosmopolitan world on this rural landscape, if only in the collective imagination. It also heightened the ambiguity of travel, as it became unclear whether someone going to Sefadu was going to the "original" site a long way off or to the clearing within walking distance of Kpuawala.

On Kpuawala "big" (upland) rice farms, too, practices of naming established homologies with physical features or units of social organization in the village, as though in recognition that without the cooperative work required in farming, and the foods that farming yielded, not much could take place elsewhere. For example, clumps of new leaves growing out of tree stumps left behind in the clearing process were referred to as *tifa mawɛɛ* ("leaf" *mawɛɛ*). This expression links them to the extended household (*mawɛɛ* is a contraction of *muaa wɛɛ*, "our house"), the key unit of social identification and labor organization in the everyday life of these farming communities. The extension of the term *mawɛɛ* to leaves sprouting anew off cut-down and burnt stumps amplified the meaning of the social unit as well, inscribing it, at least ideally, in processes of regeneration from a common root and semiotically grounding it—through its naming—in the farm and its activities.[24] These inscriptions underscore the heterogeneous, nondomestic, and potentially short-lived nature of the *mawɛɛ* as a social unit. In this regard, it is telling that its name should be evoked on a farm whose success or failure is often accounted for in terms of harmonious or conflictual relations within families (particularly between husbands and their wives, but also among brothers and kin of different generations).

Some practices reflect more direct parallels between farm and village sociality. After burning the cleared patch of forest and bush that would be the site of a particular year's rice farm—while the ground was still hot and the smoke rising off it—a farmer would "put in its heart" (*kpaa li wua*). This consisted of planting in a single spot a sampler of the crops that would be represented throughout the farm (for instance, some rice, maize, beans, cotton, cassava, pepper, and banana shoots) while reciting prayers for a good harvest. This act of foundation was explicitly likened to the more permanent and less regular foundation of towns and houses. In Kpuawala, the town's founding shrine was often referred to as its "heart" (*ndíli*), a term that drew a parallel with the farm, and with living organisms. The town's heart was the site of an old mango tree (under which medicinal substances were said to have been buried) and of two ancestral graves, which were located behind the house of the elderly town speaker.

Another parallel site in both town and farm was the *kpowa*, or cooking hut. In both town and farm, this was a more temporary shelter than houses; only a few in Kpuawala bothered to use expensive corrugated metal roofing for cooking huts, preferring instead to use mud and thatch. On farms, the structure seldom lasted longer than one or two years. But whereas village cooking huts were built on the outer edge of compounds and the settlement, near the water, gardens, and farms, where the materials for processing and cooking food were gathered, the farm hut was relatively central to this site. It was in a place where one could command a view of most of the farm, a location near its "heart." This location offered a strategic advantage: the ability to see enemies approaching—a fact that was underscored in storytelling sessions, where farm huts were always the site for surprise, lonely encounters with dangerous forces. Thus in times of need and danger the cooking hut could be a lookout and shelter—even the basis for a new community, as in the case of Kpuawala. But it could also be a lonely outpost where isolated individuals or family groups were attacked easily, away from the security of large numbers in the settlement.

A different way in which rice farming offers clues to Mende sociality is through the anthropomorphism with which the growing rice plant is described—from the use of terms describing bodily processes such as gestation and birth for different stages of ripeness, to labels such as "legs" and their joints given to the plant's stalk. Conversely, temporality in the human life cycle is described in terms of the periodicity of rice farms and fallows in particular sites. Many Kpuawala people used farming and fallow cycles to date events, and to estimate their own age. Thus a woman whose age I had asked for pointed at her uncle's farm nearby and said that this was the third rice farm made on the site since her birth (*ti kpaa laalo heima saawa*).[25] During our conversation, she also dated more recent events by referring to the rice plant's "anatomy." She had heard of her father's illness "when rice plants already had two knees/joints" (*ngombi*, the term for human knees as well), earlier in the farming season and had visited him "when they were pregnant" (grains were swelling inside the sheath)—sometime in late September.

In 1985, when I first arrived in Kpuawala, different varieties of rice were farmed on upland and swamp farms, but the latter were thought merely to supplement the former and to produce an inferior-tasting food. Imported white rice was consumed as well but was merely tolerated, in a manner similar to paddy rice. Upland rice crops were mixed with other planted foods, such as peppers, beans, corn, cassava, cotton, fruits, and vegetables that complemented the rice staple, as well as self-propagating crops like oil palms. These were of interest to other members of the domestic farming unit besides the (usually male) farm owner—for example, women and elderly relatives. They also provided most of the ingredients for cooking a complete meal. The different growing cycles of crops on the hillside plots also ensured their productive use beyond the rice harvest. This was an important time for physically and politically weaker members of households to gain access to the land and its products. The heavy clearing and burning of forest tracts necessary for the first year's rice farm was labor-intensive, and its success depended on good timing. Senior men responsible for a "big farm" tapped their social networks and used their political influence to rally enough labor to complete the job. By contrast, field preparations for the second year's crops were much lighter. At this stage, the plot was no longer a "farm"—a site by definition devoted to rice cultivation—but could be used as a garden for planting vegetables and peanuts, or left fallow while harvesting late-maturing crops sown the previous year, such as beans, spices, and cotton. The work could be undertaken by individuals such as elderly widows, who did not have access to large labor groups unless they could pay for them (though having the plot allocated to them in the first place, amid a number of competing dependents, bespoke influence at a different level).

Thus in a synchronic dimension the intercropping pattern on upland rice farms incorporated a heterogeneous household membership because people of different ages, people of both sexes, and people with different labor requirements owned and cultivated different crops. However, over time, during a second year of farming, even past its existence as a "farm" proper or when it began reverting to bush, the *practices* marking the site of a former rice plot reflected the stronger incorporation of the labor and interests of marginal members of households, who took advantage of the longer growth cycles of some subsidiary crops, or of the relatively light labor input required by others, to acquire a degree of economic autonomy.

Among the crops that are interspersed with the rice and come to fruition well after its harvest is cotton, which is a valuable commodity owned and processed by (often elderly) women. At this stage, the site is no longer called a farm (*kpaa*) but is referred to either in terms of the crop planted there—*tangɛihu* for *tanga*, cassava, or *nikiihu* for *nikii*, peanuts—or, if the land is not cultivated, as *njɔpɔ*, a word that denotes young bush in the process of regrowing on an abandoned farm site. The *njɔpɔ* also evokes the market (*njɔpɔwa or "big njɔpɔ"*), with its heterogeneous varieties of foods and plants, and like the market, this is primarily women's territory: by contrast, the organization and ownership of the farm's main crop, rice, are largely in the hands of the collective household and of its male leadership. In wartime, the *njɔpɔ* was also a crucial resource for survival in rural areas. At harvest time, rebels spread across the countryside to take possession of the rice crops, leaving the civilian population to scavenge for secondary and gardening crops in the *njɔpɔ*. Thus the *njɔpɔ* was the overlooked, humble source of subsistence for the marginalized in peacetime, and for the victims of aggression and of the theft of staple crops in wartime.

By contrast with upland rice farms, which produce one yearly harvest, wet rice paddies have higher yields (up to three crops per year) and do not require fallow periods.[26] But work is particularly tiring and dangerous in wet paddies. In Kpuawala, the rainy seasons were punctuated by accidents involving men and women who had either stepped on a thorn or cut their foot with a farming tool while working in flooded paddies. Women were particularly prone to the accidents connected with wet rice paddies, because they spent more time there while carrying out their weeding tasks. Despite the difference in productivity, then, dry rice cultivation had advantages over flooded paddies—a fact expressed culturally through people's marked preference for the taste of hillside rice.[27] Paddies were also much more exposed than hillside rice farms. Their flatness, openness, and location in low-lying areas made workers in them highly visible to ill-intentioned outsiders. These factors, along with the intensive labor requirements made Kpuawala farmers abandon paddy rice cultivation in wartime long before they gave up farming hillside rice for fear of losing their crops to the rebels.

Mende preference for upland rice must itself be contextualized, however. By the early 1990s, years of dependence, during the rainy season, on rice imported through American PL 480 and other aid programs, which had made this a key product in patronage links between urban-based politicians and their rural constituencies, had instilled an appreciation for the fact that donated rice did not require time-consuming labor. Furthermore, once the civil war disrupted farming, making local rice a rarity, any rice at all was considered a luxury compared to the bulgur wheat distributed by international relief organizations, which people had earlier been accustomed to feeding to their infants as a dietary supplement from the "under-five" clinics in rural areas. During the civil war, people began to talk appreciatively of various mixtures of rice and bulgur that could make the latter palatable, if cooked similarly to rice, and to exchange recipes for improving the flavor of this mixture.

Women's vested interest in the upland rice farm and its later uses for gardening meant that they were more willing to cook kɔndɔ, the large rice meal that was the main compensation for work parties that assisted with the heavier farming tasks. Indeed, the reputation of a particular woman as a cook could be critical in a man's efforts to recruit help for clearing, burning, plowing with hand-held hoes, and other major projects. Conversely, if a man lacked the necessary female aid in cooking and weeding, he sometimes could not even lay an upland farm. Thus, although gender roles in rice farming were temporally segregated because they were tied to different phases of the plant's growth cycle,[28] they were also interdependent—and, in fact, synchronically complementary—if one views this crop's cultivation in the context of the intercropping on the big farm and the encompassing set of practices, such as cooking and food processing, that also took place there. Many of these uses of different rice plots (upland and paddy) at different times (first year's rice farm, second year's garden; wartime, peacetime; as temporary shelter or settlement) were not immediately intelligible in their appearances. They were time-bound practices that, if not witnessed, could only relive in narratives.

CONCLUSION

The rural Sierra Leonean landscape does not lend itself to an easy reading of the history embedded in it, partly because conflicts unfold through competing claims to—and interpretations of—the landscape itself. The possibilities for transforming the landscape, and for its appropriation for political ends, are embedded in intelligible historical relics in material form. But they are embedded, too, in the ambiguity of names and in the nonmaterial, temporary practices of narration. And while telling stories in which the passage of time is expressed through changes in the landscape (e.g., the demise of the railroad; the interval between rice farms on a particular plot) may appear to be more intangible, this discursive dimension is as concrete as stone and mortar. For it is in this dimension that meanings are produced and negotiated, and ambiguous, polysemic clues to a contested history are given new life through ever new and provisional interpretations.

Remoteness itself, which the foreign, urban traveler might recognize in signs of a "receding" modernity, has long been an attribute strategically constructed by both local communities and the larger political units of which they have been part. Hence the deliberate failure to maintain paths between communities on opposite sides of a political divide and the careful upkeep of paths between others linked by close ties of patronage—both historically and in modern electoral battles. Upon this landscape is mapped an alternative imaginary topography, one related to the life experiences and encounters of particular social actors, but without obvious links to its physical landmarks. This flexible topography is continuous with practices embedded in fleeting gestures and whimsical connections to other places and other worlds. The use of the names of very distant, exotic places for local farming hamlets contributes to the ambiguity of this topography. This ambiguity is in part the result of this region's troubled history, one in which the strategic concealment of one's real whereabouts and traveling plans could mean the difference between life and death.

To this concealment was linked a parallel sense of the deceptiveness of appearances of creatures encountered on the path. *Ndɔgbɔsui*, witches, and other beings could easily overpower the traveler not cautious enough to guard his or her intentions. At the same time, an alternative sociality—one wherein every friend may become an enemy—is associated with the world beyond the settlement. On rice farms are mapped some of the features foundational to the physical and social spaces of settlements (their hearts, extended households, the measuring of time). And at another level, these sites host the integration of the capacities and special interests of people of different ages, genders, and relationships to the household. Also, the "socialization" of landmarks on the rice farm is reinforced by the fact that historically and in the present, this site can be a seasonal, and potentially a permanent, alternative settlement—one that becomes an option when village life has been undermined by war or factionalism. The shifting locations of farms and settlements are the product, in part, of political fragmentation in this region. But they also produce forms of life and modes of sociality that are themselves multiply situated, as people shift among different identities, names, and places, and assume that others do so as well.

Weaving Cloth, Hair, and the Social World

The Mende word for weaving, *f(v)ɛ*, semantically links cloth production, hair plaiting, the making of hammocks, and the making of hunting and fishing nets. Thus weaving and its products provide a crucial entry to the Mende gendered universe, as well as to the regional political economy and history in which it is embedded. In some cases, men and women separately prepare raw fibers and make and use woven objects, so that these come to stand for a segregated world of practices. This is the case for men's hunting nets and hammocks on the one hand, and for women's fishing nets on the other. Hunting and fishing, the activities for which these objects are made, appear to mark gender differences even further, but both involve common forms of entrapment, too. By contrast, the weaving of hair and that of cotton cloth stand in different ways for encompassing principles of sociality, where gender distinctions are interwoven, if not blurred. On a daily basis, hair weaving is practiced by and on women alone, and this activity is central to female beauty and values (Boone 1986: 186–192). But the condition, length, and covered or uncovered status of both men's and women's hair, at all ages, is an important indication of physical, social, and mental well-being—or of its absence.[1]

A shared feature of cloth weaving and hair plaiting is that each distinctive style is named. The names may describe patterns. For example, *stɛpi* is the name given to strip-woven cloth with a step pattern, and the *cɔnlows* hair pattern consists of small, parallel plaits braided from the forehead to the nape of the neck, like corn rows. However, plaited hair unravels and requires new styling often, whereas a blanket made of locally woven cotton can last for years—even decades or centuries—if

well cared for. This difference in durability makes hairstyles more susceptible to association with current events than is country cloth, whose patterns (perhaps because of their durability) also change less easily.[2] In this
respect, hairstyles have more in common with styles in imported clothing,
which change rapidly in tailoring and pattern to reflect the latest fashions
and thus can usually be traced back to a specific event or time.[3] Imported
fabrics have largely replaced locally woven cloth for making quality
everyday or special-occasion clothes. Though made in Europe (and more
recently in West Africa for the regional trade) for over a century, this
clothing has been earmarked for the West African market, whose tastes
have been reflected in annual pattern changes and specially commissioned designs.[4] Commemorative cloth patterns were commissioned for
special occasions, and they often showed portraits of national leaders or
international heroes with dates and insignia. In such cases, particular historical events were actually imprinted on the fabric itself![5]

CLOTH

The principal industry throughout the entire Mendi
country is the weaving of cotton into cloth. The texture
of this cloth is very durable, and the colours, being all
vegetable dyes, retain their brightness, however often
washed. This cloth is made upon a primitive native loom
in long strips only a few inches in width; of these strips
are formed the country cloths and gowns. . . .

I am sure, if these cloths were known in England they
would be much appreciated and used, especially for
portières and other hangings; but hitherto they have
been treated only as curios. This is a native industry,
which, if encouraged in England, would give
employment to thousands of people.

The up-country chiefs and people, used as they are to
cloth that will really wear, somewhat despise such cheap
and gaudy specimens of English cloth as they chanced to
see in the hands of my carriers, and they have said to me
that they were quite able to buy and pay for good cloth,
if they could get it. These Upper Mendis, if dealt with
commercially at all, should be treated honestly, and
deceived neither with regard to quantity nor quality.
This is to say, a twelve-yard piece of cloth should

measure twelve yards, and not be folded for the express
purpose of disguising its length. It would be very short-
sighted policy to do business with these shrewd people
on any other lines.
                    Alldridge (1894: 138–139; emphasis added)[6]

It is evident that the trade of Sierra Leone with the
interior is in its infancy. I saw no British calico or
muslins among the tribes I visited. They raise large
quantities of cotton and manufacture their own wearing
apparel. Until their time becomes more valuable, English
cotton goods cannot be furnished to them as cheaply as
they can make their own cloth.
                    Blyden (1872: 28)

It is perhaps paradoxical that in a book entitled *Topics in Sierra Leone
History: A Counter-Colonial Interpretation* (1976), Sierra Leone historian Arthur Abraham should agree, in placing cloth production and symbolism at the center of Mende cultural identity, with T. J. Alldridge, one
of the main and earliest agents of British imperial penetration into the
Mende hinterland. Abraham defined the Mende as "the country cloth
culture" (Abraham 1976: ch. 4). Historically, however, this strip-woven
cotton cloth (country cloth) marked the Mende integration within a
broader, regional system of relations rather than a distinctive cultural
identity. In the 1890s, Alldridge and other British colonial agents documented the use of country cloth for clothing and also as prestige gifts and
currency in Mende country. Local cotton in the form of thread on spools,
uncut strips, or blankets was sometimes preferable to money, and in the
early days of empire was used to pay taxes, fines, and debts (Abraham
1976; Edwards 1992: 143–147; Wallis 1903: 229).
   On the one hand, the economic and symbolic value of cloth in Mende
culture was linked to its ubiquitousness as a marker of social transformation, gender complementarity, and political status.[7] On the other hand,
the very objectification of country cloth as a bearer of Mende cultural
and historical values was linked first to its identity as an originally expensive foreign good made by Muslims from territories to the north of this
region, which was owned in significant quantities and sizes only by the
élites, and later to the demand for it by other, European foreigners. Thus
this most authentic product of Mende material culture marked this society's embeddedness within a larger sociopolitical and economic fabric,

as much as it represented the society's distinctive contributions to regional history.

In time, weaving also became a key element of the exhibition abroad of Mende and Sierra Leonean culture. At the 1924 British Empire Exhibition in Wembley, strip-woven cloth was central to the Sierra Leone display. Among the eight Sierra Leonean men invited to represent Sierra Leone at the exhibit, along with their wives, five were members of military, police, and local administrative bodies, and the other three were weavers. Weaving was the only activity represented live in the exhibit (Goddard 1925: 241–243; Lamb and Lamb 1984: 10).

Archeological evidence and formal similarities suggest that over the course of centuries, certain weaving patterns common in Mende and elsewhere in West Africa reached the region from northern Africa (Gilfoy 1992: 86–88). Cotton and indigo (the plant that yields the dark blue/black dye favored in many parts of West Africa) grow especially well in the savanna and oases between western and northern Africa, and thus they have been key factors in the development of long-distance trade between different regions (Brooks 1993: 55; Curtin 1975: 211–215). Historically kola nuts played a similar role on these trade routes—but in the opposite direction, because they grow in the forest region. Finally, cotton and indigo have Asian origins as, it is believed, does the horizontal loom used in local West African weaving. Thus these materials might be seen as evidence of integration within an even larger world system (Brooks ibid.).

Country cloth was the material sedimentation of centuries of interregional contacts between the forest belt of West Africa and the Mediterranean trade routes, but it also became important to relations with seafaring Europeans in the coastal West African enclaves. Both Blyden's 1872 text and the passage cited from Alldridge's observations in Mendeland in the 1890s (on page 51) suggest the keen interest British agents had in cloth. In this case, similar sentiments were expressed by a European trader-turned-administrator and by a West Indian educator and diplomat of African descent engaged on a civilizing mission to his native brethren. Both men observed how well made, attractive, and durable local cloth was and how difficult it would be to introduce Indian and British cotton imports to this potential market. Thus cotton cloth produced in the Sierra Leone hinterland was at once an object of demand by Europeans and a commodity whose production they sought to displace in order to create a market for their own trade goods.[8]

The political economy of cotton cloth in linking Mende polities with outsiders through prestige gifts, peace-making tokens (Kup 1961: 169), or currency had a gendered dimension as well. In situations where white cotton cloth was given as a gesture of peace between enemy warriors, a woman of fair complexion was said to be the preferred intermediary and carrier of this gift (Ibid.; Day 1994: 492).[9] The significance of such acts can be linked at one level to marriage: the historical record is replete with instances in which both men and women in Mende advanced their political interests by making strategic alliances wherein they "gave" female kin or dependents in marriage to powerful men (e.g., Day 1994; Hoffer 1974). But the gendered aspect of cloth's value had a lot to do with how men's and women's labor and resources were embedded in its production. Indeed, Alldridge's remark about the trickery of dishonest European traders who folded cloth in such a way as to conceal its substandard size resonates with Mende ideas about how tensions between the sexes were concealed within the folds of domestic cloth use and production. Marriage, the birth of children, and other key events in a woman's married life were supposed to be marked by a gift of cloth from her husband. Domestic conflicts often were sparked by delays in such gifts, or by the perception that a husband had "cheated" by buying smaller than standard lengths of cloth. Thus the historical role of cloth as an object of both overlapping interests and conflict between Mende and various others with whom they interacted has made this cloth an object over which both gender complementarity and difference are played out.

The phases of cotton cloth preparation, production, and consumption integrate male and female productive activities and domains. Locally woven cotton cloth is associated with Mende sociality itself, not only because of this integration of gendered symbolism and productive domains but also because of the history of cloth as prestige gift, currency, and sought-after item of trade. Women and men have complementary roles in the process of cotton preparation and cloth production. In Kpuawala, most women planted some cotton on their household's dry rice farm and harvested it in the year following the rice harvest. They also dried it, seeded, carded, spun it, and occasionally dyed it.[10] More often, weavers had to be satisfied with creating patterns out of the two natural shades in which cotton grew locally: white and light brown. During Sande initiations in Kpuawala, female elders used the labor of younger women and initiates to pick cotton in the previous year's rice farm and to seed it. Then the senior women would card and spin the cotton. Several of the prominent elderly women in Kpuawala kept spools of cotton thread in the rafters of the big houses they inhabited, as a form of wealth and as insurance against penury in hard times.

As weavers and tailors, men produced the finished cloth. This complementarity was not symmetrical, as one might argue the separate domains of fishing and hunting were. As studies in the political economy of cloth production have shown, women's ownership of, and control over, the early stages of cotton processing involves the most time-consuming and labor-intensive phases and those most easily displaced with the advent of cheap and available imported thread (e.g., Etienne 1977; Schneider 1989: 183). By contrast, men's control over the finishing stages of cloth production gives them access to greater social and economic capital.

Once an argument broke out between Mama Kema, my elderly neighbor, and Kadiatu, a woman living in the neighboring compound. Mama Kema claimed to have left Kadiatu two spools of white cotton thread before her departure, some time earlier, for her hometown in a nearby chiefdom. Upon returning, Kema went to collect her thread, only to find that Kadiatu had given one of the spools to her husband, who claimed it belonged to him. Kema was furious but said that she would not sue the man; she would let him have the cotton and "put things in front of God" for his judgment. A nearby observer of the scene commented that cotton, like chickens, was not something one could steal, because both were needed for sacrifices. Thus, she said, anyone stealing cotton would incur the wrath of beings much more powerful than its human owners. Two elderly men chimed in to explain that when one dies, one must be buried in white country cloth, and no thief would be able to find peace having stolen the thread needed to make it.

If white cloth served as a sacrificial link to the dead, white cotton thread was also used to tie a baby's umbilical cord at birth. In mourning, cotton thread also served to mark the specific relationship of a mourner to the deceased (by being worn around the neck, across the chest over one or the other shoulder, or on the right or left wrist). Thus spun, unwoven, white cotton thread conveyed specific information about the kinship and affinal ties between the living and the dead, whose body was later buried in whole, woven fabric of the same color. The links between the living were also conveyed powerfully by the weaving of thread into cloth.

One of my earliest pictures of Kpuawala shows the chief's meeting place encircled by local cotton thread, which was being wound around the building from its spools, in preparation for weaving. The weaver was the chief's elderly brother, who lived right next to the meeting place and found it convenient at that time of the day to use this public building, rather than a domestic one where people might need to enter and exit, to set up his loom and the warp's threads before beginning his work. Despite its utilitarian motivation, the symbolic import of this gesture was compelling. Here was a process, weaving, which produced a valued ceremonial and gift object, cloth, and this in turn has had a history of representation as a "key symbol" of Mende culture. But in order to produce this fabric, the community's key public space was being surrounded and enclosed by thread that had just been handed over by its female owner for this purpose.[11]

Few in Kpuawala wore clothes made of country cloth: Alldridge's century-old observation that Mende people dismissed lighter and less durable fabrics no longer held. Quite the opposite: especially in demand were ready-made clothes in synthetic fabrics that combined durability with lightness and easy care. These were bought from itinerant vendors or from traders at market towns, where they arrived after being parceled out from bales of second-hand clothes shipped into Sierra Leone through the Catholic Relief Services or businesspeople who were in the trade for profit. By contrast, country cloth blankets took much labor and soap to wash, required a whole day to dry, and in Kpuawala were available for sale only in the direst of emergencies.[12] Instead, country cloth blankets were commissioned as gifts for honored guests and for use at life cycle transitions—at initiations and weddings and especially as shrouds for burials.[13] Individual women or men who owned spools of cotton might commission a male weaver to make the cloth and would cover the food and other expenses involved in the process. Once made, however, country cloths tended to become a *collective* gift to a particular person. A household, or the matrilateral relatives, or an entire community would give a country cloth as an expression of friendship, honor, or the like. The social life of cotton, then, involved its transformation from a crop grown, processed, and owned by individual women to a male-woven and -sewn commodity sold only under duress or, more commonly, given as a gift to cement social alliances. The vicissitudes of cloth giving reflect the tensions embedded in such transformations.

On one occasion, several male Kpuawala elders approached Batoma, an elderly woman, asking her to sell them her cotton thread. They had found out through discreet inquiries with their wives and female relatives that she alone, at the moment, had an amount of spun thread sufficient to produce a blanket. They offered 40 Leones for each of three large spools (in 1985, the equivalent of some $16 U.S.), at a time when a cup of cleaned rice cost about 1.70 Leones. Batoma did not seem enthusiastic at the offer and said that she was not free to dispose of the spools as she wished, for she had already promised them to someone else. She told me in private, after the elders left, that she found their offer ridiculous in light of the cost of food and other necessities at the time. Eventually, the elders had their way and obtained the thread, putting pressure on Batoma and shaming her for her selfishness, while they wanted to make the whole community proud by giving a large, well-made country cloth as a collective gift from Kpuawala to a distinguished guest. Other women in similar situations hid their cotton spools or new blankets, claiming that these had already been given away for a relative's funeral or another important occasion. Others still preferred not even to spin the cotton into thread until it was committed for a specific purpose— and hence was beyond interception. Through these delay tactics and concealing techniques, women often could significantly interfere with social projects in which they did not have key interests and roles. On another occasion the following year, Batoma herself commissioned the making of a country cloth that she gave to a relative during an extended family gathering in which she played a key role, though her brother's entire household, with which she was living in Kpuawala, collectively participated in the gift.

Men weave cloth in Mende, and the space required to do so with the small, portable tripod looms used in Mendeland ensures that this activity generally takes place in the public spaces of settlements—the verandas in front of houses or even communal meeting places. The long cotton strip stretches across open clearings or around houses and meeting places; this is a highly visible activity in the inhabited settlement. Given this visibility and publicity, it is not surprising that someone like Travelling District Commissioner Alldridge should claim that weaving was the "principal industry" of the Mende during his wanderings in that region in the 1890s. This would certainly be the impression of a visitor who restricted his or her travels to the dry season and stayed in settlements, rather than in the surrounding territory. What did escape Alldridge, however, were the multiple, less visible strategies and labors of women embedded in this production, which were integrated into the final product and into the social relations it helped shape. Though male weavers both connected and enclosed communal public spaces with their cloth making, the fact that historically a woman was the bearer of cloth to make peace among warring parties might suggest that their less visible strategies were considered crucial to this process.

HAIR PLAITING

[T]he longest operation is the hair-dressing, which may
take some days. A woman may be seen lying on the
ground with her head in the lap of the operator, who
after combing out the wool with a strong, native
wooden comb, with little prongs, joins on other pieces of
wool that are most elaborately plaited, and continually
added to until the required height is obtained. There are
numerous designs in this hairdressing, and . . . it is quite
a science, the most common and favourite pattern rather
suggesting that curious cell-like concretion known to
geologists as the brain stone, the top being embellished
by a little silver or leather gree-gree.

Alldridge 1901: 113–114

Long, unkempt hair was considered a sign of madness in both sexes. In
this sense, then, plaited hair stood as a marker of socialization, as
opposed to madness, or "lack of sense" (*kpowa*)—a term that put the
mad in the same category as the uninitiated of either sex. As Alldridge
suggested, the pliable nature of hair, both plaited and nonplaited, also
served to secure and secrete potent objects. Like the women photographed a century earlier by Alldridge, an elderly woman in Kpuawala,
who was prone to headaches, wore woven into her loose plaits a small
pouch-encased Qur'anic amulet on a string. She seldom gave anyone the
opportunity to observe this object, because she covered her hair with a
head tie, as did most other adult women in Kpuawala. This raises an
important convergence of hair and cloth on women's head. Both were
sites for concealing small things—in the plaits of one and the folds of the
other. Many Kpuawala women kept money tucked in their headties or
concealed in a corner of their cotton wrappers. The pliability of both hair
and cotton served the purposes of concealment as well as of elaboration.
Medicinal bundles were plaited into women's hair, but in a similar manner they were woven or sewn into garments, particularly those worn by
heroic male figures such as warriors and hunters (Cisse 1964;
McNaughton 1982).[14] Thus both cloth and hair could become sites of
concealment as special objects and substances were woven into them or
hidden under them.

Cloth was woven in public spaces, but not as often as women plaited
each others' hair. This was a practice that could be observed on a daily

basis and almost anywhere women had a chance to sit down between the day's chores. A familiar scene by a cooking fire behind Kpuawala's houses, or in forest clearings, was that of a woman with her head in a friend's lap. Her woolly hair was first combed out and then transformed, under the partner's rapidly moving fingers, into an elaborate pattern of tiny plaits molded to her skull. Then the roles were reversed, or the favor was returned at a later date, in a similar manner or through other means.

Hair plaiting is the only type of weaving performed on the human body, so it has sensual dimension. As a living thread, hair grows and comes loose and hence needs to be woven again and again, thus offering repeated opportunities for this sensual experience among women. It involves oiling and massaging the scalp and is also an opportunity for relaxed gossiping. Women in Kpuawala had their hair plaited at least every two or three weeks, which made this particular form of weaving much more responsive to fashions and style changes than the two other semantically linked forms of weaving, clothweaving and net making. Each new hair-styling session was an opportunity to experiment with new designs, many of which acquired names and were associated with events surrounding their introduction to the area. When traveling to market or encountering female visitors from urban areas, women were attentive to their hairstyles and studied them in order to reproduce them at home. Thus hair weaving was more responsive to changes in style and technology (synthetic extensions, chemical products and other hair-straightening gadgets, and decorative additions such as beads) than the other forms of weaving. It inscribed the history of the moment on women's bodies, as styles took on the name of events or popular icons on the national or even global scene.

The time and attention that women spent on hair plaiting was all the more remarkable given that they then covered their heads with head ties, which made their elaborate hairdos all but invisible. Here we see at work an aesthetic of concealment at a different level. Substances with secret potency can be woven into the hair itself—in its braids—to give the head a protective or healing aura. But the beauty of the new hair design is also concealed, under a scarf, as though it did not need to be displayed to exert its attraction. Women often said that finely braided hair was one of the key elements in seducing men, but they saw no contradiction in the fact that they kept it mostly covered. On the contrary, they thought it sufficient that their beautiful hairstyles be visible only for a few moments, as they took off and rearranged their scarves, for them to have the desired effect. However, the head ties concealed the opposite of beauty too, for they covered unmade, loose hair when women did not have time to have it braided. Thus an aspect of the attraction in the dissimulation of women's hairdos was the element of unpredictability and surprise as to whether the concealed hair was plaited at all, let alone in which style.

Taming hair through its weaving into plaits, then, was a crucial move for those, like women, who tended to have it long. Another feature of hair plaiting noted earlier is that it is often a way of incorporating extraneous objects into one's hairdo. In the nineteenth century, Alldridge observed that cotton, silver gree-grees (casings for Qur'anic amulets), shells, and other objects were woven into women's hairdos in a decorative manner. The more modern and cosmopolitan Kpuawala women had plastic extensions, colored beads, or other objects in style at the time woven into their hair. But although the aim of adding these bright decorations was to extend one's hair and attract attention to it, the way in which small, black-encased amulets were woven into it (for example, to heal headaches) suggests that in other contexts things had to be concealed under hair to work effectively. In these cases, the dressed head did not act as the clothed body did, to publicly display the weaver's status and identity, but instead acted like a cap, under which things were secreted.

New hairstyles have further enhanced the possibilities of hair as both bodily adornment and cover. In Kpuawala an alternative to hair plaiting was the use of hot irons and creams for straightening purposes. The only context in which I observed this practice was in preparation for the ceremony marking the end of Sande initiation. For the occasion, initiates whose hair was straightened also wore dress styles and accessories that conveyed a cosmopolitan sophistication, after earlier rituals had emphasized their skills in traditional dance, song, and appearance (see Ferme 1994). When I commented on the fact that this appeared to be one context in which women deliberately sought to loosen their hair from the braids that ordinarily decorated their heads, and yet did not appear to be considered mad, I was told that I was mistaken in using the word, "loose" (fulɔ, also "untied"). The techniques for performing this straightening operation, with heat and substances added to the hair, made this a controlled act—one that despite its appearance did not contradict the identification among women's attractiveness, tightly plaited hair, and more encompassing Mende ideas of social order.

Hunting Nets on the Perimeter of the Meeting Place (1990)

CHAPTER 2

Ambiguity and Gendered Practices

Hindo womia a mbomɛi, nyaha ndɛi mia a gbɛhɛŋ.
Hammocks belong to men, stools to women.

Mende proverb

Proverbs embody apparently transparent declarations of cultural ideals and seek to establish the boundaries of legitimacy.[1] In particular, they enunciate the gap between the ideal order of culture and the historical contingency within which the lives of social actors unfold. Rules of propriety spell out principles of social organization in forms that mimic the cultural modalities through which groups are excluded from, and included in, particular domains. For example, the proverb about hammocks and stools quoted above lays out the rules of propriety concerning gendered objects and postures. However, normative statements often enunciate zones of ambiguity and transgression, where these same boundaries are in fact overcome in the context of practice. This apparent contradiction between cultural ideals and actual practices sheds light on how social actors incorporate social norms, but it also points to what are most likely to be ambiguous sites of contestation.

The cultural prescriptions that identify certain domains or objects with oppositional gender symbolism are ideal configurations of desirable bodily postures, moral qualities, and spatial proximity and orientations. In turn, these techniques of the body produce and reproduce a repertoire of unreflexive gestures into which social actors are socialized, which only in times of crisis emerge into consciousness and become the subject of explicit commentary (and transgression). In particular, in this chapter I look at the shifting meanings of objects such as stools and hammocks within the articulation of a Mende social space in order to grasp the temporary gestures and performances through which gender domains are made and unmade. I also examine the discourse that links cultural prohibitions to military readiness and to attributes like braveness, which are considered essential in warfare but are also deployed in the hierarchical valuation of personal attributes in peacetime. Hence the naïve division of the world between senseless women and brave men masks a cultural strategy that tends to elide these distinctions when they most matter—that is, in states of emergency where life itself is at stake.

In Wunde, women could not sit in hammocks for the duration of the men's Poro society initiations. This prohibition extended to female chiefs—that is, to office holders who in other ways had greater latitude in transgressing gender boundaries. Variants of this rule existed in other parts of Mendeland and had historical precedents as well. During his journey in the interior to secure treaties with local chiefs for the British government, Alldridge noted that one female chief, though injured in her leg, refused to travel in a hammock (Alldridge 1901: 256). The general understanding in Kpuawala was that hammocks were more appropriate for men because they were brave and attuned enough to the possibility of danger to rise instantly, even from a state of sleep, in response to animal or human aggression. People referred to the attribute that I translate as bravery as "having a firm, steady heart" (nu li longɔ). By contrast, women were said to be "senseless," lazy, or weak. The Mende word used, hawangɔ, had connotations of moral and political, and not necessarily physical, weakness. Women were said to sit on low stools near the ground because they needed to take a posture that would keep them alert at all times; otherwise, they would not have the strategically appropriate response to situations of danger. The slow response on the part of women was a matter of judgment. For example, in a court case involving a woman accused by her husband of aggressive behavior, a man argued that women didn't necessarily lack the passion, or "hot heart" (ndima gbandi), to risk life and limb in response to sudden threats but that they often lacked the judgment to make instant decisions that could save lives. Switching to Krio, the national lingua franca, to emphasize the point, the man said, "Den no gɛt sɛns"—they lack (good) sense/judgment. Thus even the most ordinary moral order and attributes were framed with a view to strategic readiness and the possibility of conflict. The fact that women have been the main victims and among the leaders in war in this region—both historically (Brooks 1993: 306) and in the present (Human Rights Watch 1999: 48, 53)—underscores the extent to which social practices both reproduce and transgress such cultural ideals.

These cultural oppositions—between gender domains, objects, and moral qualities—point to a classificatory logic whose formal opposition is more important than the actual content (e.g., see Bourdieu 1990b: 86 ff.; Lévi-Strauss 1966: 75). However, the same oppositional classification produces through its very existence an order that was not already there. It has a performative role, producing and reproducing a hegemonic order in which women's powers are subordinated. As Judith Butler reminds us, gestures, rules, and ritualized enactments make up a gendered reality; they create a social fact in the process of its fabrication (Butler 1990: 136). The performance of gender differences works in part through processes of exaggeration that, depending on the context, can strengthen gender boundaries but also undermine their clarity.

Thus the logic of "exaggerated" prohibitions regulating gendered patterns of seclusion and subordination must also be questioned, as anthropologists have done (e.g., Abu-Lughod 1990; Ardener 1972; Cooper 1997; Moore 1986). In particular, the analysis of societies where gender segregation is most visible has shown the importance of shifting the focus from the spatial domains to which women might or might not gain access, to the resources they (or other groups apparently excluded from culturally valued domains) have at their disposal to move across, and challenge, social boundaries of a higher order. The fact that women's physical mobility may be restricted in some settings does not necessarily hinder their social and political mobility—for example, as owners of capital and of expensive, rent-producing urban properties—in spaces that might be inaccessible to others with fewer visible constraints (Cooper 1997: 218; White 1990). The exaggerated performance of female absence from certain social spaces reproduces their exclusion but also dissimulates the extent to which they might be otherwise present.

In Wunde, examples of the tension between the production of gender boundaries and processes that undermined them were legion. Soon after my arrival in Kpuawala, the women's Sande society began its initiation session, and at one point during the following weeks, women took over the "B.B.C.," the largest and most frequented meeting place in Kpuawala.[2] This was an unusual gesture: women could be found in meeting places at the center of the five Kpuawala compounds, but their own socialization in groups took place in cooking huts and big houses located on the perimeters of the village's inhabited spaces. The fact that in the course of the initiation they occupied a meeting place visibly, in large numbers and while explicitly declaring them off limits to men, must be seen in relation to the situations in which such was not the case. By this I mean not only that one must analyze situations in which men were visibly in control of meeting places, which were quite common, but also that one needs to ask how this exaggerated display of gender exclusiveness might mask contexts in which the occupancy of meeting places centered around different axes of social differentiation. In this case, the occupation of the meeting place had as much to do with political strategies linked to the concept of chiefship as it did with gender politics, as was suggested by the idiom deployed in the context of initiation. For the duration of the initiation, Sande women kept the B.B.C. meeting place occupied, and eventually the newly initiated girls were brought there from the initiation bush on the margins of town, to sit as "new chiefs" (*maha ninɛi*) for the last three days before the final coming-out ceremonies. During this permanence in the meeting place, different seating arrangements pointed to hierarchical distinctions among women: though named new chiefs and showered with admiration and gifts by families and friends, the new initiates sat or lay on mats on the ground. By contrast, senior Sande women sat in hammocks.

Thus the fact that women occupied Kpuawala's main public space pointed at one level to their appropriation of an ordinarily male domain. However, this event also indicated that hammocks and public meeting places had polysemic meanings that were not exhausted by gender symbolism. These meanings encompassed gender symbolism but also pointed to a range of covert associations that could be appropriated by either men or women, depending on the context.[3] Hammocks and meeting places were the sites where political, administrative, and legal disputes concerning the community as a whole were apparently negotiated and resolved. This required skills of political mediation that extended far beyond the visible and public confines of these open spaces into the concealed sites where deals were more openly discussed. Despite the strategic location of these public sites in the center of village quarters, where everyone could see and hear sociopolitical and legal transactions, effective political mediation required constant displacement between these spaces and less visible ones. For example, as I have discussed elsewhere, the local outcome of the 1986 national elections, in which a relatively less experienced politician unseated a powerful incumbent, must be understood in light of this tension between overt and covert political mediations (Ferme 1999). Despite the fact that most public statements of support uttered in the constituency's meeting places were in favor of the incumbent, the challenger managed to strategically marginalize the political consensus around his opponent by rendering ineffective that visible space of the political. He successfully manipulated sites and social alliances that were marginal and less visible with respect to the centers of power to build strong, unpredictable political support. His ascension to power was the result of a deep understanding of mediations between visible and less visible orders of power.

The ceremonial occupation of the meeting place (and of its hammocks) by Sande women was a symbolic statement about the effective nature of female power over sites identified only partially as male domains. The shifting meaning of meeting places had to do with the fact that they were also sites of sacred and sacrificial practices, where unexpected transgressions could take place. It is within this conceptual order that one must understand the exclusion of all dangerous weapons from the meeting place, encapsulated in the formal prohibition against bringing cutlasses and guns within its perimeters. Thus the deception, or ambiguity, of the sacred—namely that it tends to defer the violence within its confines by making itself appear to be the only site of practices that can lead to the avoidance of violence (see Girard 1972: 386). Indeed, the explicit goal of most sacrificial and political practices that unfold in the meeting place is to achieve social cohesion, mediate conflict, and hence avert violence. And yet this was a site where violence commonly erupted. Thus one of the dimensions of the gender ambiguity of spaces and objects such as meeting places, hammocks, and stools is their relationship to cosmology and a political economy of the sacred, which situate ambiguity at the very core of these symbolically loaded sites.[4]

In this way gendered practices become strategically centered on meeting places, even outside of ritual contexts, and on objects associated with them, because they share with them the ambiguity and potential violence embedded in all sites linked to the realm of the sacred. At the same time they are sites for performing a polysemic array of significations around the understanding of a hierarchically ordered social world. However, the social world can be both made *and* unmade by the play of polysemy that undermines univocal meanings of stable gendered and hierarchical identities. Hence the role of the meeting place as a site where violence can be unleashed *or* contained.

The strategic uses of polysemy have emerged at the analytical center of debates from the perspective of symbolic anthropology and of a historically informed political economy (i.e., "the social life of things").[5] From these perspectives, objects and spaces are not to be seen as empty containers into which social actors infuse meaning but, rather, as sites whose material conditions of production also resist interpretations. To pursue this kind of analysis, it is necessary to follow objects through their production and up to their concrete, historical circulation. However, the historical circulation of objects, at both the discursive and the spatial level, invests them with new layers of meaning, including gendered ones, which render the very social world in which they unfold more permeable and fluid. The point, then, is to follow the analysis of objects and spaces through the temporary and fleeting gestures that shape them, without reducing them to intelligible and totalizing (synchronic) units of analysis (see Certeau 1984: 97).

THE MATERIALITY OF GENDER

Once produced by elderly men—often under commission by younger men, who provide the raw materials for the project (mostly palm leaves)—hammocks were generally hung in the meeting place, though they could also be located in the verandas and parlors of houses. In these places, hammocks were generally stationary and reserved for their own-ers. By contrast, stools were mobile objects carried by their owners from the residential compounds to meeting places, to cooking areas, and beyond the village to the farm. In the meeting place hammocks were available to anyone who came by and wanted to rest in them, even though each had a recognized owner. But men who owned hammocks in the meeting place were not free to do as they pleased with them: they were responsible for maintaining them (keeping them safe and usable for other members of the community) and for replacing them once they had frayed beyond repair. This was true of hunting nets as well. These were stored in the rafters of the meeting place so that they would be available to the community as a whole in case of need. Each extended household had at least one net—something that would assure it a part of the prey regardless of whether members participated in the hunt or not, because it was customary to give the net owner a share. Thus, although meeting places were at one level a male socializing place, at another level they were considered a space for collective conduct of affairs—whether politi-cal, administrative, or legal.

By contrast, stools had no fixed associations with a particular site. Women took stools with them, even on journeys and, when needed, to augment seating capacity in meeting places. However, the one place in which stools looked incongruent was the meeting place, outside of the con-text of large political gatherings and of major disputes. Like old hammocks, aging stools were moved out of town to the temporary cooking huts built seasonally on rice farms. The spatial removal of aging hammocks, stools, and other domestic furniture and implements from meeting places to residential areas and eventually to village cooking houses and farm huts (both of which share the same name) put them on a trajectory that linked the primary sites of social life in the inhabited settlement to those where sociality was inscribed in a more temporary and unstable manner, if not reversed.

Women commissioned the making of stools from elderly men in a manner analogous to the way men of all ages commissioned hammocks. They provided materials, unless they chose to have more durable, wooden stools, which were often gifts from male relatives who had access to leftover materials and tools from carpentry work. Husbands often made stools with rattan and cane from the swampy areas near rice paddies. Unlike hammocks and women's fishing nets, however, stools were not woven, but made (*gbatɛ*). As a process of production, then, making stools was not placed in the same category as weaving hammocks and hunting and fishing nets.

The association of gendered attributes with different objects implied an oppositional distinction between productive and reproductive practices. This link was made strongly through the juxtaposition in language between these objects and others classed with them, which were used in gendered practices. Hammocks belonged to the same category as hunting nets used in the bush and the large nets used by men for deep-water fishing. These nets were made with techniques similar to those used in crafting hammocks, except that knots were made at every hole to keep a net's dimensions fixed and prevent the animal's escape. However, although each meeting place had at least one hunting net, fishing nets were more rare. The latter were individually owned, usually by men who lived near large rivers. Also, the preferred material for making deep-water fishing nets was nylon, which lasted much longer in a wet environment than raffia but was expensive and hence was within reach of only a few. Like hunting nets, however, these fishing nets could be deployed effectively only by several people and in the context of communal fishing parties. This, we shall see, distinguishes them from the sociality and technology of women's fishing.

Thus, the semantic link with hunting was built into the production of hammocks and nets. It was a practice that took place at the center of the village, and hence at a remove from the bush. The symbolic weaving together of village and bush in the production of hunting nets underscored the intimate relationship between these sites. This linkage had a distinctively political nature as well, for the success of this particular kind of hunt—unlike that involving the use of guns—was predicated on collective goodwill. When men did not respond to the town crier's call for a hunt, it was taken to be one of the first signs of political dissent and potential instability. Consequently, the failure to show up for a hunting expedition brought on serious punishment, as did any negligence in the course of an expedition.

FISHING NETS

On my very first visit to Kpuawala, I was sat down in the evening by a group of women, and made to try my hand at this activity. You are a woman—I was told—so of course you must know how to *mbembei vɛ*, how to weave a fishing net. That and spinning cotton thread—which was indispensable to a different kind of weaving, the men's weaving of cloth—were the two practices that rural Mende women considered central to their everyday worlds.[6] In contrast with the simplicity of men's net- and hammock weaving, the women's making of scoop nets was recognized as being a technically more complicated achievement.

Scoop nets gradually took shape by being woven in the form of a basket onto a skeleton of pliant cane slivers, which were broken and extracted once the desired size was reached. The basket grows from its narrower bottom, or anus (*tokpula*) toward a wider mouth (*nda*), which gets permanently stretched onto an oval rattan frame once the net is woven. This frame keeps the net's mouth open, and its aperture can be adjusted by tightening or loosening a string connecting its waist, or middle section (*nd/lia*), which also makes it possible to carry the net on one's shoulder. The string for making fishing nets is the *mani*, which is made into twine in a manner similar to what men do in preparation for hammock making. However, it comes from a shorter leaf, that of the oil palm leaf, and remains green even after it dries. Like the hammock, women's scoop nets have hardly any knots that might keep holes at a fixed size. Instead, their stitches are made up of several passages around the reed and into string loops, and the sheer density of this intricate weaving limits the capacity of the net's small holes to expand; they can efficiently trap even small fish and crabs.

Individual women made, owned, and used their particular fishing nets, which came in two sizes. The smaller, more common size was intended to be handled by a single person, whereas the double, "twin" size (*fele*) was intended to be used with a partner. Unlike hunting nets, women's fishing nets were tied to individual owners. Women spoke of the "marks" on their nets and used these to identify their own among a pile of nets left to dry after a fishing expedition or in disputes over ownership. They would point to a small colored bead in a hidden spot toward the net's bottom or to the strands of a different vegetal fiber that created a distinctive, though subtle, color pattern against the darker green of *mani*, the palm leaf string used in this process. These identifying features were seldom obvious to the casual observer and thus were all the more effective as markers of rightful ownership: only the person who had devised them knew how they were patterned. Women also smeared the net's inside with their own secret medicines, a combination of esoteric substances and spoken formulas. These had the purpose of bringing them luck by drawing in and entrapping fish. Here too, because invisible, potent medicines needed to be activated through particular gestures and words, they worked via an order of concealment to visibly identify their legitimate owners.

Fishing nets were shared, but one had to be granted permission to use someone else's net. Some women went to considerable lengths to prevent others from taking their nets without asking for them. On one occasion, I was shown a trap built into the bottom of a fishing net and designed to render it ineffective in the wrong person's hands. One Kpuawala woman had made her net so that its anus would open under the weight of any catch unless a hidden string was tied properly before a fishing expedition. Anybody who took the net without its owner's permission would find it useless for its purpose, and at the same time, her transgression would be publicly unmasked. Though the fact that she was the only woman, to my knowledge, to have made such a device, suggests that this concealed trap may be an individual technological innovation rather than a widespread feature of fishing nets, it was consistent with other, more widespread techniques for concealing identifying features that could expose illegitimate users.

The anthropomorphic language attached to the *mbembei*,[7] its individuality as an object marked with identifying features, and its status as the property of particular women, link it to individual female identity. In this, women's scoop nets differ from men's hunting nets. There were some parallels with hammocks in the meeting place: men often checked the point where a hammock was connected to the ropes hanging permanently in the meeting place to make sure that it was well attached. A trick sometimes played by a man's enemy was to loosen the knot or twist the knob through which his hammock was secured to the rafters, so that his weight would make the hammock collapse to the ground. But in its relationship to the activity for which it was made, the fishing net stood in opposition to the hunting net.

The opening of the fishing net's concealed trap makes it useless as a tool for fishing, as well as unmasking its illegitimate user. In one of the *Ndɔgbɔsui* tales I heard in Kpuawala, the fishing net acts similarly, as a trap to unmask the shape-shifter's trickery. One of the ways to escape the *Ndɔgbɔsui*'s entrapment was to reply appropriately to its riddles. To the question "how to carry water?" one had to reply, "with a scoop net." This would make the task of carrying water endless, and the *Ndɔgbɔsui*'s identity would eventually be unmasked—a knowledge that could save its potential victim.

The concealment of a string (*ngeyei*), which can cause the net's unraveling, echoed the Mende cosmology of the female body. Other concealed strings and nets were crucial to controlling the flow of life-giving (and conversely, life-threatening) agencies over the thresholds of women's bodies. This was particularly the case when these bodies were in the reproductive and sexually active stages of their lives. Thus Sande elders, through the powers of their concealed medicines, controlled the fertility and sexuality of initiates by "opening" their bodies, by performing clitoridectomies at the beginning of initiation. This operation was referred to as "cutting the string." Indeed, the emphasis on water and fishing was central to both Sande initiation and childbirth. Songs performed during the first night of Sande initiation spoke of "crossing the water" to reach the whitest clay. This was a reference to the water holes where white kaolin clay was found, which was the visible marker of the Sande initiate's status, because she kept her body smeared in this substance from face to feet for the duration of her initiation. Furthermore, the associations among women's initiation, water, and fishing in particular was underscored by the fact that the initiates' excised labia were called with the same name as a small, common fish caught in traps and in women's nets.

The link between fishing nets and fertility was made even more explicitly in the context of childbirth, where the image of controlled unraveling, or untying, was joined by that of the fishing net as a container sealed with potent medicines. Mende midwives, who operate in the secrecy of Sande, are called *mavulɔmɔ*, a term that means both "to speed up" (*mavulɔ*, "quickly"), and "to untie" (*f/vulɔ*). With her medicines, the midwife lubricates the woman's bodily threshold in order to speed up—to facilitate—the delivery of a child. But here too the flow over bodily thresholds must be controlled, so that in the process, needed vital substances do not leave the body or dangerous ones enter it. In one difficult delivery after which midwives had trouble stopping the new mother's internal bleeding, a fishing net that was judged to have particularly effective medicine in it was removed from its frame and placed under the recovering woman as she lay on a mat on the ground. Thus, although in some contexts nets may conceal traps in their bottoms, and thus unexpectedly lose control over their contents, in others they can act as solid containers, through which even fluids do not pass, or, in the very passing of their contents they can help reveal masked realities of a different order—as in the *Ndɔgbɔsui* story.

HUNTING AND FISHING

I have earlier discussed the links between hunting and warfare in the figure of the *kamajɔ*, who wanders in the forest with his gun in search of prey, often alone and at night. Such a hunter seeks to control the threshold between the visible and the invisible orders. However, the *kamajɔ* is not associated with net hunting, which is a diurnal, collective practice involving, at different levels, the whole community.[8] By contrast with the isolated practice of the nocturnal hunter, daytime hunting with nets was organized at the village level whenever the Paramount Chief requested food contributions for visiting dignitaries. One such occasion was the visit to the chiefdom of the District Officer for the annual tax collection; another was the hosting of census officials (1985) or of electoral commissioners (1986). Thus both the occasion and the mode of carrying out hunting parties further strengthened the links between these practices and the community's integration within a hierarchical order of political and social networks.

By contrast, women went fishing collectively during the day, but each individual had her own scoop net (*mbembei*) and kept what she caught for domestic consumption. Scoop nets are placed with their mouths up against the bank of streams or water pools. Women hold them in place with their upper bodies, while their hands explore out front the muddy hiding places of fish, crabs, and other water creatures to push them into the net. This is a dangerous endeavor, for harmful thorns or water snakes can be concealed in muddy waters. At the slightest motion the net is scooped up, and after all the water runs out, the solids left in the bottom—trapped by its anus—are examined. Live creatures are picked out and tossed in the hourglass-shaped basket (*piye)* that women sling for this purpose around their shoulder and then the dirt that also got scooped up is thrown out before the fishing resumes (see page 80).

Just as Sande midwives applied esoteric medicine to pregnant women's bellies and inside their vaginas to control the birthing process, so secret substances properly smeared inside the net—its "belly" (*kohu*)—were believed to enable it to contain more fish. The fish catch could then be picked out from the net through its mouth, unless it was lost uncontrollably through its anus in the hands of a thief. In an analogous manner, only the net whose mouth was open, and whose anus and loops were sealed by potent, esoteric medicine, could effectively control the body of a woman after childbirth. The potency of fishing medicine was activated in water, through a process of dissolution and dissimulation. Thus, although dry fishing nets could be stored in different places, wet ones could not be brought into the village or inside houses, because they were believed to retain some of their potent effects and hence to endanger humans. Wet nets were left to dry behind cooking huts, along the paths leading into villages, and even hanging in trees. Like hunting nets, fishing nets were stored in places where they were easily accessible. But whereas the exposed location of hunting nets truly had to do with accessibility in the sense that the object could be used by anyone, women's fishing nets were only apparently accessible. Their casual storage along the settlement's perimeter reflected the knowledge that invisible identifying features and powerful medicinal protections bound them to individual owners as securely as if they had been locked inside houses.

Fishing and hunting expeditions entail different interpretations of the social world of practice. Whereas hunting is tied to the vicissitudes of the political and social hierarchy—the demands of chiefs on their subjects and on these subjects' extended households—fishing is organized informally. The implications of hunting for social exchange are underscored by the location of nets in the meeting places where *anyone* can grab them to join in an expedition, by contrast with the individual or paired use of fishing nets. Ownership patterns are different as well, for even though individual men commission the making of hunting nets, they are considered the responsibility of entire households.

Both net hunting and fishing expeditions were predominantly collective affairs. However, only women participated in the latter, and the atmosphere was very different. Women would sing, gossip, and joke, often at the expense of men, as they waded into ponds and rivers in search of fish. By contrast, collective hunting was done in absolute silence, and communication took place through gestures so as not to alert the prey of the party's presence. Eventually, noise was needed to scare the prey toward the waiting nets, but this took the form of loud shouting in a limited section of the large circle formed around the animal's lair, and it was orchestrated by the beater. The lot of making noise by shouting and shaking branches fell to younger boys, elderly men, and the rare woman who went along on the hunting expedition. The beater or "land person" (ndɔlɔ mɔ) went ahead into the bush with dogs to identify animal lairs. His specialized role was the closest one to that of the kamajɔ in the domain of net hunting, because he was supposed to have special knowledge of animal habits and superior skill in identifying their traces in the landscape.

Indeed, Joe, the man who usually took this role in Kpuawala hunting expeditions, was also a skilled kamajɔ who went out at night to hunt on his own, with his dogs and a borrowed gun. During the civil war, when the Paramount Chief in the neighboring chiefdom organized men into a hunters' militia, Joe became the leader of the Kpuawala group. Thus skills in different forms of hunting were not mutually exclusive, because all hunting activities required similar skills in vision and dissimulation—in identifying the whereabouts of animals while disguising one's own. Besides being the local beater, Joe also owned and controlled the dogs used for collective hunts. But his hunting dogs were not considered particularly good, so sometimes a "dog person" (ngila mɔ) with his own animals was called in from a village farther south. This man, who was known as a particularly skilled animal handler, went along with Joe to explore a potential hunting site. Once the scouting was done, the beater/dog person returned to the village and called on people to follow in silence—first the able-bodied and agile men who were assigned to the nets (mbomabla) and then the "noise people" (sɔlɛbla), mostly elderly men and boys. In the bush the beater was in charge. Men walked in single file with nets until they were motioned in silence to take up positions at regular intervals in a large circle. Each had to deploy his net, propped up from the ground to about waist level with sticks and low branches—the gɛgbɛwuli of Vandi's riddle (see Chapter 1)—and then stay alert with his cutlass, ready to fall upon any animal that might head his way. Other men made barriers with cut branches to fill in gaps between nets, and these sections were often occupied by noise people, who tried to scare the prey toward the nets. Once the circle was closed, the dogs were let loose in it, and the hunt was on.

This careful division of labor was reflected in how the prey was partitioned when it was *not* turned over whole to town or chiefdom authorities for important collective events. The beater and dog owner shared parts of the animal's back. In the human anatomy, this part of the body was associated with kin and ancestors who were "behind" people (*poma*, "back, corpse"). Thus this particular allocation of the prey suggests a link between the beater's thorough familiarity with the bush and animal habits, and the ancestors buried in the land, whose intervention was crucial to acquiring such knowledge. By contrast, the net person who had actually killed the animal received its internal organs, belly, and head. These parts, which in all animals were considered the tastier ones, were shared with the net's owner, if he happened to be a different person. The rest of the animal was divided in small pieces among all participants in the hunt, although often an entire leg was reserved for the town leadership.

The hierarchical organization of hunting, and the partitioning of the game captured, contrast starkly with fishing expeditions. These are more common and are organized on an almost daily basis during the early weeks of the dry season. Women of every status and level of expertise participate, but each woman fishes for herself, unless she is sharing a double scoop net with a friend. Women join and leave the group at their pleasure, without incurring any sanctions. The instruments for their fishing are more directly and individually linked to them than the fewer, collectively owned hunting nets, but by the same token, the organization of this activity appears to be more egalitarian, informal, and spontaneous than the hunting expedition. Thus the differentiation of the social world through the material properties of hunting and fishing practices—how they are carried out, how the prey is allocated, and so on—contributes to the formation of gender distinctions, by reaffirming the moral qualities presumed to reside in specific gender attributes.

In the next section, I show the concretization of gender ambiguity in the *maböle*, a ritual role in which the porousness of gender boundaries becomes visible. The *maböle* stands for a cultural "middle region" that contains "messily combined elements of both sexes" (Bledsoe 1984: 465) without resolving the dialectical tension between them. Here gender boundaries are zones of indeterminacy where stable identities are up for grabs.

"BOTH MAN AND WOMAN": THE *Maböle*

The *maböle* complicates the picture given thus far of cultural prohibitions about gender domains and the oppositional classification of social practices linked to them. Here is the one woman who in the midst of Poro initiation can and does sit in hammocks and who may go unchallenged on hunting expeditions with men, without ever fitting comfortably in with them in any straightforward manner. For at the same time, she goes fishing with women and makes her own fishing nets. However, she is perceived as a marginal member of both the fishing community of women and the hunting community of men. As I show in what follows, there are both social advantages and disadvantages in the *mabɔle*s identity as a sign of "gender trouble." On the one hand, she can use her marginality to be a powerful mediator between opposing parties. On the other hand, she can be unpredictably excluded from the most sacred events for the community, and her belonging in any particular setting is often a matter of contestation.

Walter Rodney has suggested that the role of the *mabɔle* as a high-ranking female official within the men's Poro society was linked to a shift during the seventeenth century in women's political role in the Upper Guinea Coast:

> Mobora, the sister of Farma Bouré, was one of the most outstanding political figures in Sierra Leone during the early seventeenth century. Her authority was attributed partly to the fact that, had she been a man, she would have been king, and partly to her own personal qualities. Recalling that the Mane movement was at the outset supposedly led by a woman, it could be that behind the Mane kings there was a female figure in the capacity of "queen mother." Whether there was any such institution or not, very high status was obviously accorded to some Mane women, which would have strengthened the female secret societies, as well as allowing them to play some role in the preponderantly male societies.
>
> (*Rodney 1970: 66*)

Rodney traces an etymological link between thie title *mabɔle* and the name of the sister of Farma Bouré, a leader of the Mane invasions at the origin of the Mende occupation of the region they currently inhabit (see also Little 1951: 245). There is in the scholarly literature no consensus on the origin and status of the *mabɔle*. For one colonial official, she was a woman initiated into Poro after having accidentally learned the society's secrets (e.g., Alldridge 1901: 133), whereas others have seen in this role little more than that of a substitute mother who cooked and cared for Poro initiates (Bellman 1980: 64). Caroline Bledsoe has noted in the *mabɔle* the very manifestation of the "messiness" of the boundaries between Sande and Poro in practice, despite an ideology of clear-cut oppositions (1984). The gist of her argument is that the reason for such ideological clarity is the absence of transparent gender distinctions in practice, where ambiguous zones of overlap are abundant. The role of the *mabɔle*, however, raises more intricate questions about the performative dimension of gender, to which I now turn.

In the 1985 Sande initiation in Kpuawala, Hawa, one of the initiates, was taken before the end of the seclusion period and handed over to men in the bush, for initiation into Poro. Having gone into the Sande bush, she never was "pulled out" of it.[9] Hawa came from a family of *mabɔlesia* (the plural form), which included her paternal grandmother Jenne, who also lived in Kpuawala. Part of the reason why she was being initiated into Sande was that she was going to marry a prominent local Poro man, who was rumored to be a skilled performer of the *Gɔbɔ* masquerade.[10] Hawa entered Sande and thus underwent the clitoridectomy that marks this first stage of initiation. She also appeared with her Sande cohort in the *Gani*, the first public appearance of initiates after their induction, marking the end of full seclusion. The timing of Gani is shaped by cosmological and pragmatic reasons, the latter being the conclusion of the healing process in the aftermath of clitoridectomy. However, this is never articulated, because excision belongs to the register of Sande secrecy. After the Gani, initiates may come and go from the bush during the day to work on the farms of families or Sande elders, but for the purpose of recognition they must wear white clay smeared on their bodies and white head ties. At night they return to the seclusion of the Sande bush until the final pulling-out ceremony. Sometime during this period, Hawa was "taken" by Poro men for them to initiate her among their own. This was the language used by some of the female bystanders who noticed Hawa's absence from her cohort at the end of Sande initiation, but in fact the society's elders would have had to hand her over to Poro officials consensually. At the pulling out of Sande initiates, Hawa was not among the girls who were sitting in state for three days in one of Kpuawala's meeting places.

Instead, upon returning to the village from the Poro bush, Hawa was treated like male initiates of that society, who sit for *four* days in their best finery to be admired, praised, and showered with gifts—a "male" number explicitly contrasted with the three days spent in a similar manner by Sande initiates. Because Hawa was alone, the men had set her up in the veranda of a senior man's house in the village. Men visited Hawa in her separate space, addressing her as *ndakpɛi*, the familiar term of address used among male age-mates. By contrast, women (including myself) were explicitly prohibited from seeing her at this time, *jifa hindo mia angie*, because she was a man. However, although the distinctive bodily feature of male Poro initiates was their shaved heads, which they covered with caps or scarves at the end of initiation, Hawa's hair was left intact. She thus maintained a key marker of femininity despite her incorporation within Poro. *After* this event, Hawa married, had children, and joined her senior co-wives in their everyday productive practices. The only contexts in which she was distinguished in any way from the rest of her Sande cohort was on ritual occasions involving Sande secret knowledge. Thus, for example, during later Sande initiations in Kpuawala, Hawa never approached the enclosure inhabited by initiates and society elders, let alone participated in their celebrations.

Although she lived in one of the "big houses" occupied by the village's women and children, Hawa left this space when secret meetings were convened there or when it became the site of activities concealed from men, such as childbirth. The paradox here was that she herself eventually went through the experience of childbirth and yet was not allowed to witness Sande elders practicing midwifery and using secret Sande medicine. This instance points to yet another way in which a distinction is made between the register of immediate experience and that of esoteric knowledge, which is not presumed to derive from the former in any direct way. The fact that Hawa had given birth did not imply that in that context she would have learned the secrets of midwifery.

The distinction drawn in Mende between the register of experience and visibility on the one hand, and on the other hand the practices of dissimulation and esoteric knowledge that imparted depth of meaning to that register, was embodied in the *mabɔle*'s paradoxical position. I was once in a Kpuawala big house with a group of Sande women assisting Jebe, a young girl who was going through labor for the first time. We suddenly realized that Jenne—also a *mabɔlɛ* and Hawa's grandmother— was resting in her bed not far from where we were. A woman called Batoma addressed her as *ndakpɛi*, the term used among young male age-mates, and said, "Go smoke your pipe outside! You know that men cannot be in here." After meekly protesting, Jenne left, muttering, "We men hate this sort of crowd." Batoma turned apologetically toward us, explaining that the only reason Jenne was allowed to sleep in the big house at all was that there wasn't a bed for her elsewhere. Another female elder approached and assured me that Jenne "did not come to the *kpanguima*" (the enclosure erected for the women's Sande initiation) because she was a man. Later Jenne returned, begging to be allowed to rest, and was told to lie facing the wall, away from the events unfolding in the center of the room, and to stay concealed behind the dark cloth that served as her mosquito net. By the time I came back just before dawn for the delivery, Jenne had been told to rise and leave once more and had already gone for a walk.

Jenne's interaction with other women bespeaks more than the cultural differentiation of gender roles and domains. For one thing, *mabɔlesia* like Jenne and Hawa participate in the social roles typically associated with both genders: they are excluded only from women's ritual domains and from the spheres of ordinary practices on which secret knowledge bears most directly. Within Poro, they bring feminine elements. For example, they bring the cooling capacities historically linked to female mediators in wartime, and they splatter medicines over the "hot-hearted" *Gɔbɔ*—the Poro masquerade that comes to town at the end of male initiations. In addition, *mabɔlesia* are said to have quasi-maternal roles in the Poro initiation bush, ensuring that young members are properly fed and cared for. In their ordinary lives, *mabɔlesia* (as we have seen) share with other women the experience of marriage and childbirth, as well as carrying out the same daily chores in farming, food processing, and cooking. Thus it is impossible to clearly identify the gender of the *mabɔlesia*, for male and female attributes blend into each other in a way that does not permit the resolution of tension.

The analysis of the *mabɔle*'s role in Poro suggests that she is a figure of gender mediation and tension. Men may very well bring along a *mabɔle* on a hunting expedition, but she also makes fishing nets and goes after fish with the rest of the women. She may be addressed as a man by both men and women, but she brings feminine qualities to her Poro role—she keeps her braided hair. Conversely, she is excluded from female rituals and secrets but undergoes some of the same experiences she is forbidden to witness. She joins Sande and belongs to one of the society's initiation cohorts, and yet she never gets "pulled out" of it. By contrast, in the context of Poro she literally stands out—she alone is pulled out of the society's initiation without being inducted within a male cohort to which she might fully belong. Thus the *mabɔle* embodies principles of overlapping gender qualities and of gender indeterminacy itself. However, at the same time, she cannot be perceived as a model of emancipated woman within the Mende gendered universe, for she is the only woman who can enjoy these shifting boundaries from one domain to the other. She is the visible manifestation of the arbitrary construction of gender boundaries, but what she manifests cannot be freely appropriated by just any woman.

Historical contingencies militate against neat distinctions between ritual and everyday domains. There was no permanent Sande house in Kpuawala to which midwives could retreat with a woman in labor, so *mabɔlesia* like Jenne and Hawa could find themselves in the wrong place and thus accidentally witness things that should be off limits to them.

And as one of the midwives mentioned, there were not enough sleeping places in town, so Jenne slept with other women, increasing the chances of such "accidental" occurrences. Though the barring of *mabɔlesia*'s access to Sande events and enclosures might seem, at least ideally, to produce a clean separation, the fact that Sande controls aspects of everyday life and knowledge (childbirth and midwifery) that *mabɔlesia* also experience makes this a tricky process.

Ultimately, like the *Ndɔgbɔsui* whose trickery is circumvented by suggesting that one can carry water with a woman's fishing net, the *mabɔle,* visibly woman but in many ways male, enunciates the very principle of gender dissimulation. It is perhaps the apparent randomness in how gender qualities overlap in the *mabɔle* that constitutes her particular form of entrapment. She also embodies a principle of mediation consistent with a more widespread Mende resistance to dyadic models of person and world. As we shall see, this model even resists the apparently perfect dyad of twinship, a relationship based on complete identification in the case of same-sex twins and devoid of age-based hierarchical differences. And yet in Mende, the key twinship role is held by the third member of this relationship, the child born *after* a set of twins and yet inseparably linked to them.

Like the third "twin," the *mabɔle* is a gendered embodiment of the Mende search for principles of mediation—that is, for a way of managing a regime of ambiguity without resolving it dialectically into a stable order of meaning. Her gender ambiguity allows her to move freely and play a mediating role among conflicting contexts at different levels of the social order. As a woman leader, she mediates among Poro men and between them and the community. She guides Poro initiates over the threshold between ritual and ordinary space, as they leave the meeting places at the end of initiation. She leads the Poro procession in town and "cools" the society's wild masquerade in its performance. Thus, in a sense, she mediates potential conflicts that might erupt from the excesses of the masked performance. Conversely, as a ritually male-identified woman, she experiences on a daily basis the tenuous nature of her relationship with the everyday practices typical of her sex, from which she is always on the brink of exclusion. In the rice fields at work with other women, she might be abruptly singled out and sent away if someone goes into labor. Asleep at night in her bed in the big house, she can be unceremoniously awakened and told to find other accommodations for the night. At the same time, these very gestures underscore her distinctive status within the community as a whole and the ambivalence that her ambiguous identity instills in others.

Mama Kema (1990)

CHAPTER 3

Strategies of Incorporation

Marriage and the Forms of Dependence

Although modern Sierra Leone owes its existence in large part to the abolition movement in eighteenth-century Great Britain, domestic slavery in the Protectorate was formally banned by colonial authorities only in a series of ordinances drafted between 1926 and 1927 (Grace 1975: 240–249). In 1928 a District Commissioner noted the "calm bordering on indifference" with which this event was greeted in the rural countryside and the fact that not much had changed in the organization of labor and social relations (Grace 1975: 251). There were, however, "minor incidents" in this transitional period; "some wives tried to leave their husbands on the grounds that they were not wives but slaves" (Ibid.). Indeed, some four years earlier, one of the Sierra Leonean rural chiefs had argued that there was no need for formal antislavery legislation from the colonial government, because intermarriage was already ending slavery. He offered as evidence his own redemption of two slave wives before the District Commissioner so that their children could inherit from him (Grace 1975: 240).[1] Thus, in the interstices between marriage, slavery, and other relations, along the continuum of interdependence, were created spaces for the perpetuation of relations of inequality under new guises, such as the familiar idiom of kinship that turned slaves into "cousins" through the politics of marriage. At the same time, as the case of wives seeking divorces implied, formal emancipation also opened new avenues for challenging these relations in modern Sierra Leone.

THE EMERGENT LEGACY OF SLAVERY

No, we don't have slaves now, we have *cousins*.
Sierra Leonean chief, quoted in Lewis (1954: 67)

This chapter argues that without understanding the emergent legacy of slavery embedded in the idiom of Mende marriage and kinship, one cannot make sense of the ambivalence with which many people approach these intimate relations. Many of the older people I met during fieldwork had personal memories of slavery but were uncomfortable expressing them. Their reticence was due in part to the perception that slavery was an institution frowned upon by outsiders like myself and to the fact that acknowledging it meant distinguishing masters from slaves. After all, who wants to be recognized as a descendant of slaves? Who is entirely free from suspicion of having slave ancestry? The unwillingness to talk about domestic slavery was also linked to the fact that it had become increasingly difficult to distinguish it from other forms of dependence shaped by practices of fosterage, adoption, and marriage over successive generations. Herein, this corner of Muslim West Africa was no different from other parts of this region that had been affected by both the Atlantic slave trade to the south and the slave raids from northerly Muslim peoples, and that share a considerable degree of categorical and linguistic ambiguity in matters concerning dependents, strangers, and certain kinship relations.[2] Thus this chapter in Sierra Leonean history was not openly discussed in Wunde villages for strategic reasons, to conceal a family history of servitude, and also because of the transformation of the idiom of slavery into one of dependence forged through the bonds of marriage and kinship.

However, it was precisely in the idiom of marital and kin relations in Kpuawala that the emergent legacy of slavery surfaced—for example, in the notion that a maternal uncle was master of his "slave" nephew or that a particular alternative to matrilateral cross-cousin marriage had the purpose of "ransoming" a nephew from his mother's brother. Like other people in the region and in Africa, the Mende distinguish the mutual relationship between a maternal uncle and his nephews and nieces by using specific terms of address: a person refers to his or her maternal uncle *kenya* and is referred to by him as his *njagbe*. By contrast, most other relatives of one's parents' generation are addressed as "father" and "mother," and those of one's offspring's generations as "children." The especially political nature of the relationship between *kenya* and *njagbe* is underscored by the fact that in this region, hierarchical relations between different social groups are described through this kinship idiom. Among the Kpelle of Liberia, who are neighbors of and culturally related to the Mende, the hierarchical relationship between maternal uncles and their nephews expresses the links between ruling and dependent lineages and provides the rhetoric for their competing claims to legitimacy (Murphy and Bledsoe 1987). "Matrilateral ties and cross-cousin marriages . . . are not always constituted by strict genealogical reckoning, but by a form of political reckoning that assigns kin groups and individuals to dominant and subordinate rank" (Bledsoe and Murphy 1980: 155).[3]

Wherever the political order is legitimized in terms of inherited rights, marriage and kinship ties tend to be differently construed, depending on the interests at stake (Comaroff 1982: 150 ff.). However, in the West African case, the articulation of kinship relations and politics goes beyond strategies internal to a society. The idiom of kinship shapes accounts of relations between different societies in the context of a history of warfare and slavery. Thus when talking about other Sierra Leonean peoples, Mende in different settings sometimes referred to the Loko—a linguistically related, smaller group to the north—as their *njagbe*, "nephews" (sister's sons) as well as "slaves" (*nduwɔ*, sing.). They might add to such expressions the comment that the Loko (or Landogo, see Speed 1991) were culturally less sophisticated, militarily weaker, and more recent settlers in the region, with more questionable claims to land and other resources. Some Loko people argued the opposite—that they were maternal uncles, *kenyani*, and the Mende their slaves. Regardless of the respective Mende and Loko roles, these statements indicated that the link among political hierarchy, ownership of persons and their labor, and kinship ties—especially the relationship between a woman's brother and her sons—operated between groups as well, as a strategy both of alliance and of hierarchical incorporation.

To take an even broader regional perspective, the slave/master model informed relations between different populations in the Upper Guinea coast rain forest belt and peoples from the savannas to the north who were often involved in the slave trade. The relationship between rain forest coastal region and peoples of the interior savannas and desert articulated with the hierarchical distinctions between dark-skinned and fairer people, between decentralized polities and states, and between indigenous religions and Islam. In Sierra Leone, local lore still echoes with accounts of the incursions of Samori, the Muslim Mandinka warrior who in the 1880s waged holy wars in this region, along with his Sofa cavalry

(Fyfe 1962: 448; Person 1976). Fula and Mandinka Muslims from the north were also prominent in the slave trade along the Sierra Leonean rivers (Fyfe 1962: 270–274). However, the Fula and other peoples of the Guinée highlands to the north of Sierra Leone were in turn subordinate to the light-skinned Arabic and Berber speakers of the desert (Labouret 1929: 251). In a context in which slavery was still condoned, Labouret noted that among the Fula, uterine cousins addressed each other respectively as "slave" and master, or "Arab."[4] Slaves could be seen, then, as giving way to cousins because the two categories had a potentially overlapping history.

Thus, in spite of local variations, in a large area of West Africa the idiom of kinship and marriage expresses—and shapes—specific positions in the political economy, both past and present. The hierarchical relationship between Mende *kenya* and *njagbe* is modeled in part on that between master and slave, wife-giver and wife-taker. Historically, marriage and slavery were linked in the Mende household. First, there was a correlation between the numbers of slaves working on a household's farms and the wives overseeing and complementing their labor; second, these two groups had similar dependent roles in relation to the senior male members of the patrilineages controlling their households. And finally, enslaved women often became wives (Crosby 1937; Grace 1977).

The links between marriage and slavery help place in context the degrees of dependence that underpin the Mende notion that everybody is under someone's patronage, or "for" somebody (*nu[mɔ] lo va*), and within which we must consider not only marriage but also the practices whereby dependents, strangers, and other sociological figures of alterity are incorporated within a familiar universe. In particular, I examine the links among inequality, marriage (especially between matrilateral cross-cousins) relations among in-laws, and relations between maternal uncles and their sisters' children.[5] These are relationships wherein discursive and behavioral practices are overshadowed by references to enslavement, to ransoming, to a vaguely defined set of "troubles" through which wife-takers have to go in order to marry, and, after marriage, to the maintenance of good relations with in-laws.

In Mende, as we shall see, jural rights and inheritance are by and large transmitted patrilineally, and residential patterns at marriage are virilocal, at least ideally. However, a wife's family—especially her brothers—maintain important rights with respect to her progeny, and there is a stated preference for matrilateral cross-cousin marriage. Leach argued, in response to Lévi-Strauss's contention that a key feature of matrilateral cross-cousin marriage was its egalitarian nature (Lévi-Strauss 1969: 235–254), that in fact this form of marriage produced an asymmetry between wife-givers and wife-takers and that, although it was impossible to know from the outset which side might have higher status in any given situation, the inequality between them made this type of marriage highly *political* (Leach 1961: 101–102). In Kpuawala, conflicts that divided relatives by marriage sometimes triggered the threat of breaking up the relationship that brought them together. However, it was usually a woman's maternal relatives, rather than her paternal ones or her husband's relatives, who made these threats. In other situations, the same bonds of marriage and kinship were invoked to justify political loyalties. The anthropological literature on kinship has emphasized the supportive role of matrilateral kin toward their nephews, and maternal uncles in particular, in patrilineal African societies where, by contrast, agnatic ties were more hierarchical and competitive (e.g., Comaroff 1982; Radcliffe-Brown 1952: 28). This bond between a maternal uncle and his nephews in particular, especially in contexts where there was also a preference for matrilateral cross-cousin marriage, was linked to this relative's identity as a male equivalent to the mother (e.g., Radcliffe-Brown 1950: 34; 1952: 28).

Scholars of kinship have noted that regardless of the jural norms governing descent and marriage, people in practice always had the option of emphasizing their bonds to maternal or paternal kin (e.g., Evans-Pritchard 1951). However, a historical perspective on this question has shown the strategic uses of such choices over time (Comaroff 1982). In the Mende case, this historical approach must also integrate an understanding of the links among marriage, enslavement, and emancipation over time. This approach helps explain why relations between maternal uncles and their nephews are characterized by hostility as well as by support and mutual obligations (Radcliffe-Brown 1952: 91–92; Wilson 1950: 127). Furthermore, it contextualizes the coexistence of behaviors that imply egalitarian relations and other behaviors that point to hierarchical differences instead.

In Mende, to marry is to sit (*hei*), a word that situates this relation in the public domain of stools and hammocks. Thus the idiom of marriage also evokes political hierarchy; as we shall see, chiefs are those who are said to "sit on" their subjects and territories (*mahei*).[6] However, the metaphorics of sitting in the politics of marriage—and in politics more generally—is contested at different levels by practices developed around the institution of the *heimɛi*, the home.

KENYANI AND RANSOM BRIDES

Kema and Abdule, her brother's adult son, were sitting on the low perimeter wall of my house's front veranda, resting while keeping their eye on drying cocoa beans in the clearing before us. Kema eyed Abdule's seven-year-old daughter, Satta, who was playing nearby, and began to tease her nephew about giving her the girl in marriage for her absent son, Morie. "Give me a 'goat's-head wife' for Morie," she told Abdule, who grunted noncommittally. "Let them spoil their siblingship by marrying." Satta was considered Morie's matrilateral cross-cousin (MBD), and as the daughter of someone in a "mother's" relationship to him, she was a kind of sister. Hence the "spoiled" siblingship: The marriage entailed the loss of a sibling for the sake of the more advantageous gain of a spouse who could bear children. The reference to a goat's head reflects the fact that by marrying off Satta to Morie, Abdule would put an end to his obligation to share with the latter the head of any game he captured or of any animal he slaughtered (cf. Crosby 1937: 251). Kema went on to say that marrying a goat's-head wife was ideal because it promised greater stability than other marriages. She grinned and said, "That way, there are no arguments, no noise. Let's say that I am the boy's *kenya*. Even if they have disagreements, my nephew (*njagbe*) would not be able to sue me (for divorce or damages), because I'm his *kenya* (maternal uncle)." She pointed over to the veranda across the clearing where Jami was spinning cotton and added, "Jami, *Kamo* Jussu's wife, is his *kenya*'s daughter," as though referring to this, one of the most stable and apparently happy matches in the village, were enough to illustrate her point. Indeed, most matrilateral cross-cousin marriages in Kpuawala seemed to be characterized by relaxed negotiations over bridewealth (often accepted in lower amounts than for other marriages) and a great deal of flexibility in living arrangements. When they did not work out, for example, spouses were more likely to separate *de facto* without formalizing the arrangement.[7] One old man who had several wives told me that his junior one was a "wife born within (the family)" (*ndehu nyahɛi*), adding with a smile that he was sure she would stay married to him. Even if she wanted to divorce him someday, her father was his "mother," *yie*, his own mother's brother, and would not agree.

However, as I suggested earlier, the same matrilateral uncle who displayed such support toward a nephew and potential son-in-law also "owned" him to some extent. In the past, he was said to have had the right to sell his nephew into slavery, a feature shared with other neighboring people (see MacCormack 1983: 286) This legacy was flagged by the next part of the conversation between Kema and Abdule. Kema reflected that perhaps her son Morie might prefer to give his *kenya* his own daughter in marriage, as "ransom" (*gumawɔ*), instead of further sealing his subordinate role vis-à-vis Abdule by taking a wife from him. In this new scenario, Abdule would be receiving a wife from his nephew instead of giving him one, a form of marriage that seemed fairly hypothetical in Kpuawala. But what was it that needed to be ransomed through this marriage? Both Kema and Abdule replied that Morie was his maternal uncle's slave (*nduwɔ*), that he was at his *kenya*'s beck and call, and that in the past Abdule could have sold him into slavery, if he had wanted to do so. In this case, marriage could make the difference between freedom and enslavement: a maternal uncle was unlikely to sell into slavery a nephew who was also a son-in-law, because the latter was already a subordinate through the labor and other support obligations that made up his "in-law troubles." On the other hand, Morie could seek even stronger protection against potential enslavement by giving a wife to his uncle and thus reversing their roles in the hierarchical relationship linking maternal uncle to his nephew—by causing them to be related as wife-giver to wife-taker.

The ambiguous mixture of proximity and hierarchical distance in the relationship between a woman's brother and her children was also exemplified by another case that involved Abdule. Abdule and his brothers owned the house where I lived in Kpuawala and had assigned Abdule's eldest daughter Fataba, Satta's older sister, to assist me in domestic chores. After some time, I realized that Massa, the girls' mother, could not do without, or did not want to do without, the assistance of her eldest daughter in her daily domestic chores. Massa continued to assign Fataba time-consuming work in their own household so that the girl was never available when she was needed at my place. Uneasy with the double burden this situation placed on the young girl, I gradually stopped asking Fataba to do chores and informally found someone else to replace her. However, Abdule noticed and, probably aware of his wife's role in this situation but unwilling to confront her directly, came calling with Massa, Fataba, and Massa's brother—Fataba's *kenya*. The *kenya* dominated the discussion, telling both Fataba and her mother that he wanted the girl to attend to my needs alone. Things gradually went back to where they had been, but Fataba and her mother were much more careful to conceal their lack of compliance, now that the uncle had been made aware of the situation.[8]

This situation contrasted with the picture of easy familiarity and mutual obligations between matrilateral relatives put forth in the anthropological literature on kinship in patrilineal societies. As we shall see, it also generated some debate about the nature of corporate kinship and more encompassing domestic arrangements. Along with the mutual liberties and obligations embedded in the notion of "goat's-head wife"—a term that evokes the *kenya*'s obligations toward his *njagbe* and reverses them through marriage—is the darker memory of slavery and the ransoming of men through marriageable women. Indeed, as I discussed earlier in this chapter, the language of matrilateral ties and cross-cousin marriage was often more a form of political reckoning of relations of inequality than a matter of genealogical reckoning, or even a prescription for expected behavior.

This legacy gave important bargaining rights to marriageable women and to women who participated in negotiating marriages on behalf of their husbands or of their male relatives. It was not, however, a legacy immediately apparent in the idiom of marriage, one centered on giving and receiving wives and hence situating the latter as objects of these transactions. True, women as sisters and daughters of men contracting marriages included themselves among the active subjects of this giving and receiving, but in so doing they distinguished themselves from wives. And though feminist anthropologists have shown the pitfalls of assuming that this language tells the whole story about marriage transactions, reducing women to mere means for establishing alliances between groups of men without paying attention to their actual roles in society (Rubin 1974), it is nonetheless significant that the source of legitimacy for powerful Kpuawala women was usually their relationship to particular male figures of authority.

WIFE FINDING, WIFE TROUBLE

In what follows, I look at the common forms of marriage in Kpuawala and the social expectations involved in this process. The idiom of giving and taking wives suggests that the bride's own perspective is not central to marriage transactions. However, this is true only at the rhetorical level. In practice, a prospective bride's approval is crucial to the completion of marriage negotiations, and men's anxiety over their chances of success in this process are reflected in the notion of toil and trouble embedded in the expression *nyaha monɛ*, "wife (or woman) trouble," with which they refer to it.

In Kpuawala, the younger the woman, the more concern there was over whether she would actively participate in making a marriage work or would undermine it. Childhood betrothal was seen as ensuring a more stable outcome to marriage. It usually took place between families that already enjoyed close bonds of friendship or joint interests. According to some Kpuawala men, there were advantages in beginning marriage discussions when a prospective bride was still a child, discussions such as the half-joking exchange involving Abdule's young daughter. The suitors had more time to win over their prospective bride with presents and visits. The wives eventually obtained through early childhood betrothal were called "sprouting seedling wives" (fale gbua nyahanga), for the relationship began when a girl was a mere seedling and was nurtured until her maturity. A wife chosen so young had a chance to grow into a relationship with someone she would know well by the time the marriage took place, and hence she was less likely to unexpectedly change her mind about her husband.

A more common form of marriage in Kpuawala was one involving "finding/picking a wife" (nyaha gɔɛ) who was reaching puberty and was therefore about to be initiated into, or had just joined, the Sande society. Girls at this stage were thought to be more definite in their tastes regarding potential husbands. For example, Momoh first noticed Massa during a visit to Yawaju and spoke to her for some time over the following days. Then he gave her a small present, told her that he liked her, and asked whether she felt she could return his interest. Her assent prompted Momoh to go to her parents, and in a meeting with them and Massa—to which senior matrilateral kin were also summoned as soon as the nature of the visit became clear—declared his liking and gave the customary token kola money to show the earnestness of his intentions.[9] From then on, Momoh visited Massa regularly, often bringing her small amounts of money, food, and other gifts, while making arrangements with her parents to initiate her into Sande (wua la Sandehu).

Despite Massa's and her relatives' assent to his marriage proposal, Momoh did not feel certain of the outcome ahead. After he had begun fulfilling the formal prerequisites to marrying Massa, and throughout the duration of her Sande initiation, he spent what for him was a fortune consulting diviners and purchasing love potions made by a renowned local Muslim healer to ensure that Massa would fall in love with him, and that he would appear to her in erotic dreams. Furthermore, he made every effort to ingratiate himself with his future in-laws by willingly submitting to his "wife troubles" (nyaha monɛ), the work necessary to raise the money to pay for marriage expenses and to keep in-laws happy. He showed up at Massa's parents' farm with his friends to help clear, burn, and hoe the rice farm. He also brought them choice parts of game he captured in traps or while hunting, a share of the palm oil he produced, and so on. Momoh's anxiety over whether this marriage would work out subsided only after the end of Massa's Sande initiation, once an official marriage license had been obtained from the chiefdom clerk, and he had been living with her for several weeks.

In the end, it became clear that Momoh's anxiety had another, concealed source—one linked to the double bind in which young men like him often found themselves when trying to please the myriad constituencies who had some interest in a couple's marriage arrangements. Momoh's hard work in pursuit of money for Massa's initiation and for marriage payments, and to assist in the farming activities of her relatives as well as his own, aggravated a hernia that he had successfully concealed in the past. However, Momoh's hernia had become more pronounced over the months of his wife troubles, and because it had descended into his scrotum, it was now causing an abnormal enlargement of his genitals. Momoh took to wearing baggy clothes to conceal his condition. Eventually, despite his almost mortal fear that something might go wrong in the process, he asked me to arrange for a surgeon friend of mine to operate on his hernia in the Provincial Headquarters town of Bo. At his young age, Momoh could not tolerate the thought of the scorn of other men, and women's sexual jokes, that would be directed at him once knowledge of this condition got out. He reminded me of how a senior man in the village had recently been mocked in public by his political enemies over the same ailment, and he confessed that he was afraid Massa would leave him if he became a laughing stock in a similar manner, or if his condition interfered with his sexual potency, attractiveness, and fertility. Because neither of Momoh's previous two wives had had children, he was very worried on this score.

That marriage was a potentially fragile arrangement was underscored by the care with which transactions were recorded, for the explicit purpose of future returns in case of divorce. All initiation expenses and marriage payments in Kpuawala were scrupulously recorded by the groom and his family, and several told me candidly that this was so there would be no argument over what needed to be refunded by the bride's parents in case of divorce. Conversely, if parents sponsored their daughter's initiation before a prospective groom had come forth, they passed on their expenses when she married. Expenses for initiation included specific fees and gifts requested by Sande elders; rice, oil, meat, and other food items to support both the initiate and the society elders for the duration of the proceedings; and what amounted to a *trousseau* for the bride—specified numbers of cloth lengths tailored into clothes, underwear, and accessories like shoes, bags, umbrellas, costume jewelry, makeup, and perfume.[10]

Not all marriages, however, coincided with a woman's Sande initiation; many unions involving adult Kpuawala women seemed to derive from other, more or less informal arrangements. These unions could be both formed and dissolved without much family involvement. When Momoh was left by his senior wife Alimatu, I asked whether she had filed for formal divorce papers with the chiefdom clerk, an act referred to as "getting papers" (*kɔlɔ mbumbu*). He responded that this had not been necessary, because he was not the man who had initiated her into Sande. His answer reflected the fact that formal marriages were usually linked to Sande initiations. This was due not to any "traditional" preference or to any greater legitimacy of such marriages over others but, rather, to the fact that Sande initiations were well-publicized events held with the permission and paid license of chiefdom authorities. Thus these marriages were more easily registered by government clerks in the chiefdom administration, who showed up when closing ceremonies were scheduled and wrote out licenses in exchange for fees. Though fines were imposed by chiefdom clerks on those who were later discovered to have married without taking out a license, it was easy in practice to avoid this additional expense in any form of marriage other than those that took place immediately following a prospective bride's Sande initiation. Some families preferred paying the license costs in order to have the marriage formally registered in the chiefdom books, in case marital troubles down the road resulted in divorce. Experience suggested that in such circumstances, the parties with marriage licenses and written documentation of all transactions and agreements had a better chance of being awarded damages or at least of protecting themselves from punitive fines.

In the case of Alimatu and Momoh, there had been no formal marriage. Alimatu was older than Momoh, whom she had met after having left a previous husband. Though no single event attended by their kin appeared to have marked formally the union between Alimatu and Momoh, over time the expectations of their families had become the same as those characterizing marriages that had been contracted more formally. For example, Momoh's widowed mother often praised her daughter-in-law Alimatu for taking good care of her, even when her own son ignored her. Momoh and Alimatu had not had any children, and their hometowns were very far apart. Every year, Alimatu visited her father and his relatives near the Liberian border, but one year her visit extended beyond two months. Momoh went to Alimatu's hometown to pick her up, but she refused to follow him. When he found her, Alimatu had begun to live with another man, so Momoh returned to Kpuawala alone. When we talked, about a year after this event had taken place, Momoh felt that their relationship had ended. He still missed Alimatu and would have liked to get her back, but he felt he had no way to force her to return against her will.

In other cases involving remarriages, and in which there were children and close relations between the kin groups involved, there were money exchanges and licenses as well. For example, Mussu had been initiated into Sande by her former husband Suare. When they separated and she decided to marry Lamin, the latter made marriage payments to her family, some of which were used to compensate Suare for the original bridewealth. Suare and Mussu had children together, so Lamin was not expected to reimburse initiation expenses. Lamin also paid the costs of getting official divorce papers and, later, a new marriage license. Thus some years later, when Mussu decided to leave Lamin, she had to pay to obtain divorce papers from the chiefdom authorities. Lamin also sued her for the reimbursement of bridewealth and of the costs he had incurred in getting their original marriage license.

Although it was important in all kinds of unions that the woman explicitly express her "liking" of her husband-to-be in the presence of her kin before they would accept his gifts, in practice genuine attraction and fondness often seemed to characterize marriages between people who knew each other relatively well and who had already formed several previous attachments. Adults who had previously been married subsequently sat (were married) in ways that involved fewer formalities and less significant exchanges of wealth, but women in these contexts had more freedoms and a chance at a more egalitarian, companionable relationship than those who married very young. When I returned to Kuawala three years after my first stay there, two women who during my earlier visit had been living with their respective husbands and children were remarried to other men, whom they had known for a long time. One of the women, Mariama, had been widowed and had subsequently married a man who, as her lover, had fathered her oldest child before her previous union. In other words, after her husband died, she went back to an old lover who had fathered her eldest child and who had lived in the same community as she had throughout her marriage, without remarrying.

The other woman, Aisattu, also had resumed an affair with Braima, a former lover, after returning from an absence of several years. Both she and Braima, were married. When Aisattu finally left her husband, Braima wanted to marry her, but his wife Miatta—who was younger and had not been able to conceive—objected to the idea. Miatta threatened to leave her husband if he carried out his plan to marry a woman who was older than herself and hence in a position to undermine her status as a senior wife. Her childlessness put her in an even weaker position. Despite Miatta's ultimatum, Braima married Aisattu, who had been his lover on and off over the years, was older, and had been married several times. He did so because he liked her and because she had proved, in his words, "good at/able to hold children" (*ngi bɛngo a ndopo houla*). Miatta, the wife he had initiated into Sande, left him and returned to live with her family in a neighboring village.

Among domestic relations ranging from several forms of marriage to more informal unions, those resulting from genuine attraction were recognized as being potentially the most durable. Attraction was *nyande*, a concept that encompassed physical beauty but was not limited to it (Boone 1986: 138–143). One young woman told me that her aging husband was *nyandengɔ*, attractive, because he took good care of himself, was clean, and wore nice clothes. More important, she said, he took good care of her: He fed her adequately, bought her new clothes when she needed them without waiting for her to beg him, and appreciated her work. He complimented her cooking, gave her money for tobacco snuff when she had a particularly heavy day at the farm, and said nice things about her to her family. People in Kpuawala recognized that it was difficult to have good marital relations and that in the context of polygynous marriages, it was unlikely that a man's relations with all his wives would be equally good. But having a favorite wife, a *ndoma nyaha* (from *ndomɛi*, "love, liking"), meant trouble among her co-wives. Thus the men who had more than one wife never publicly acknowledged a preference for one over the others. When asked, they said that it was against the Qur'an to have a preference and cited the town *imam* to the effect that it was permitted to have up to four wives, but only if a man could afford to support them and if he was able to treat them all equally.[11] However, the amount of joking among men, and in stories told to larger village audiences, over the preferential treatment of wives, especially the newest and youngest, suggested that this was one of the main sources of tensions and breakups in polygynous marriage.

CUTTING THE TIES THAT BIND

Levirate accounted for yet another form of marriage in Kpuawala, one that revealed in a particularly stark manner people's ambivalence toward this institution and the bonds it created, and severed at the same time. Widows could become inherited wives, or *po nyahanga*, by marrying a dead man's brother at the end of the 40-day mourning period. However, this practice in Kpuawala was more common when the widow in question was part of a large household comprising resident adult sons and their families, who were an attractive source of labor and dependents for aging male relatives of the deceased. This marriage snatched from the jaws of death was symbolically closer than any other to the ideal first marriage envisioned by most young men and women in Kpuawala—one between a girl just initiated into Sande and a young man with no other wives.

When Francis M. died, Hawa, his elderly widow, became the object of intense courtship by several of his surviving brothers. The latter brought her kola money, told her that they liked her in public speeches filled with praise for her talents, and proposed marriage. The aspiring husbands informed her grown children and matrilateral relatives of their intentions in fervent perorations. The advanced age of the suitors making these passionate declarations generated more than a few snickers from the otherwise solemn gathering. Nonetheless, a symbolic parallel was drawn with Hawa's first marriage, through the ceremonies marking the end of her formal mourning and those immediately preceding her remarriage, which echoed those held at the end of Sande initiation.

The last day of Hawa's 40-day mourning period began with a display of grief that matched the immediate aftermath of Francis's death. Women's sustained, loud wails echoed through the whole village. The handful of older women, all widows like Hawa, who took charge of the day's events took a jar of dirt that had been collected at the site where Mr. Francis's corpse had been washed, some 40 days earlier, and turned it into mud once again by mixing it with water and pounding it in a hole in the ground. Three times Hawa, whose head had been kept shaved during the mourning period, got down on all fours and brought her face and mouth down to the mud in the hole, stood up, walked to a corner of the meeting place, and returned to face the house she had occupied with her dead husband. There she addressed him each time: "Francis, you and I once sat together (we were married). Now you have died, and I am no longer your wife. Even those children we had, they are no longer your children. Today you are leaving them to me." Then the elderly women smeared the mud on Hawa's body, tied dried strands of plantain leaves on her limbs, and sat her on a mat placed over some fresh leaves, cordoned off in a corner of the meeting place by a rope made of plaintain leaves. Only other widows like herself entered the area, where a meal of plantains cooked in oil was prepared. This non-food, in the sense that it was not the rice that constituted the only Mende "food," was off limits to all except widows and widowers, and especially to women of child-brearing age.

The measures taken to separate Hawa and her children from her dead husband, and the tone (ranging from the authoritative to the angry) with which she addressed his *jinɛi*, his spirit, asking it not to be jealous, and to stop roaming close to her, were only some of the symbolic manifestations of the ambivalence with which people regarded marriage—and its relationship to death.[12] Although spouses of both sexes went through similar mourning rituals, there were gendered differences that pointed to a different relationship between each sex and the other's body. When Sallu, a young man, was widowed at the death of one of his wives, he went through rituals similar to those of Hawa, but in his case there were no parallels drawn with initiation. One key difference in how widows and widowers mourned their spouses in Kpuawala seemed to center on processes of identification and mimicry, which characterized women's behavior toward their dead spouses or brothers-in-law, but not men's mourning of wives.

When Morigwa died a widower, one of his surviving sisters-in-law (a brother's wife) dressed up in his gown and cap, picked up his water kettle, and parodically imitated his departures for the farm, occasionally breaking into mourning songs, taunting and cajoling him in conversation, and mourning his loss. Other sisters-in-law, also dressed in drag, made off with the money and food contributed to the funeral and memorial ceremonies; their behavior angered some male elders presiding over the events and amused others, who implied that this was predictable behavior by referring to it as "sister-in-law business," *semɔ hinda*. But Hawa's body—the wife's body—coated in the dirt that had been in contact with her dead husband's corpse pointed to an impersonation of an entirely different order. It was a gesture that performed a kind of reconstitution of the dead man's body by inverting the process that had transformed into dust the mud formed under the corpse at the time when it was washed. Now water was added, transforming the dust back into mud, which was smeared on the widow's body. Thus Hawa's final day of mourning began by her own body being encased in a layer of mud that brought her back to the moment of her husband's death.[13] When dry and hardened, this mud formed a second skin over Hawa's own and was animated by her, as though to bring Francis to life one last time before washing him off for good. From this perspective, the bonds of marriage were being recognized as strong ones—as surviving even death. However, as Hawa's words to her husband implied, it was bonds of jealousy that ensured this survival, not those of affection and tenderness.

Jealousy was further evoked in a subsequent, less public stage of the rituals involving the end of the widow's mourning. After eating the cooked plantains with other widows and widowers, Hawa was taken by the female elders to a stream outside the village. They sat her naked on a log resting in the shallow stream's bed and held a divination session. A few rice grains were placed on each one of Hawa's hands and feet and on her tongue, head, and back, and a white chicken was made to peck at them. The chicken, to their apparent relief, ate everything. Had it not, it would have been taken as a sign of Hawa's imminent death. Then Hawa was made to confess all the lovers she had had during her long marriage to Francis. A pebble for each of five names extracted from Hawa was placed in a basin containing a medicinal leaf concoction, which was being kept afloat on the stream's surface. Then the women cut the dried plantain ties on Hawa's limbs and threw them downstream, behind her back, as they waved leaves and shooed away bad *jinanga* and "sins." Then new ones were placed at the same spots, and Hawa's whole body, including her head, was washed with soap. All the materials that had been used to cook the plantain meal consumed earlier, including the remaining wood embers and debris swept up from the hearth, as well as the mats and plantain leaves on which Hawa had been seated, were also thrown behind her back to be washed away downstream, to remove *hinda nyamu*, "evil things," from the town. The old rags Hawa had used in mourning were washed, and her body was smeared with scented palm oil and dressed in new clothes.

I use the passive tense advisedly in describing the steps to end Hawa's mourning: through all proceedings, other women handled her body, made her assume different postures, and fed her as though she were being molded anew—a passive, plastic entity in their hands. Not until she was escorted back to the village, radiant in new clothes and in her well-oiled, shiny skin, did she again take an active role in the proceedings surrounding her. At this stage, women made explicit parallels between Hawa's transformation and that undergone by young girls initiated into Sande. They pointed to the mud that had covered Hawa and reminded me of the white kaolin clay that covered the bodies of Sande initiates until the final coming-out ceremony. At Sande initiation, too, the final ceremony began with a ritual wash and the discarding of the old rags worn during the seclusion period, now changed for oiled skin and new clothes. In both cases, these bodily transformations marked a transition from a state of seclusion, a death-like stage of dangerous communion with powerful agencies, to a return into the community as *Sande yoisia*, as new Sande initiates, "new chiefs," and desirable, marriageable women.[14] For a woman, a spouse's death was the only case in which an ended marriage could be followed by a repetition at some level of the experience of Sande initiation that, in most cases, coincided with her very first wedding. The abruptness with which death interrupted the ordinarily unfinished business of all marriages—the unacknowledged resentments and jealousies beneath the surface—made this clean break with the past a requirement, but also a fiction. At the end of mourning, Hawa had to acknowledge her past lovers to her dead husband's spirit even decades after the affairs had taken place. But she never would have done so if she had predeceased Francis, just as surely as he went to the grave with concealed offenses of his own.

After returning from her symbolic cleansing and re-initiation, Hawa consulted with her relatives to decide which suitor she would select. She and her children chose the husband who in their opinion would best look after them and their interests, even though that decision did not involve any change in their living or working arrangements. When I asked Hawa whether she would not move in to live with her new husband, she responded that this was the kind of marriage where she only "prayed for him" (*ngaa sɛli wie*), where she visited him after morning and evening prayers in the mosque, to pronounce blessings and pay her respects. She was too old, she went on, to be interested in sleeping next to her new husband. It was time for her to look after her grandchildren, while her new husband's younger wives took care of his daily needs. In this case, then, marriage did not even involve "sitting" in the sense of co-residence between husband and wife.

SPLITTING AND JOINING

Sande elders came to see me and said, "Joadi Modima, you must turn to Sande matters now." So first thing in the morning, I lay down in the main meeting place. I pulled out a "Sande hammock," hung it facing the

Kpanguima [the Sande initiation enclosure], and turned
on my side in it so I was facing toward Sande matters.
The *Soweis* asked again, "Joadi, won't you turn your
attention to Sande matters?" And I told them, "Don't
you see, I've been lying in this hammock for a hundred
years now, turned toward Sande matters. . . ."

> *Joadi Modima, storyteller,*
> *Kpuawala, performance on March 1, 1986*

In a comic reversal, Joadi the storyteller portrayed the predicament of
men who had to sponsor a Sande initiate in order to marry as a restful
spell in a hammock, facing the Sande enclosure. In later lines, the storyteller rattled off at breakneck speed a list of successive farming activities
he purportedly engaged in after constant prodding by the same Sande elders. Joadi spoke in rapid succession the words for tree cutting, brushing,
burning, weeding, sowing, hoeing, and harvesting, as though the activities they evoked had been carried out with as little effort and in as short a
time as it took to enunciate them. Of such hilarious material were a
man's marriage troubles (*nyaha monε*), or Sande troubles (*Sande monε*)
made though the physical labor required to cover initiation expenses and
bridewealth was considerable, the troubles referred to in the expressions
surrounding marriage, and which include in-law trouble, were of another
kind, too. They revolved around the ambivalence toward marriage as an
institution that "split off" a woman from her kin, even though this separation created bonds of a higher order between kin on both sides.

Marriage brings sets of in-laws in relation with each other. The tension embedded in a relationship created through the separation of a
woman from her family of descent in order to join her husband's household is reflected in the term for male in-law, *mbela*, whose homophone is
the verb for "splitting." The idiom of giving and receiving wives/women,
which permeates talk of marriage, stresses the unity of a higher order
created by this relationship. It also implies that the parties who give and
receive wives are corporate descent groups identifying with the male
point of view, regardless of whether it is female members of those groups
who speak of these wives. By contrast, the focus on "in-lawness"—on the
condition achieved through marriage—puts men (for it is only men who
address each other as "splitters") in the position not of unifiers but of
separators. At the same time, this terminology implies that out-marrying
female members of patrilineages are considered essential to the integrity
of their kin groups.

Though marriage may separate a woman—and especially her children—from her own lineage, at another level it also expands that lineage
to encompass the newly acquired in-law and his labor and gifts. For a
man, finding a wife is virtually synonymous with paying bridewealth for
her, as the use of the expression *nyaha gɔɛ* for both processes suggests.[15]
Men become indebted to their in-laws: they must offer gifts, work presta-
tions, and take on financial burdens in case of family crises. Thus the ritual
splitting and sharing of kola nuts, which start off marriage payments, may
mark an incipient cleavage in one group, but it is also the formalization
of reciprocal socioeconomic obligations, particularly on the groom's side.

In a way, marriage is not even the beginning of what one Kpuawala
man once referred to as in-law trouble (*mbela mɔnɛ*). If his intended wife
has not been initiated yet, his Sande troubles (*Sande mɔnɛ*) precede all
others. As we noted earlier, a prospective husband provides a substantial
amount, if not all, of the money, food, and gifts required for his future
wife's initiation. In order to raise the resources for initiation, a man will,
with the help of his household, lay a special "Sande farm" (*Sande gbaa*)
during the preceding farming season. If he is already married, his senior
wife or wives play an important role in planning the additional labor and
in setting aside resources for another wedding. The preferred timing of
Sande initiations and weddings is toward the end of the dry season, when
oil palm fruits ripen.

In addition to the expenses of initiation and bridewealth required by
Sande leaders and families, chiefdom authorities exact a marriage license
fee to be paid, usually, at the end of Sande initiations. In 1985, the cost
was 50 Leones per licence—a sum vastly inferior to all the other expenses
of marriage and initiation, but ten times the amount of the yearly government tax.[16] However, initiation and marriage expenses do not normally
reach amounts that make them "the most significant transaction in the . . .
economy," as is the case elsewhere in Africa (Turton 1980: 67). They
undoubtedly constitute one of the most significant transactions, along
with funerals, but bride service and gifts to in-laws throughout the marriage generally have greater value than the initial expenses.

Cloth gifts mark the key moments in establishing and developing marriage relations. In Kpuawala a groom was expected to give an "in-law
gown" to his prospective father-in-law (*mbela lomei*). After consumma-
tion of the marriage, he presented his mother-in-law with cotton cloth to
thank her for having trained her daughter well.[17] This training encompassed the supervision necessary to ensure that the daughter remained a
virgin until marriage. I was told that if Sande officials, upon performing

the clitoridectomy that is part of initiation into the society, saw evidence
that an initiate was not a virgin, they would sue and fine her parents, who
then would have to scale down their expectations regarding bridewealth
and marriage prospects.

Gbesse and Mariama had been married some eight years, and they
already had three children together. Mariama also had two other children from a previous marriage, one a married daughter with a nursing
infant of her own, the other a boy of about ten years of age. Both of them
lived with their mother in Gbesse's compound, though eventually they
moved away to their father's hometown on the Liberian border. In 1990
Mustafa, Gbesse's father-in-law, had a disappointing rice crop. Mustafa
attributed his crop's failure to the fact that his young wife had left him for
a lover and that, as a result, he had trouble marshaling enough help at
critical periods in the farming season. Mariama's mother had long since
died, and Mustafa had the regular assistance of only his elderly widowed
sister, Kadi, who had come to live with him since the death of her own
husband. As a result of his crop's failure, Mustafa was unable to return
the seed rice he had borrowed from an agricultural development scheme.
Gbesse stepped in and paid his father-in-law's debt, but in order to do so
defaulted on his own. By the end of the dry season, in April, the official
from the government rice loan scheme was regularly visiting the village to
collect outstanding debts. Gbesse had also experimented with new money-
making schemes, such as a fish nursery, to help support his two daughters, who were now going to school in Bo, the provincial headquarters,
and living there with his older sister. He seemed a highly unlikely candidate for defaulting on the loan scheme, given his outstanding entrepre-
neurship and hard-working habits. It became apparent that the reason
why Gbesse had defaulted on the seed rice loan scheme was that he had
felt obliged first to help his father-in-law repay his own debt, which consisted of seven bushels of rice in the husk—and only after fulfilling this
troublesome in-law obligation could he turn his attention to his own
business. Thus, well into his marriage Gbesse steadily provided his father-
in-law and neighbor with farming and financial assistance, as well as
doing skilled carpentry work to improve his house. This pattern of "troubles" that Gbesse gave himself on behalf of his father-in-law did not
change in later years.

The parallels drawn in women's lives between their first marriage as
new Sande initiates and their remarriage as widows is strengthened by
their families' expectations of sons-in-law upon the death of a wife's parents, especially that of her father. When his only father-in-law died,

Braima was responsible for a large share of the funeral expenses as part of his "in-law's crying/mourning" (*mbela wɔɔ*). Braima bought a goat to be sacrificed at the funeral and shouldered a considerable share of the logistical burden of feeding and housing visiting mourners. He also offered one of the largest monetary contributions to be partitioned among the family of the deceased at the funeral. If mourning a single father-in-law was a troublesome burden, prospects were all the more daunting for Kpuawala men who had several wives. One man who had six wives living with him had produced 6,000 Leones' worth of palm oil in a single day—the equivalent at the time (1990) of four 50-kilogram bags of clean rice—all of which was to be contributed for the funeral expenses of two of his fathers-in-law.

If in-law relations among men—those addressing each others as split-ters—were fraught with a sense of toil and obligation on the part of the son- and brother-in-law, those across gender lines were marked by avoid-ances as well. In particular, sons-in-law avoided close contact with moth-ers-in-law and their domestic spaces. In Mende storytelling, an outra-geous narrator only had to speak of men sitting on a bed with their mother-in-law, or hugging her, and having sex with her to elicit consid-erable embarrassment among men in the audience. In Kpuawala breaches in mother-in-law avoidance had to be "washed" by the Humoi society, whose primary concern was to heal breaches in the pro-scribed behaviors among certain categories of relatives (see Harris and Sawyerr 1968: 56, 94–95).

However, the term *demia*, which mothers-in-law used to address their sons-in-law, also had connotations of familiarity and support, by con-trast with the toils and troubles associated with "splitters." For example, brothers-in-law also tended to address each other as *demia* instead of *mbela*, implying that even in-law relations between men of the same gen-eration could be more supportive and familiar than those across genera-tions. As we saw earlier, women of all ages also might address a man as *demia* when requesting a favor, a fact that underscores the friendly qual-ity of this term of address.

There is an encompassing politics as well to the relative indebtedness of wife-takers toward wife-givers. Though generally it is the former who are beset with in-law troubles, this is not the case when they are of higher status than their wives' families. A son-in-law who is an important chief is not expected to do bride service, and he might also be a poor economic provider for his wives' relatives. The higher the chief's status, the greater the number of his wives, though some might be of the "praying" kind discussed earlier, with whom there are no sexual relations. Some of the section chiefs and paramount chiefs in the Wunde area had as many as 30 wives and were constantly offered more by subjects and allies who wanted to strengthen political ties with them. Having many wives, chiefs reasoned that they could not possibly support all of them with their children. In these cases, wife-givers expected mostly patronage from their in-laws, a fact that reversed the typical relationship between the two sides (see Bledsoe and Murphy 1980: 149).

Despite the perception that wife-takers were indebted to wife-givers, this relationship in practice had reciprocal dimensions, as was implied by the fact that *mbela* and *demia* were reciprocal terms of address. On one occasion, a section chief in the neighboring Pujehun district came to Kpuawala to sue his wife's brothers in court for not having behaved as in-laws were expected to. This suit suggested that wife-takers could legitimately have expectations of wife-givers too. The plaintiff in the village chief's court began by summarizing his own track record as an in-law, an account that revealed a model picture of in-law troubles. Despite his chiefly status, this son-in-law had contributed to funerals in his wife's family, most recently to that of his father-in-law, the former Kpuawala town chief. He also had visited several times when called to help solve family crises. By contrast, he pointed out that his brothers-in-law had failed to come when summoned on three different occasions involving in-law obligations: (1) a serious illness of his wife, their sister, (2) the death of her newborn baby, and most recently, (3) the meeting to arrange a daughter's upcoming Sande initiation. In his accusations, the chief was not referring merely to the failure of his in-laws to attend the funeral. More important, he was addressing the fact that they neglected to contribute financially to the costs incurred on those occasions, an aspect included in the idiom of physical presence and participation that he used. In this sense, money and other goods play an important role as material markers of participation. One can "come" by simply sending an emissary with a monetary contribution. The outraged chief won his case and received a financial contribution to defray the costs of his daughter's upcoming Sande initiation.[18]

THE MOBILITY OF DEPENDENTS

I often heard Kpuawala men express anxiety over the stability and durability of their marriages.[19] Over a period of several months, my neighbor was transformed from a cheerful man to a sad and quiet shadow of his former self. Eventually, I discovered that this was due to his suspicion that his only wife was having an affair. He was so worried that she would leave him for her lover that he did not have the courage to confront her with his suspicions. Another man with one wife and two young children, a strong and respected headman of the town's male working force, did not dare question his wife's constant trips back to her mother's home-town with their children, even though he wanted to enroll his daughter in the local primary school. On another occasion, for several days he showed up at his friends' houses at meal times to be fed, because his wife had refused to cook for him since he had slapped her during an argu-ment.[20] She sued him in the chief's court (*mayiage*), which found him guilty and demanded that he apologize and pay her a punitive fine.

It would be tempting to attribute this apparent failure of husbands to enforce their authority over their wives to the relative powerlessness of younger men with a single wife, who were entirely dependent on the lat-ter for domestic and farm work. However, other cases undermine this assumption. Upon my return to Kpuawala in 1990, I was amazed to find that the head of one of the two town wards, a "big man" and former member of the town council, had been left by the three wives who had been living with him during my previous stay. In 1985–1986, ten people had lived in his house, including his wives, children, and several depend-ent strangers. His house was a village meeting point, where in the evenings one could always find groups of people in lively conversation, entertaining each other while making baskets, seeding cotton, or playing games. Now it was a semideserted household occupied only by the man, a wife he had married years earlier, when his occupation as a lorry driver kept him always on the road—and who had until now lived in Bo, the provincial headquarters—and their two children.

The three wives I had known during my previous visit had gone back to their native villages and towns. They all came from communities in the same chiefdom or the neighboring one. One of them had already begun divorce proceedings before I left Kpuawala in late 1986, in spite of the fact that she was pregnant with her husband's child. All three had had between one and three children with him, and they took these children with them. They were among the 19 women who since my earlier visit had left the village for one reason or another—about 17% of the 91 mar-ried women I had counted in 1985. Some of these women had been wid-owed and left instead of marrying one of their husband's surviving broth-ers; others had officially divorced; and some had separated from their husbands without taking any formal steps toward a divorce.

Several of the 77 adult men whom I had counted in my 1985 census had also left by my second Kpuawala visit in 1990. Most of these men were relatively young, productive members of the community, and nearly all had been dependent outsiders, or strangers (*hotanga*, pl.), in Kpuawala households. Several had left after their marriages with Kpuawala women had dissolved. For these dependent young men, a marriage breakup triggered mobility, just as it did for women who left their husbands. Moinina, who had been married to and had a child with his Kpuawala host's daughter, returned to Wunde, his hometown, when his wife divorced him.

The modality of this marriage's breakup sheds more light on the cases outlined at the beginning of this section, where two husbands were hesitant to question or limit their wives' movements and affairs. Moinina too had only one wife, and when he suspected that she had become pregnant during an affair, he forced her to confess her lover's name in court (*ndawo*). Moinina's wife confessed her lover's name, but then declared that she no longer wanted to return to her husband. Instead, she asked to stay with the younger man, whose baby she was expecting. Her lover was fined, but he also helped her raise the money to obtain a divorce and later married her.

The outcome of this case depended in part on the willingness of the woman's relatives—particularly her parents—to support her bid for a divorce. In her case, she wanted to divorce a "stranger," who was her father's dependent, to marry a young man who belonged to the lineage in which her own father had in the past been a dependent guest. What had begun as an accusation of adultery and a request for damages became a divorce case, with the aid of family members who perhaps thought that the second man's younger age might make him a more compatible husband or that they might enjoy better relations with him and his family than they had with their dependent. However, in Kpuawala people seemed more often to fear and expect that unattached male outsiders to the community (especially young ones) would be likely to have affairs with married women, as was made clear whenever new strangers were formally introduced.

A young man named Ibrahim had come to Kpuawala to visit a friend, and later he decided to stay. When he made this decision, he had to be introduced formally to the town elders and gain permission to settle. In the town meeting at which this event took place, Ibrahim first was asked whether he was running away from something, such as economic troubles or criminal infractions, to which he answered no. Then Ibrahim's host gave a brief account of the place and family of his guest's origin and of the history of their friendship. Finally, the Kpuawala elders explained their roles on the town council and listed local rules of conduct (*sawa*, "rule, law"). There were two main rules, they said: a stranger must remain attached to his host family and not go around working for just anyone, and he should not bother "the wives of his friends/peers" (*mbaa ti nyahanga*). This twin concern with the labor and the sexual habits of strange men highlighted at once what made them desirable *and* feared. Healthy, young men were a source of potential labor, but also a sexual threat to the stability of marriages, and these two rules sought to exercise some control over them on both counts.

Ibrahim paid the appropriate greeting kola to the town council through the head of his host family, who again warned him not to bother married women. Instead, Ibrahim was told publicly that if he saw a woman he liked, he should let the head of his host household "pick him a wife" (*nyaha gɔɛ*) or help him acquire the resources to marry. Thus, echoing an established pattern in the region's history, marriage was presented both as a solution to the potential threat that strange men posed to local women and as a means to incorporate them into the community. Marriage was conceived as an essential element in the community's social and physical reproduction—a means for both retaining potentially mobile young women and recruiting new male dependents from the outside.

Ibrahim's host had good reasons for warning his new dependent; as his patron, he would be held responsible for the young man's conduct vis-à-vis the rest of the community. Within a month of this event, the town elders were again convened to hear Ibrahim's official host repudiate him as his guest, alleging that he spent too much time cutting palm fruits with another young man's household. Ibrahim was also accused of taking some of his host's money and gambling it away. The outcome of this meeting was that Ibrahim transferred into the household of his new friend, under the patronage of the latter's father. This time the Kpuawala elders warned Ibrahim that they would be watching his behavior, over the next few months, before reaching a final decision about permitting him to continue residing in the community. Over the following months and years, Ibrahim continued to be a problem, and yet the threat of evicting him was never carried out.[21]

The treatment of Ibrahim and other problematic guests in Kpuawala seemed to conform to Simmel's classic argument that strangers, though defined as outsiders, fulfill a key need *within* their host communities (Simmel 1950: 402–408). For example, the combination of proximity and distance embodied by a stranger made him or her a target for confidences that would not be shared with more integral members of the community. Consequently, the notion that a stranger would someday return to a home of origin remained in large part a fiction. This appeared to be the case with Ibrahim as well: he eventually married and settled in Kpuawala. But his mobility among Kpuawala households suggested that at the very least he might someday leave, if not to return to a putative home of origin, then to settle in another community where he might have made new friends. Indeed, given the constraint of having to occupy a dependent status—to be "for somebody"—until deemed qualified to become in turn patrons of others, junior men and wives at least could choose whom to depend on. As the case of Ibrahim and that of the wives discussed earlier suggest, this mobility could yield considerable leverage and was a key difference between slaves and other dependents.

Just as unattached young men posed a potential threat to the community, as well as being among its key resources, so did unattached women in their reproductive years. Several Kpuawala Sande elders said that they thought girls should be initiated when their breasts were "ripe" (kpelangɔ, a term used both for ripe fruits and a girl sprouting breasts), at puberty, because otherwise they would have to wait to marry. Otherwise, in the interval between puberty and initiation, a girl would be more likely to become sexually active, thus spoiling her chances at a good marriage. In Kpuawala, once a woman had been widowed, or if she was a single stranger, she was expected to "show" a (new) husband (hindo gɛ) before a year was out. When I asked the reason for this rule, I received an answer that resonated with the argument the town elders had given when warning Ibrahim that he should work only for his host household and not for others. I was told that men and households might get into fights and jealous arguments among themselves for access to a single, unattached woman. Kenneth Little documented this rule elsewhere in Mendeland during World War II (Little 1951: 167), although he also provided evidence that the remarriage rule for husbandless women became codified and more widespread as a result of interventions by the Native Administration system set in place by the British colonial government (Ibid: 169). In addition to the concern over the "social evil" presented by unattached women, rules governing their remarriage—which included the levirate in cases of widowhood—were justified by the need for women to have someone who would "stand surety for them" (Little 1951: 144). The crucial point, then, was that everyone must be accounted for by someone else—that everyone must be linked in a relationship of patronage or clientship—and husbandless women, as well as strangers, were perceived as elusive and noncompliant agents in this system.

NIGHT AND DAY

The *kpakali* was an old-fashioned Mende chair. It consisted of a tree section with three branches splitting off at narrow angles and at roughly equal distance from each other, which formed a tripod when turned upside down. A short wooden section was then added transversally between two of the tripod's legs close to the ground, to form a narrow seat. For the inexperienced like myself, it was easy to upset the *kpakali* in the process of sitting in it or standing up out of it. The use of the *kpakali* as both sitting and tripping mechanism was also familiar to more experienced Mende users. A commonly heard proverb in Kpuawala claimed that "In the night, the *kpakali* trips those who have wives/women" (*Kpakali kpindihu nyahamɔ mia a gɔla*). In other words, jealous husbands rushing out of the house in the dark to catch their wives having trysts with their lovers were likely to trip over chairs on the way. The night was the time when husbands were most unsure of their wives' doings, the ideal time for concealment. The fact that husbands did not know what their wives were doing at night might seem a paradox, but in polygynous households, husbands in fact cohabited with only one wife at a time. The institution of polygamy, then, enabled women to conceal extramarital relations more effectively than in monogamous marriages—a fact of which Mende husbands were well aware. The *kpakali* and the proverb it evoked were material reminders of the potential for betrayal in marriage. However, as we shall see, polygyny was also desirable in other ways, for the acquisition of social and political power.

This uncertainty about the covert activities of married women extended beyond sexual affairs to a whole range of illicit nighttime practices carried out under cover of darkness. During the dry season in Kpuawala, when rice and palm fruits were harvested, "night rice" (*kpindi mbɛi*) and "night oil" (*kpindɛi gulɔ*) became the object of a surreptitious, small-scale trade carried out by wives under cover of darkness. This night trade provided a contrasting parallel to the open transactions of its daytime equivalents. To be sure, many men and women of different ages were not particularly public about their purchases and sales, regardless of the time of the day in which these occurred. However, certain features set apart the goods marked as nighttime commodities.

When a woman came to my door whispering that she had some night rice or oil for sale, it was understood that these were amounts she had surreptitiously subtracted from the produce processed earlier in the day. The amounts involved were small, perhaps two pints of oil or three to five cups of rice. My visitors often kept these commodities concealed on their person, or, in the case of oil, they would make sure I agreed to the purchase before retrieving the goods from a hiding place. Though women were usually compensated for their processing labor with a portion of the resulting goods if these were subsistence crops like rice and oil, or with money in the case of coffee and cocoa, the night trade involved additional, stolen amounts.

A woman engaging in night sales was also in a hurry to acquire money, though this could be done only in small amounts, given the limited quantity of goods involved. As a result of the conditions under which these goods had been acquired, and under which they were sold, they were offered at lower prices than their current market value. Low prices and flexible terms of payment were another generally recognized feature of women's nighttime trade. Kpuawala men and women often indicated their willingness to negotiate reasonable prices by saying that what they had to sell was like "night rice." In other words, they were willing to part with the goods for a relatively low price. Finally, night trade was carried out with a trusted person, but one, like a stranger, whose relative distance made it unlikely that she would reveal the transaction to a woman's kin or husband.

The fact that goods sold at night by women were concealed implies that their acquisition and sale belonged to the register of transgression, but this was only partly the case. Everyone in Kpuawala seemed to be aware of these "thefts," and the fact that they were openly evoked in other kinds of business transactions suggested as much. On different occasions when men were telling me about their crops, they deliberately ignored questions about obvious discrepancies between harvested amounts and what was actually measured after processing—after the rice was cleaned of its husk, the oil extracted from palm fruits, and so on. It was as though men's vagueness about what happened between the harvest and the production of processed foodstuffs mimicked women's ambiguous activities in the same spatiotemporal interval. Once the collective work of harvesting rice in tied bunches, or harvesting heads of palm fruits, was over, men's supervision gave way to women's processing work. The work site shifted from rice fields or scattered collection points for palm fruit heads in the bush, to the processing clearings and cooking huts on farms where women and children were the only permanent presence, while men dropped in intermittently between other activities. The very nature of processing work, which was more time-consuming and drawn out than the bursts of collective energy invested in harvests, made it easy to escape notice when one was siphoning off small amounts of goods. But the vagueness of men's accounting for their produce, coupled with a general awareness that some of it was subtracted at this time, suggests that this was a sanctioned practice.

When confronted with straightforward questions about this practice, some Kpuawala men half-heartedly called it a form of theft but did not seem particularly concerned about it. On the contrary, they seemed amused at my suggestion that they might want to stop it. Everyone did this, they claimed, and they expected it. This was how women got money for tobacco snuff and other small expenses. Men also disagreed that the practice might stop if they awarded their wives a higher compensation for processing work in the first place. On this everyone seemed to agree: subtracting a small amount of the product of one's processing labor had nothing to do with the amount of compensation awarded for that same work. Rather, it had to do with a kind of entitlement that came with the form of work, which women brought to most stages of farming and domestic life. Women owned the rice left "stuck to the pot" after cooking, which even had a special name, *manyɛ*. This food was seldom restricted to the burnt remainders suggested by the idiom of *manyɛ* and could in fact add up to as much as a third of the pot's contents. However, as with night rice and oil, it was considered mean to try to account for this "accursed share." As Bataille suggested, surplus, or the excess beyond what was necessary for sustaining a system or an organism, was an amount destined to be lost without profit or calculation (Bataille 1989: 60). Everyone knew about it, but nobody wanted to quantify it. Indeed, resistance to measuring such purloined goods in part created the conditions for their subtraction. Once processed food was measured, weighed, and accounted for, its theft by anyone became a serious offense that warranted compensation or prosecution in court. But in the interval between the harvest and the processing of food for consumption, variable amounts could disappear through ruses that made both husbands and wives complicitous in the endeavor. Wives adopted covert tactics to subtract and dispose of night produce, and their husbands participated in shaping a spatiotemporal window in which their crops were unaccounted for. Perhaps this was due to a strategic—if unwitting—calculus that this kind of oversight might prevent the enactment of other women's nighttime tactics, sexual entanglements that might drive husbands to jealous surveillance. Like the chair in the proverb, this surveillance would inevitably trip husbands up, so the night was best left to the concealed tactics of their wives' income-generating activities.

CONCLUSION

One of the first questions I used to be asked by Mende people testing my proficiency in the language and culture was a tongue-twister that translates as "Are you here on your own?" (*Bi mbei a bi mbeilo?*). The correct answer, even if one has come alone, is that one is always "for" someone else: one's host or landlord, one's husband, the local chief, all the way up to chiefdom and government authorities. Being for someone else (*numui lɔ va*), as mentioned earlier, is the Mende way of phrasing these relationships of dependence between juniors and seniors, women and men. It is a valued affirmation of interdependence, but it also points to the potential transformation of dichotomous relations, such as the splits brought about by marriage, into productive and fertile unities of a higher order, such as those represented by large farming households.

Individual autonomy and independence threaten these larger units with infertile and unproductive splits, such as those represented by husbandless women and by strangers who have less at stake in the domestic groups in which they are dependents. Those who are on their own are liable to be suspected of antisocial behavior, such as witchcraft. But it is not only potential dependents, those "for someone," who can become ostracized for showing too much autonomy. Big people (*kpakoisia*) who are very successful in farming, politics, or business are liable to be equally suspect, particularly if there is a perception that they do not use their wealth and status to help dependents and instead seek only their own profit. Thus the system is one of thorough interdependence, albeit within a hierarchical social order.

As wives, women are dependents *par excellence* and are the subjects of an idiom of giving and owning. Like young strangers who might turn out to be womanizers, drinkers, and gamblers on the run, women must be controlled and remarried if husbandless, lest they pose a threat to the social order. However, I have shown that this language of ownership equally reflects women's historical role in both shaping and obliterating relations of slavery. Women managed slave labor on farms, but they were also the intermediaries, through marriage, for incorporating slaves into domestic groups and transforming them into kin over time. When women themselves were slaves, they could use to their advantage the overlap between their dependent roles as slaves and wives, declaring themselves either one or the other at abolition.

Thus women share the same status with strangers and other figures of alterity, who are reminders of both the existence of an order of concealment and the social instability of power. The forms of dependence within Mende patronage networks point to the fact that the idiom of hierarchy masks the potential for reversals in these relationships. The very idiom of dependence conceals the extent to which these relations are part of a system of *inter*dependence. The historical frequency with which dependents have become patrons, and vice versa, shows both the ambiguity and the unpredictability of social relations. Hence the coexistence of multiple registers, which blur the boundaries between licit and illicit practices, and where the day's visible economy gives way to the night's occult circulation—thereby rendering the hierarchical system highly unstable and reversible.

Splitting Kola

But the principal fruit, in the estimation of the natives, is the
colá. . . . [I]t divides into two parts, and is either of a purple
colour or white. . . . Those who can procure it chew it at all
times and at all seasons. It is presented to guests at their arrival
and departure—sent in complimentary presents to chiefs—
is a considerable article of inland trade, as well as with the
Portuguese . . . , and [is] frequently made the token of peace
or war.

Matthews (1788: 59–60)

The value of kola in West Africa can scarcely be over-stressed.
The kola nut is associated with religious rites, initiation
ceremonies, and property rights; it is used as a stimulant, a
yellow dye, for medicinal purposes, as a symbol of hospitality,
and in diplomatic relations between rulers; and it was
particularly highly regarded among Islamicized peoples.

Rodney (1970: 206)

In July 1993, I was standing in a line at the Lungi airport, waiting for my
turn to be interviewed by army soldiers before boarding a plane out of
Sierra Leone. The soldiers, a conspicuous presence at the airport since the
previous year's military coup, were demanding money and gifts from
departing passengers. Some of the people in the line tried to argue; others
fearfully complied. When my turn came, I opened my carry-on luggage,
the hand-woven basket I had brought from Kpuawala. Fatoma had
woven it for me as a present, making a pattern out of natural and dyed
rattan fibers. The latter were red, and to obtain this color, Fatoma had
used shavings from the red camwood tree—a time-consuming dyeing
process to make the basket "just like in the old days," something by
which to remember him once I was "beyond the sea." Already the two
soldiers inspecting my belongings were aggressively asking about my foreign and Sierra Leonean currency. They fingered a leaf-wrapped bundle
in my basket and opened it to reveal the kola nuts inside. Suddenly the
tense atmosphere in the terminal dissipated: the uniformed men burst out

laughing, and immediately, to the great relief of the other passengers, the atmosphere became palpably more relaxed. Turning to me and now addressing me in Krio instead of English, the soldiers "begged" for kola in the traditional manner. They were incredulous that I should be taking kola abroad with me and that anyone living that far away should have a taste for something that reminded them of their rural origins.

Having freely rifled through the pockets and luggage of passengers ahead of me in the line, the soldiers now refused to touch any of my kola nuts unless I took one, bit off a piece, and offered them the rest in the manner customary in rural Sierra Leone. They lost all interest in my money too, and jokingly engaged in an exaggerated performance of the polite behavior normally associated with the ceremonial distribution of kola nuts. One of them, a Mende, upon discovering that I spoke his language, began referring to me as yiemɔ—as "mother-in-law." The soldiers' reaction evoked the historical links between money and kola in Sierra Leone, as sometimes mutually exclusive, sometimes equivalent commodities. Furthermore, the joking reference to mother-in-laws pointed to the certrality of kola symbolism in instantiating marriage alliances. The point of all this is that, like my peasant basket, the leaf-wrapped kola nuts evoked for this particular group of men a rural world that contrasted starkly with the circumstances of our encounter. Hence their exaggerated, absurd performance of courtesies. But, as we shall see, the performative aspects of kola exchanges in all contexts sometimes cloak in amity more ambivalent intentions.

In rural Mendeland, kola was consumed and exchanged on a daily basis. Kpuawala men kept whole nuts or fragments in their pockets, and women tucked them in their head ties or secured them in knotted corners of their lappa, the cotton wrappers they wore as skirts. On the farm, or while traveling, resting, and chatting in the evening, sooner or later someone reached for a whole or broken nut, bit some off, and shared it with others. Alternatively, she or he would ask, nya gɔ toloi, "give me kola." The acts of reaching for kola, "begging" for it, biting off or splitting it, and sharing it had the automatic frequency, the taken-for-grantedness of the shared gestures that made up rural Mende everyday life with scarcely a trace of conscious acknowledgment. Men and women, young and old, valued it for its stimulant properties, and particularly because it kept hunger and thirst at bay during the physical exertions, and in the heat, of farming (see Brooks 1993: 52). Kola was essential to keep one going until the afternoon, when the bulk of the day's work was done, and one could sit down to rest and eat a proper meal of rice.

Kola nuts come as irregularly shaped, roundish fruits varying between the size of a thumb nail and that of a large peach nut. They can be cleanly broken into their two constituent, asymmetrical halves. They come off the trees inside green pods, and they are encased in a white, soft skin that is kept on the nut to keep it fresh in the short term but must be peeled off fruits for long-term storage, to delay deterioration. The nuts themselves may be creamy white, pink, or a purple-red and are carefully separated according to shade and size, for different uses.[1]

Like cloth, kola nuts of the *Cola nitida* variety have played a key role in integrating the forest belt of the Upper Guinea coast into an encompassing set of regional economic, political, and cultural ties. Like woven country cloth, kola has functioned as a currency and has historically served as a material expression of key aspects of Mende sociality. In the case of kola, this link is more strongly marked by the continued use of *to(lo)i*, "kola," as a term for certain kinds of money. In regional exchange networks, kola often moved in the opposite direction from cloth, but on the same routes. In precolonial times, cloth made its way south into the forest belt inhabited by the Mende and was exchanged for kola, for which there was great demand among northern Muslim peoples. These two commodities overlapped in cloth production, where kola has long been, with indigo, one of the key natural dyes used in making cotton clothing and blankets.[2]

The very name kola (or cola) by which this nut is known in European languages is a variant of the northern Sierra Leonean (Temne) term for it, and Sierra Leone has the highest concentration of kola trees in the region (see Brooks 1980: 3). Thus kola nuts have long represented a specific contribution of this area to the broader regional economy. As early as the thirteenth century, Arabic sources documented the importance of kola in trade relations between the West African savannah and desert regions, and the forest belt to the south where they originated (Levtzion 1973: 181). Ethnic enclaves specializing in the kola trade spread across West Africa in precolonial times but expanded their range considerably with the pacification and common currencies ushered in by nineteenth-century colonial regimes (see Amselle 1977: 189ff; Cohen 1966: 20; Lovejoy 1973). In the 1970s, one could trace members of a single family of a specialized kola-trading group centered in Mali over a territory that encompassed Bamako, Madina (a village on the Mali–Guinean border), Côte d'Ivoire, and Blama, in Sierra Leone (Amselle 1977: 87), which was the market town closest to Kpuawala.[3] Thus to this day, Fulani and

Mandingo traders travel throughout rural Mendeland to buy kola, and the nut's symbolic connotations echo its role as historical mediator between indigenous landlords and visiting strangers, between invading, trading, or (Muslim) proselytizing northerners from the savannah and farming, forest-belt southerners (Brooks 1993).

The act of splitting a kola nut into its two constituent parts is symbolically central to Mende rituals that signify both unity and separation. As a token of peace or war, kola nuts both create and bridge distances between different groups. At the same time, their productive cycle makes them bridge the temporal gap between different seasons. When kola is scarce, it is the object of intense desire and endless conversations. To ensure a steady supply between the two annual harvests, owners of kola trees take care to periodically cull, wash, and repackage their nuts in fresh leaves for storage in cool places inside houses. In the Wunde region, these harvests coincided with "burnt farm time" (*mɔtu kpee*), in April–May, and with "rice-cutting time" (*mba lee kpee*), roughly in November. Thus the kola tree's bearing fruit marked an important transition in the annual rice farming cycle: between rainy and dry seasons, the preparation of fields for sowing and the harvest, and the social activities linked to these critical moments in the Mende calendar. Indeed, work on the economic history of this region has shown that kola and rice cultivation are integral to each other: farmers contributed to the diffusion of kola trees by planting them on farms for shade, as well as for their fruits (Ford 1992). The practice of shifting rice cultivation meant that kola trees were also continuously planted at new sites, which contributed to the creation of forest islands in farming regions.[4]

As I mentioned above, the Mende historically sealed friendship or peace by offering kola, and they did so in language that often explicitly referred to *splitting*. In Kpuawala, requests for kola often took the form "come, let us *split* kola" (*wua mbei a mu toloi mbla*). The nut is both one and two. It is difficult to split (*mb[e]la*) with one's hands, even though it has a clear fault line where the two halves are joined. Once separated, each half is unique in its curved, asymmetrical joining surface, which matches only its original partner. Thus the act of splitting kola suggests an affirmation both of wholeness—of "one word/voice," the Mende term for unity (*ngo yila*)—and of breaking down into separate, different units. Kola nut halves fit together in ways that suggest an asymmetrical complementarity, which parallels certain social relationships. In particular, gender and marriage relations display a complementarity that mirrors the forms of kola sharing. As we shall see in the next chapter, kola is used metonymically and metaphorically in the grammar of local language and social relations. Historically, marriage has mediated some of the same relations characterized by kola nut exchanges, such as those between former enemies, between humans and spirits, and between mobile and settled communities. During the eighteenth-century wars in the Sierra Leone hinterland, kola was offered along with white cloth as a gift, through women intermediaries, to initiate peace negotiations between male warriors (Day 1988). Furthermore, the gendered intersections of kola use were symbolized in their numbers during sacrificial offerings. In Kpuawala, sacrifices to ancestral and other spirits on the occasion of funerals, child-naming ceremonies, and marriages displayed clusters of three or four kola nuts, numbers that were understood as female and male, respectively (cf. Sawyerr and Todd 1970).

The politics of kola circulation in Kpuawala was redolent with the history of this area's exploitation in the processes that brought it within a larger regional economic system. As with other products that were consumed and valued *locally*, in addition to having economic value elsewhere, kola was the object of an ambivalent trade with variously identified foreigners. Kola nuts were at once a material expression of values at the core of "Mendeness," *and* of the historical interdependence of rural Mendeland with non-Mende outsiders. Again, kola shares with cloth a feature that further specifies the nature of this historical relationship with outsiders: both commodities were important items in long-standing trading partnerships that were primarily oriented to the north and the trans-Saharan relay trade, but later marked the economic and political reorientation of this region toward the south, and the coastal trade with Europeans and other foreigners, such as the Lebanese, whose presence in the region was linked to colonial occupation. Kpuawala people often expressed their ambivalence about marketing kola nuts to foreign traders such as the Fula living among them or the Lebanese who dealt in kola on a larger scale in important towns.[5] Villagers unwillingly mortgaged their kola crops for credit during the rainy—and hungry—season, and thus tended to see these trading relations as exploitative. However, when kola was scarce and its price doubled, tree owners played this game to their advantage, by concealing their stored stock of nuts and selectively circulating them within the community or selling beyond it. In Kpuawala, rites of passage that took place in the midst of the rainy season, which was

already under the shadow of rice scarcity, were preceded by—and predicated on—their main sponsors' efforts to find appropriate amounts of
kola nuts by following rumors about who had hidden stores of the precious good. Thus the meaning of kola as an offering of peace and friendship was magnified both by the historical resonances of a regional political economy and by local tactics in managing supplies through times of
plenty and scarcity.

The kola nut's value was underscored by the fact that the gifts and
exchanges required for certain occasions involved "giving kola" (*toloi
ve*), although it was not kola but money that was actually given. When
arriving at a place anew or after a long absence, one was expected to give
"greeting kola" (*fama loi*), a small fee to be distributed among local
authorities. In general, giving kola was a sign of greeting to respected ritual specialists—for example, members of the "medicine," or secret, societies. Kola—that is, money—was also given in appreciation of esoteric
knowledge imparted by such specialists. Other contexts in which kola-
money was given were specifically linked to conjugal relations and the
language accompanying such exchanges suggested that these sought to
bring unity and peace to marriage, and multiplication through reproduction. The act of "laying down kola" (*toi la*) marked the beginning of
bridewealth payments by the groom and his kin to the bride's family.
Once married, a man gave his wife "nursing mother's kola" (*koima loi*)
in the wake of childbirth. In both of these cases, the money given was
seen as a token of appreciation, rather than being connected in any way
to expenses, such of those of marriage, for example, or of rearing a child.
Furthermore, in both of these cases kola exchanges marked phases when
the marital union was especially fragile: before the existence of any real
bond, and at the beginning of a long period of sexual separation between
husband and wife, until their child is weaned.

When people gave money but called it kola, they made—at least ideally—clear distinctions between these transactions and those involving
plain currency.[6] One of the first points most people made in trying to
explain the distinction between money used for payments and that which
changed hands as "kola" was that the amount of the latter could not be
questioned. By contrast, all payments and prices (*pawɛi*) were negotiable,
and hence the object of intense negotiation, regardless of whether a fee
was attached to a court fine or a commodity for sale. Indeed, kola almost
had to be a small amount of money, which was accepted with blessings.

Kola, in other words, signified the intention of establishing a long-lasting relationship characterized by more important and sustained exchanges, as in trading partnerships or the peace offerings mediated in the past by this gift. It did so by making the money form convertible into a range of intangible values collected under the polysemic umbrella of kola: into peaceful greetings when offered by a visiting stranger to a host community, into respect when given in exchange for ritual knowledge, or into happiness in the context of marriage.

However, the very status of kola-money at the nexus of such important manifestations of individual and shared sociality made its opposition to payment money contingent. The clear distinction between the two forms was muddied as soon as the relations that kola was supposed to auspiciously inaugurate soured. Thus on the occasion of my send-off from Kpuawala, members of a faction that opposed the Paramount Chief whispered criticisms of the greeting kola amounts that were being handed out by his representative to performers in the celebration. These comments underscored the stinginess of the kola-money amounts, given the importance of the occasion, thus contradicting the purported incommensurability of such tokens. Likewise, in divorces that I witnessed in Kpuawala, bridewealth kola was invariably reclassified as part of the payments that had to be returned by the wife's family to the groom and his kin, rather than as the gift that preceded such payments. Thus as "extension of the self" and of particular social relations, both kola and money can be identified with those relations because they concretize the most abstract of values—happiness, respect, peace, and unity. The flexibility of money "is only that of the extremely liquid body which takes on any form, and does not shape itself but receives any form it may possess only from the surrounding body" (Simmel 1978 [1907]: 326). However, in Sierra Leone, kola encompasses and extends the flexibility of the money form, by signifying the elusive boundaries between payments and gifts.

My exchange with the military at the airport was shaped in part by the notion of kola as an alternative medium of social exchange to the "hard" currencies the soldiers were seeking to extract from harassed passengers. But it also had to do with the possibilities of converting one form of value into the other—with the recognition that ultimately cold cash, too, was destined to the social projects that elsewhere were still mediated by kola exchanges. Indeed, the change brought over the soldiers by the sight of kola nuts in my luggage—their laughter, where amusement mixed with surprise and awkwardness—had to do with their recognition that I shared with them the knowledge that our encounter belonged to the same register of vulnerable social interactions (e.g., efforts at peace-making in times of conflict.

Jina (1986)

CHAPTER 4

The House of Impermanence and the Politics of Mobility

Maybe it is a good thing for us to keep a few dreams of a house that we shall live in later, always later, so much later, in fact, that we shall not have time to achieve it. For a house that was final, one that stood in symmetrical relation to the house we were born in, would lead to thoughts—serious, sad thoughts—and not to dreams. It is better to live in a state of impermanence than in one of finality.

Bachelard (1964: 61)

The minuscule, a narrow gate, opens up an entire world. The details of a thing can be the sign of a new world which, like all worlds, contains the attributes of greatness.

Miniature is one of the refuges of greatness.

Bachelard (1964: 156)

In this chapter I explore a place, the people and objects occupying it, and the alterations produced by their movements in and out of it as they strategically shape the social relations that brought them together there. The material world—in which these relations unfold—participates in social processes through its dense, polysemic meanings. Objects and places are indeed related metonymically with social actors, groups, or events. Looking specifically at the configuration of metonymical relations requires moving between different analytical scales, between large and small, part and whole. Yet, as the intersection of social, political, and economic circulation of kola suggest, it is a movement well worth undertaking: the miniaturization of the whole, or its condensation in a fragment, makes for an even denser meaning (Certeau 1986: 101).

Thus I focus on the smaller objects, on enclosures within larger spaces, to understand different social networks and imagined socialities. Much of importance in Mende daily sociality is prefaced by the adjective *big*—big person, big farm, big house, etc.—and yet these sites of "greatness" are in practice impermanent and vulnerable to social and physical reduction if not outright disappearance. I examine the small things out of which large ones may come forth because, as Bachelard points out, the work of the social imagination lies in augmenting the small, and not vice versa;[1] the process of finding clues to an encompassing world in the apparently insignificant details of material life is simpler than its inverse.

It is a tricky project, which (like all analyses of the material world) risks devolving into an overly structured discourse that pays insufficient attention to agency and intentionality, even when objects and spaces are contextualized in relation to social practices (e.g., Bourdieu 1990; cf. Ortner 1996: 11). By contrast, paying excessive attention to human intentions and practices, their temporalities and historicity, would leave little room for understanding how these are constrained by material conditions, as well as shaping them. A constant juggling and switching of analytical scales is required: one must move from the analysis of objects and places—their production, circulation, transformations, and valuations—to human practices and forms of sociality.

To discuss the formation of gendered perspectives on and strategic positions in the *mawɛɛ*, the "extended household"—the most important unit of social identification, labor organization, and co-residence in the everyday life in rural Wunde chiefdom—I found I had to begin with the big house, even though only its women and children lived there. Why begin with the big house, given that men tended to have leadership roles in the *mawɛɛ*? Because I was told that this was the main *place* with which members of a *mawɛɛ* identified, along with the big farm outside it. The big house, a Kpuawala woman once told me, *is* the *mawɛɛ*'s house.[2] More people lived in big houses than in any other buildings in rural communities, so this was a place where many different activities were concentrated. The big house was also historically the place from which slave farm labor was organized. Notwithstanding their conceptual and social importance, big houses were also physically marginal to village space and associated with ambiguously valued processes. The reasons for this ambiguity have to do with the social and physiological processes that unfold in the big house. My argument is that at some level, the big house has a metonymical relationship with the *mawɛɛ*—it is a part that stands for the social whole. Furthermore, within big houses, objects such as beds and cooking pots—their uses and how they are interwoven with particular social identities, relations, and occasions—are vital to understanding both the big house's imaginary centrality to *mawεε* identity and strength and its historical impermanence. Tied to this big house dynamics is the tension between the crucial role of women and their children in agricultural production and physical reproduction at the core of *mawεε* life, and often conflicting options for residential and social affiliation, which account for the mobility and impermanence of these household members.

For here is the irony: although big houses were said in Kpuawala to be the *mawεε*'s main residential site, there were only half as many of the former (five) as of the latter (ten). To explore what accounts for the range of residential arrangements grouped under the single category big house, as well as its absence altogether in some cases, I offer in the following sections a "biography" or "social life" of the Kamara big house in Kpuawala. If the core site of identification of the *mawεε* is such a place of impermanence, what are the implications for the social unit to which it is so central?

BIG (WOMEN'S) HOUSES

During my first rainy season in Kpuawala, in 1985, I used to love visiting the Kamara big house (*pεε wai*) next door to me in the evenings, when most people were at home keeping the damp out with a large fire in the middle the room. The large, elongated room had nine wooden beds around its perimeter. Some beds had canopies of makeshift mosquito nets made of solid cloth scraps sewn together. Others had combinations of mats, towels, and extra cloth hanging from their wooden frames. Whatever materials protected sleepers from nighttime mosquito raids were hanging on three sides of the bed, and the fourth flap—facing the room's interior—was pulled back. On this side, the bed's occupants were sitting conversing with neighbors or preparing for the night. I felt warm and comfortable in the semidarkness of this large, single room teeming with young children and women of all ages. Had I been a man, though, I might not have felt the same way. Adult men in the community certainly did not seem at ease in this space, as evidenced by the fact that whenever one of them needed to contact a wife or female relative in the big house—or perhaps only wanted to buy tobacco snuff from the elderly Mama Kema, who made the best in town—they called from beyond the threshold or sent in a young child to carry out their errand.[3]

The big house's thresholds were not just imaginary boundaries reinforced by unarticulated, embodied habits that stopped adult men outside
them. Senior women held the keys and controlled the flow of people in
and out (their direction and timing) through selective closings and openings of the house's doors, from both inside and outside.[4] The front door
was normally closed from the inside during the day, when most people
were gone to the rice farms, and the few remaining nursing mothers or
older women used the back entrance to move between the building and
the cooking huts beyond. However, during the day it was difficult to keep
big house entrances under control, given the large numbers of people
residing there. At night, while women and children slept in the house,
only occupants in need of relieving themselves opened the back door.[5] By
contrast, the front door was open whenever the house was occupied—for
example, in the morning before women left for the fields, and on moonlit
evenings in the dry season when they gathered on the veranda to seed,
card, or spin cotton, sell kerosene or snuff, and socialize.

After many subsequent visits, I remember thinking that from the middle of the big house each bed looked like a little self-contained world as
women and children prepared for the night in the dim light of small
kerosene lamps hanging from their individual canopies. This perception
was my own; no practices or words of the beds' occupants triggered it. It
was due in part to the fact that each canopied bed enclosed not only
human occupants but also their personal possessions—clothes, strip-
woven cotton blankets, head ties, and other small items—which carved
out a personalized place in the cavernous, ill-defined collective space.
Objects worn on the body were stored within the enclosure formed at
night by the canopied bed, and other possessions (such as cooking pots,
utensils, and durable foodstuffs) were stored immediately beyond its
perimeter. Food was locked away in wooden boxes made specially to
protect it from theft and animal pests (sɔbɔxi). But it was not so much the
static location of these objects in and around individual beds that created
the kind of boundary that made me think of box imagery. Rather, it was
the relationship between the storage of possessions and their circulation
among other inhabitants of the big house that seemed to create shifting
social boundaries. In a place where everyone could see what one possessed, the patterns of object use made big house sociality—but could
unmake it too.

One of my worst memories from the first two years spent in Kpuawala
was of the growing resentment between two of my favorite female
friends, who occupied contiguous beds in the Kamara big house. Mama

Kɔɔ (Fig. 1, A3)—the reserved but fiercely loyal woman who cared for me and cooked and shared my meals—became increasingly hostile toward Mamì (Fig. 1, A4), her husband's niece. Neither woman admitted that there was anything wrong, but the tension was palpable every time the two were in the same place, and eventually Mamì moved out of the big house and into another compound. This outcome was personally upsetting because Mamì was more of a friend, but also because her keen intelligence, wit, and disregard for social expectations made her a critical interlocutor in my research. Neither woman acknowledged that anything had happened, and it was only when I grew so frustrated that I stopped accepting Mama Kɔɔ's food—and through this act inadvertently caused a public embarrassment to her husband's extended family—that a formal inquiry into the matter was held. It revealed that trouble had started many months earlier, when, upon divorcing her elderly husband, Mamì had to return to him the mosquito net and bedding he had provided for her and their infant daughter. Feeling sorry for Mamì, who was thus left without protection from insects at the height of the rainy season, I had given her my extra mosquito net. I had asked Mamì not to reveal the source of the gift, but my naïveté in assuming that this could remain a secret was brought home on my next visit to the big house by the visual impact of my sparkling white, gossamer-thin net (obviously a quality import) side by side with the homemade, heavy patchworks of cotton and synthetics, salvaged from worn clothes, that shielded neighboring beds. I heard occasional comments about the attractiveness of Mamì's new net, and a few jokes about how permeable to mosquitoes the local equivalents were, but no public speculation about the object's origin. During the inquiry held several months later, it became apparent that Mama Kɔɔ—and probably everyone else, too—had immediately guessed that the mosquito net was my gift to Mamì and had become hostile and resentful ever since, out of jealousy. Other contexts in which big house residents refused to share their good fortune, appropriated each other's belongings without asking permission, or stole them outright, also led to resentment and enmity.

Another reason for my perception of beds as distinctive enclosures, which while partaking of the big house's intensely public and social "feel" also remained the *particular* space of individual women and their children, was that their general appearance varied considerably. The degree of care and expense with which beds and bedding materials were maintained, as well as the quality and quantity of objects stored around the former, spoke volumes about their occupants' personal and social position at a particular moment in time. Thus, ironically, the least physically enclosed of beds—one unadorned with mosquito net or hanging clothes—pointed to its occupant's relative social isolation and poverty. The bed on which Satta slept during a month-long visit had neither protection from mosquitoes nor a lamp; and her light, worn clothes were her sole defense against the night chill; and only the ragged remains of a blanket partially covered her palm leaf bedding. Satta cut a rather forlorn figure amid the busy evening hubbub in the big house. She sat somewhat apart, an elderly semi-invalid, and when she did say something, her toothless, tobacco-filled mouth produced such slurred speech that she was often ignored by the uncomprehending audience. Her only close relative in Kpuawala was a half-brother, an elderly, childless widower who lived alone in a neighboring compound. Satta's isolation—and the poverty of the bed she occupied—underscored the extent to which my impression of camaraderie in the big house was temporary and partial at best.

One rainy season evening in the Kamara big house, Mama Kema, its senior resident, was sitting on a wooden stool by her bed (Fig. 1, A8), farther along the same wall where the entrance to the room was located. As the sister of the senior man, who was also the town chief, Kema, herself a grey-haired elder, exuded an easy confidence and authority. Her fine-featured face often broke into smile as she directed younger women and children to do chores around her, gave advice, or displayed her subtle sense of humor in conversation. Kema sat low on the ground on her small stool, her slight body bent over the tobacco snuff she was selling. She chatted with Sao, her sister-in-law, while counting change and bending over the glass jar at her feet, from which she dispensed tiny capfuls piled high with tobacco and lyme powder into the open palms of her female and child customers or into the small glass vials they brought with them. Sao was a loud, stoutly built, and hard-working middle-aged woman— the second surviving wife of the town chief, Jussu. Her appearance was slightly disheveled, and she seldom bothered to have her hair braided, instead keeping it concealed under a head tie. Both Kema and Sao seemed to get along with most of their big house neighbors; the former was also a precious asset because of her knowledge of midwifery, her familiarity with Sande ritual and medicine, and the excellent tobacco snuff she produced. Sao made up for her occasional obtuseness with her easy, no-nonsense demeanor and lack of malice. Her laughter—often at her own expense—revealed a front tooth gap that, I was often told, was considered a sign of female beauty (see Boone 1986: 99–100). Sao shared her bed, which was located next to the house's back door (Fig. 1, A1), with

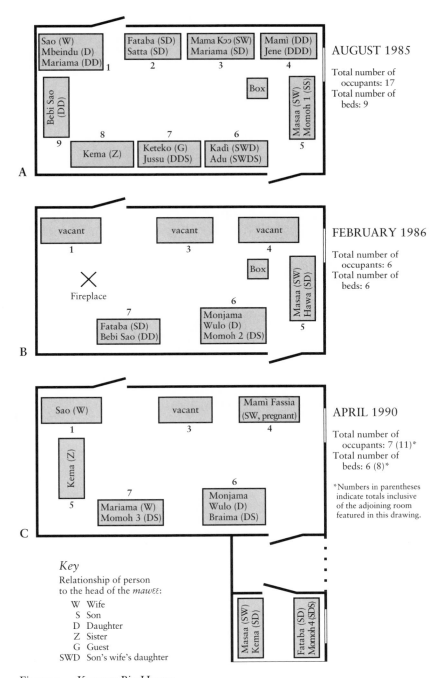

AUGUST 1985

Total number of
occupants: 17
Total number of
beds: 9

FEBRUARY 1986

Total number of
occupants: 6
Total number of
beds: 6

APRIL 1990

Total number of
occupants: 7 (11)*
Total number of
beds: 6 (8)*

*Numbers in parentheses
indicate totals inclusive
of the adjoining room
featured in this drawing.

Key

Relationship of person
to the head of the *mawεε*:

W   Wife
S   Son
D   Daughter
Z   Sister
G   Guest
SWD Son's wife's daughter

Figure 1.   Kamara Big House

her daughter Mbeindu and the latter's newborn daughter, Mariama. Addressing Kema as "my husband," (*nya hini*), she told her how she found the arrangement crowded but could not trust Mbeindu to properly care for the infant alone. Along the short wall separating Sao's and Kema's beds was another one on which two girls were playing. These were "Bebi" Sao, daughter of another one of Sao's adult daughters, and her cousin Fataba, whose father was the chief's eldest son from his senior wife. Fataba and her younger sister shared a bed diagonally across from Bebi Sao's (Fig. 1, A2).

On the bed next to the big house's front entrance, Kadì was changing her firstborn baby, Adu (Fig. 1, A6). While grooming the baby, with whom she shared her bed, Kadì was cheerfully talking to her mother, Mama Kɔɔ, who was also nursing an infant daughter in the bed across from hers (Fig. 1, A3). The body of Kadi's baby boy displayed the telltale signs of malnutrition: he had a bloated belly, bald head, large, serious eyes that made him look older than his 20 or so months, and skinny legs on which he still could not walk. His quiet demeanor matched that of his small, lightly built grandmother Mama Kɔɔ, who was married to one of the chief's three adult sons living in the village. Her daughter Kadì—born from a previous union—followed the common practice of returning to live with her mother for her first childbirth.

Eventually, all the women joined Mama Kema in a heated conversation about bedbugs, the bane of *pɛɛ wai* inhabitants here and elsewhere and a common topic of discussion among Kpuawala women. The battle against bed bugs in Kpuawala big houses periodically preoccupied their entire population and was a catalyst for creating alliances or tensions among women, as well as testing marital relations. Bedbugs could be found in men's beds as well, but because there was only one bed to disinfest (and doing so was the responsibility of a single individual), it was easier to accomplish.[6] By contrast, it took a concerted effort among all big house inhabitants to get rid of bugs, which otherwise would migrate to other beds. There was a direct correlation between the cost of disinfestation methods and their effectiveness. The best and most expensive method consisted of spraying beds and everything on them with cans of *Shelltox* from the Blama or Kenema Lebanese stores, but I was just about the only person who invested money in such a luxury. The next best option—and the most expensive one in Kpuawala—was hiring the services of traveling "bedbug people" (*kpengbeyalui bla*), who periodically came through with their home-made, kerosene-based chemicals. The most common solution, however, was to take apart every bed, move it outdoors, boil the palm leaf bedding, pour boiling water on the wooden frame, and hunt for the remaining bugs one by one as they tried to escape the heat by leaving the joints where they hid during the daytime. Stools, benches, clothes, and all bedding had to undergo the same boiling-water treatment too. Given the scale of any operation mounted against bed-bugs—especially the latter method, which typically lasted a whole day—all big house residents had to participate in the disinfestation project for it to be successful.

Even when a big house undertook the concerted effort to eliminate bedbugs, the high mobility of its residents, and the regular visits from women and children who normally lived elsewhere, made it virtually impossible to prevent a reinfestation at some later date. Occasionally one could hear women accusing either each other or their husbands of being too selfish to contribute money for a disinfestation project. I often heard men talk about the need to raise money for "bedbug medicine/poison" (*kpengbeyalui hale*) for their wives, so that their infant babies might be spared the painful bites of these ubiquitous nighttime raiders. The stan-dard reason that nursing mothers in Kpuawala gave to get money from their husbands for their personal expenses was the need for bedbug med-icine and kerosene. Attention to these details and the expenses they entailed was considered by both husbands and wives to be a barometer of the closeness of their relationship. Women, especially nursing mothers, could shame their husbands into paying for kerosene and bedbug medi-cine by complaining publicly about their failure to do so. Mama Kɔɔ began complaining about her son-in-law when he failed to provide kerosene for nighttime lighting for his nursing wife. She thought this lack of attentiveness was a sign that he was not interested in his son's well-being, arguing that the baby's failure to thrive was in part due to this and other, similar acts of negligence. Eventually, she initiated a lawsuit against him for failing to provide for her daughter. This concern with men's role in providing sleep-related comforts (relief from bedbugs and lighting for nighttime safety and infant care) is particularly striking in view of the expectation in many other domains that women be self-suffi-cient in providing for themselves and their children; they were often responsible for more expensive requirements, such as foodstuffs, school fees, and even health care.

Thus the issue of bedbugs helped bring into focus not only the collec-tive goodwill of women in the big house—their cooperation and invest-ment in the common well-being—but also the status of marital relations, in as much as it became a pivotal gauge of a husband's involvement in or negligence of the welfare of his wife and children. Two features of the bedbug's *modus operandi* made this creature a metaphor for spoiling relationships at other levels: it attacked at night during peoples' sleep, and it "ate" them, feeding on its victims' blood. This made it a particularly hated pest, even though it was far from being the most dangerous to human health.

Another source of complaints among big house occupants was the misuse or damage of a resident's possessions. Theft was rare in the big house and, when it did happen, was assumed to be the work of an intruder from outside. As Fassia once told me, "We Mende prefer to beg than to steal: one only costs us a few blessings, the other gets us cursed." But the unauthorized loan of a big pot belonging to another big house was once the source of a major intra- and inter-house diatribe in Kpuawala. At particularly labor-intensive times in the agricultural season, such as when trees were cut and brush was cleared to establish a big rice farm, the *mawɛɛ*'s women, often with the assistance of friends and relatives, cooked the *kɔndɔ*, a large rice meal with cassava leaf sauce, which was the main reward for farm work parties. Like bedbug hunts, the preparation of this major meal depended on the cooperation of the *mawɛɛ*'s women, and it was one of the main contexts for using a "big pot," or *fɛ wai*. Furthermore, because not all *mawɛɛsia* owned big pots, the pots' circulation between larger and wealthier big houses and poorer ones (or members of *mawɛɛsia* that had no big houses) was an indicator of patronage and exchange networks among big houses and households. This large, heavy, cast aluminum cooking vessel could measure about three and a half feet in diameter and half that in depth. Cooperation was needed in the very act of lifting it, once it was weighed down with food. The big pot was often one of the most expensive items stored within the big house—its most prized and durable collective possession. The house's senior woman, who also supervised its usage and the lending of it to other big houses on special occasions, stored it.

Large meals for ritual occasions such as funerals and male and female initiations were cooked in big pots. For village-wide events, several big houses would put their pots to work, and their senior women would coordinate cooking activities for feeding dozens and dozens of additional visitors. During the 1985 Sande initiation in Kpuawala, society elders requisitioned two big pots for several weeks, until the end of final ceremonies. Thus the big pot underscored the centrality of food for occasions ranging from the mundane (farm work parties) to the ritual and esoteric. What was common to all occasions in which big pots were used for preparing meals—as opposed to the ordinary, smaller cooking pots in which women cooked on a daily basis—was that these were collective events that brought together larger groups within and beyond the community.

On this particular evening, Mama Kema was going on in a vaguely accusatory tone about someone who had been allowed to sleep in her bed during her absence from Kpuawala, leaving behind bedbugs. Her reasoning pointed to another key element in relations between humans and bedbugs in the big house: infestations were the inevitable by-product of the great mobility of women and children into and out of the big house, and of this place's role in accommodating visitors from outside. At the same time, more permanent inhabitants in the big house used bedbugs as an excuse to decline hospitality: a bed might be denied because it was deemed too badly infested to be used by a visitor, and hence an embarrassment to the community. Conversely, the threat of infestation could be used as a reason to turn down a potential occupant. Women were frustrated, but they were also humorous when comparing notes on their dealings with bedbugs. Much amusement was generated by different individuals retelling the tale of my first morning in Kpuawala on each one of my stays there, when I inevitably inherited someone's bug-infested bed and emerged from my room after a sleepless night, covered with red bites. During the embellished and detailed account of the ailment and its cures for particularly tender-skinned *puu bla*, "white" people,[7] women kept on working, sharing tobacco snuff with each other, or carrying on business while participating in the general conversation.

"The bed" also stood metaphorically for sexual relations, and hence figured prominently in the discourse about permitted intercourse, especially in relation to women. If a man had a single wife, she would live with him until advanced pregnancy and then normally return to her mother's big house—especially for the birth of her first few children. Women were not supposed to have sexual intercourse until their infants walked and were weaned, which meant that they could spend up to three years in the big house. Transgressors were said to have "jumped behind the baby's back" (*i windea ndopo woma*), situating themselves between sleeping baby and mother in their shared bed and hence distracting the latter from the former's care. Mothers caught up in romantic entanglements were thought to lose interest in their baby's well-being, and hence to risk causing them to fall ill and die. During my time in Kpuawala, several husbands sued their wives to discover whether a baby's ill health was due to an extramarital affair. Sometimes husbands themselves were the culprits—especially when they were married to only one woman—and convinced their wives to resume sexual relations while still in the big house with a nursing baby. When Massa (Fig. 1, A5) became pregnant while still carrying around her nursing infant son, Kema jokingly referred to her husband's impatience and suggested that Massa must have really liked him to go along with his wishes.

Abdu, Massa's husband, had not yet "taken apart the nursing mother's bed, or bedding" (*kuima kpukɔ vaya*), Kema noted, referring to the practice that marked the transition back to normal sexual relations after abstinence during a child's infancy. Once a child was weaned and could walk, husbands normally had to ply their wives with presents and new clothes to replace those worn out by the baby's constant soiling to persuade them to leave the big house and resume sleeping with them. When faced with dismantling their big house beds after having spent between two and three years there, women often stalled to renegotiate the terms of their marriages. Though some, like Massa, were close enough to their husbands not to mind if he was unable to give her the requisite presents, others took advantage of the extended separation to leave their husbands permanently. Mami made the decision to divorce her husband, which led to the mosquito net incident mentioned earlier, when her baby girl began walking and she faced the prospect of having to resume living with him. When women did decide to return to their husbands, if they had no co-wives (as in the majority of Kpuawala marriages), they stripped their bed down to the wooden frame across which straight sticks supported the palm leaf cushioning or took them apart to store them for future use. If there were co-wives in their reproductive years, the big house bed continued to be in use during a woman's nights off, when another wife slept with their husband in his room.

Thus the pattern of assembling and disassembling, or of setting up occupancy and vacating, women's beds is related to the practice of polygamy, and the big house residential arrangement shares some features with segregated female living in northern African or Middle Eastern societies.[8] However, it is an unusual arrangement in this region and is unique even compared to other parts of Sierra Leone. It is more common, even in parts of West Africa where some degree of polygamy is practiced, to find individual wives with their own house or shelter, whom the husband visits in turn. It is also uncommon for settled, agricultural societies so closely to identify women's residence with the location of their belongings and beds, though it is not uncommon in situations of greater mobility—for example, among pastoralist or trading groups.[9]

Thus beds in Kpuawala big houses—the way in which they were decked and outfitted, their location, their infestation by bedbugs or freedom from them, and their assembled or disassembled condition—conveyed much about the occupants of those beds, their age and status, and their relationship to larger social groups. The conflicts arising out of sharing property or managing pest infestations in the big house also articulated with women's strategic management of relations among themselves as well as with husbands, in-laws, and kin. These conflicts, or their avoidance and resolution in forms of collaboration, were also key in the formation of bonds that cut across all such groupings, if only for a limited time and in a particular context.

By contrast, men's beds were not central to anchoring male property and position within the household, nor to the discourse on male sexuality or on transitions between different stages of the life cycle. Like women's beds, however, they could convey information about their owners' wealth, personal taste, and so on through the quality of their manufacture and bedding. Some of the men who had worked for some time as tailors or carpenters in towns, or as alluvial diamond diggers, had brought back with them Western-style spring bed frames that they decked out with mattresses made of rice bags filled with dried chaff and stalks and covered with imported Chinese cotton sheets. I was surprised by my first visit to Sellu's bedroom, when I was asked to bring him medicines during an illness. Sellu's room was in a house whose outward appearance was similar to that of most Kpuawala mud houses—a bit rundown, its clay whitewash fading in patches, or stained with brown mud where a repair had been necessary. He himself looked like most other village farmers—though perhaps somewhat more cheerful and friendly with me—and spent his days on the farm in tattered clothes, alongside his two wives and young children. By contrast with his house's ordinary exterior and mud surfaces, Sellu's bedroom had cement floors and walls, and the walls were painted and decorated with framed pictures. The bedroom was furnished with European-style furniture, and magazines, newspapers, and suitcases spilling over with imported commodities were neatly stacked around its edges. Except for a few details (such as the absence of windows), this was the kind of room one might find anywhere in urban Sierra Leone, complete with the decorative objects of the aspirant bourgeois the world over: handmade doilies, statuettes, and pictures. The contents of Sellu's room were collected when he worked as a public transport driver in the diamond-rich Yengema area to the north.[10]

The kind of dichotomy between the exterior of Sellu's house or its common spaces, and his bedroom could not be kept concealed in the big house, whose many occupants bring in frequent visitors, and where the difficulty of concealing anything is underscored by the presence of locked boxes in which women put their most important belongings. If an adult man had a whole bedroom in which to keep what he did not want others to see, a woman in the big house only had a wooden box. But only upon reaching a degree of self-sufficiency did a man even acquire a room and bed of his own. Young boys in Kpuawala usually slept on a mat on the floor in the bedroom of the adult men to whose care they were entrusted—usually a father or grandfather, but sometimes an unrelated teacher or mentor—whom they in turn assisted with daily chores such as fetching water and wood. Later, they might share a bed with another teenage boy or young adult, until they were ready to support themselves and marry. Thus adult men in Kpuawala tended to have their own individual rooms and beds, which they shared with their wives or, temporarily, with male friends in need of short-term accommodation. Like their owners, these beds tended to stay in place, in marked contrast to the regular dismantling of those belonging to women. Furthermore, because virtually all bedrooms had padlocks on their doors and were locked when their owners were gone, property in men's rooms did not need to be restricted to a box or to a bed's immediate vicinity, as it was in the big house shared by women and children.

Big houses ranged in form from free-standing, single-roomed structures (of which there were four in Kpuawala), to enormous rooms attached to houses that also had smaller quarters, to ordinary bedrooms at the back of houses. Some households had none of their members in big houses. The Kamara's big house was the one "hybrid" big house in Kpuawala—a large room attached to a structure with other, smaller units that were occupied by men as well as women. Its entrance from the house's veranda made it to some extent a separate entity, and any mention of the Kamara big house in Kpuawala was immediately understood to refer to this room alone. We have already met a number of big house residents. Before looking at the changes in big house arrangements over time, I shall now briefly discuss the Kamara *mawɛɛ* members who lived elsewhere.

Kaamɔ Jussu was the elderly and ailing head of the Kamara *mawɛɛ*.[11] He had handed over daily responsibilities and farming duties to his oldest resident son, Abdu(lai), though he still represented this group vis-à-vis the community at large. *Kaamɔ* Jussu lived in a single-roomed house (Fig. 2, C)

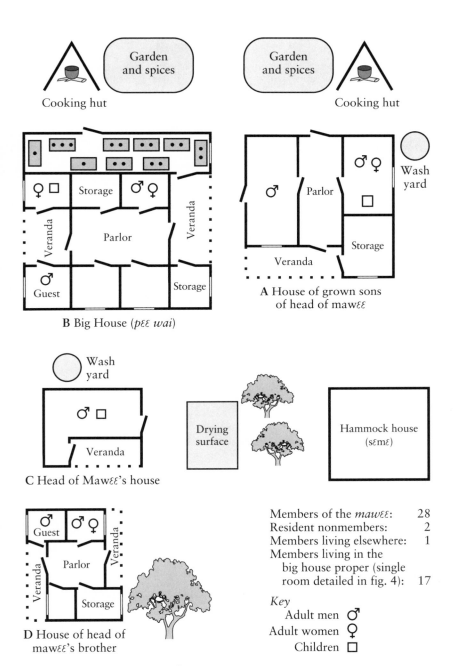

Cooking hut

Garden and spices

Garden and spices

Cooking hut

Wash yard

A House of grown sons of head of mawεε

Parlor

♂ ♀

□

Storage

Veranda

♂

♀ □

Storage

♂ ♀

Veranda

Parlor

Veranda

♂
Guest

Storage

B Big House (*pεε wai*)

Wash yard

♂ □

Veranda

C Head of Mawεε's house

Drying surface

Hammock house (*sεmε*)

♂
Guest

♂ ♀

Veranda

Veranda

Parlor

Storage

D House of head of mawεε's brother

Members of the *mawεε*: 28
Resident nonmembers: 2
Members living elsewhere: 1
Members living in the
big house proper (single
room detailed in fig. 4): 17

Key
Adult men ♂
Adult women ♀
Children □

Figure 2.   Kamara Compound

with his grandson, who slept on a floor mat in the same room. His senior wife Mariama lived with her daughter's young son in a room attached to the *mawɛɛ*'s big house (Fig. 2, B), and she usually stayed in town to take care of *Kaamɔ* Jussu and his frail brother and sister-in-law (Fig. 2, D). Mariama periodically lived in the big house itself, generally when Mama Kema was not around, and on these occasions she took on the senior role there. Mariama's only remaining co-wife, Sao, whom we met in the big house conversing with Kema, spent her days in turn on the farms of her three daughters and sons-in-law. The Kamara big rice farm was worked by Mariama's three grown sons and their families; it supported them, their mother and father, and their unrelated dependents. The three sickly elders spent most of their days in town, mostly weaving (the men), and spinning cotton (the woman). Two of the town chief's sisters—Mama Kema and another widow, who had no children in the area—also came to stay in *Kaamɔ* Jussu's big house for several months during the year. But they were quite active and mobile and spent their days on the farms of various relatives. This was often the case with elderly widows who did not have children to support them on a daily basis; they had to make themselves useful on their relatives' farms in order to be assured of a meal and other support.

Dependents of other *mawɛɛsia* lived in houses owned by the Kamaras as well. One young male stranger connected with a *mawɛɛ* in the neighboring compound occupied the veranda room off the house of chief Jussu's brother and sister-in-law (Fig. 2, D). The other visitor was hosted by the chief—in a veranda room of the Kamara building to which the big house was attached—on behalf of the community as a whole. Eddie "Bo-Pujehun," as he was called, was an extension agent from a Bo-based agricultural development project.[12] He spent his days on different Kpuawala farms to assist on improvements in rice cultivation techniques, and he provided pest-resistant seed varieties as well.

Kaamɔ Jussu's three adult sons in Kpuawala were between their mid-thirties and their early fifties. In June this year, Abdulai, the eldest son, had married Hawa, a young Kpuawala girl whose Sande initiation he had helped pay for. His first wife Massa had provided crucial help in this effort, which required laying an especially large plot for the required payments, gifts, and ceremonies. Massa lived in the big house with the couple's third child and had been the object of Kema's joke about those who could not wait to wean their infants to return to their husbands (Fig. 1, A5). Hawa started working on her future husband's and co-wife's farm before the end of her Sande initiation, even though she did not begin living with them until after the marriage.

Ambulai and "Gbesse" Kamara were Abdulai's other adult brothers in town.[13] Each had one wife and two children, but they had sent the eldest child away in fosterage to "be trained" (*makɛmi*). Ambulai's boy was with a Qur'anic teacher in his maternal grandmother's village 3 miles away, and Gbesse's daughter lived with his sister in Bo, the provincial headquarters town some 70 miles away, while attending an English-language government primary school. Gbesse and his wife, Mama Kɔɔ, helped pay for their daughter's school fees, books, and uniforms by periodically supplying Satta with palm oil, rice, and other local foodstuffs that could be sold for a profit in a large town like Bo. This connection also offered an opportunity for Mama Kɔɔ and Gbesse to visit the town, while Satta used the winter school holidays to spend several weeks in her paternal village stocking up on foodstuffs to bring back to Bo.[14]

Gbesse alone occupied another room in the building annexed to the big house, where Mama Kɔɔ and their nursing daughter lived (Fig. 1, A3). Ambulai lived in another room with his only wife and their toddler girl. Both Gbesse and Ambulai had a swamp rice farm to feed their own wives, children, visitors, and dependents. Among the latter, Gbesse counted his wife Mama Kɔɔ's two children from a previous marriage, Momoh (Mohammed) and Kadì (Kadiatu—Fig. 1, A6).

The overlap between Mama Kɔɔ's pregnancy and that of her daughter Kadì, along with their joint residences as adult, reproductive women in the same big house, was not unusual in a context where girls married soon after puberty. During the years in which I followed the circulation of Kamara big house residents, other such mother-daughter pairs came together at various times. Given the common practice of sending children away in fosterage to be trained, this was an opportunity for mothers and daughters to reestablish a close relationship with each other and with the big house where together they cared for their infants. Thus big house living brought together female kin of different generations who would normally be separated by their marital situations, as well as women of the same generation who elsewhere might never develop a close relationship—like sisters-in-law Kema and Sao. At the same time, social and personal cleavages were made apparent by the conspicuous absence from the big house of women like Mariama, who as the senior wife of *kaamɔ* Jussu was entitled to live there but instead chose to live in a separate room.

Mussa, Kadì's husband, sporadically helped his wife and in-laws with agricultural tasks in Kpuawala, while spending most of his time either hunting or on his father's upland farm in Mendama, some four miles away. His frequent and extended absences (usually to the Liberian border area, where he sold the game he hunted for hard currency) eventually convinced his mother-in-law and wife that he lacked commitment to them, their family, and his infant son. He was said to spend much of his money on *jamba*, marijuana, and alcohol. This feeling was partly due to Mussa's failure to provide Kadì with money and the supplies that nursing mothers required, such as kerosene and bedbug medicine. In this respect, Mussa was not unlike many other young men in the area, who were trying to raise their own family while still being subject to continuing demands from their paternal households *and* those of their in-laws.

Another resident in the Kamara big house was Mamì, *kaamɔ* Jussu's granddaughter, who lived there with her nursing daughter. Mamì was a beautiful, tall woman, whose thin body hardly betrayed the fact that she had six living children. Only the youngest, her nursing daughter Jenebu, was with her in Kpuawala. Her husband was a "stranger" trader related to the chiefdom's ruling lineage, who was under the patronage of another Kpuawala *mawɛɛ*. Instead of staying with her husband's host *mawɛɛ*, Mamì took up residence in the big house where the women under the protection of her maternal grandfather and her uncles lived. She also "begged" her mother's brothers for a tract of swamp to set up a rice paddy, which she farmed herself with the occasional aid of hired labor. Whenever *mawɛɛ* membership was listed in this period (for example, for the purpose of paying dues for a funeral), Mamì was counted as a member of the Kamara household. She identified with this group and stressed that this was where her grandfather and her mother's brothers lived. She often addressed her favorite mother's brother (*kenya*), Gbesse, as "mother," and she turned to him for support in her relations with other members of the community.

Unlike Kadì, who was connected to the *mawɛɛ* through her mother Mama Kɔɔ, who had married into the Kamara lineage, Mamì's links to this group were her maternal uncles and grandfather. Her mother—a daughter of *kaamɔ* Jussu's deceased senior wife—had long ago reached the end of her reproductive years and lived permanently in her husband's compound in a nearby village. Nonetheless, most of Mamì's working and socializing time, as well as her economic transactions, revolved around the female kin and affines and around the children living in the Kamara big house. Occasionally, she and other women in the big house pooled

their cash from the sale of surplus peppers, beans, and other farm ingredients to buy flour so that they could make and sell fried sweets in town.
Though there could be tensions among big house members, they also
shared foodstuffs, cooking utensils, and fishing nets, and they relied on
each other for help with farming and domestic work.

THE BIG HOUSE—TAKE II

August was the heart of the rainy season—a season when food was scarce
and when people spent a great deal of time on their farms, because the
heavy rainfall limited their travels. Once the dry season returned and the
harvests were in, people began to travel to discharge social obligations
incurred during the rains or to attend the many political, ceremonial, and
ritual occasions. Furthermore, the postharvest period coincided with the
Christmas holiday schedule of schools, government, and private employment, and this enabled those who had departed for the cities and overseas
to return on holiday to their rural areas of origin.

In January 1986, when I returned from a brief absence and entered the
Kamara big house to greet friends, the place felt desolate and empty. In
contrast with the full house a few months earlier, only a handful of
women and children were now living there, and there were fewer beds—
six, compared to nine during my earlier census. Even some of these were
obviously vacant; their bedding was scattered, no "country cloths"
(kɔndi gulɛi) covered the bed's palm leaves, and no mosquito netting or
personal belongings hung about it. The big house had been transformed
from the warm, crowded place of a few months before into a hollow,
cavernous room with only two adult women and their children huddled
around a fire in the early morning chill (Fig. 1, B). However, this impression of mine was not shared by the big house's occupants, for whom the
transformed surroundings were a normal part of the changes that took
place in this big house over time.

Massa, Abdulai's senior wife, was still in the big house, this time with
a new baby, a daughter born a month or so earlier (Fig. 1, B5). This was
the baby that had triggered Kema's ironic remarks about the husband not
waiting until the previous child was weaned to get his wife back in bed
with him. Another bed was occupied by Monjama Wulo, whose mother
Sao had been there in August with a different nursing daughter (Fig. 1, B6).
Neither Sao nor Mbeindu was now in the big house. Both had left town
to visit relatives in a nearby chiefdom. Monjama Wulo was nursing her
second child, a baby boy. The third and last occupied bed was shared by

Massa's and Monjama's older daughters (Fig. 1, B7). The big house's population had been reduced by two-thirds, from 17 residents 7 months earlier (23 if one counted the women temporarily living in nearby rooms), to 6.

Different factors accounted for this population exodus. During the dry season, at the height of social and ritual activities, Kema was always in great demand as a Sande elder at society initiations in Telu, her hometown in the neighboring chiefdom. Kema spent several months of each year in Telu. Most of the younger women who had been nursing their infants either had moved out because their babies had been weaned or had temporarily left with them to visit their mothers' hometowns. Kadì had gone to visit her father near the Liberian border, and though we had heard back in Kpuawala that her son had begun to walk, she was not planning to return until her husband gave signs of taking to heart her own well-being and that of their child. Thus the population movements among big house dwellers were due in part to seasonal travels during the year, in part to changes in women's reproductive and marital lives, and in part to more lasting ruptures between them and their husbands, kin, or other big house residents.

THE BIG HOUSE—TAKE III

In April 1990, four years later, I returned to Kpuawala. *Kaamɔ* Jussu had recently died, his death having been preceded by that of his brother, whose widow was now living in a pathetic state of neglect with a niece in another compound.[15] The houses that had been occupied by the deceased men were taken over by Abdulai, who was now head of the Kamara *mawɛɛ*, and Gbesse, respectively. After his grandfather's death, Jussu, his young Qur'anic student, had left town to be a tailor's apprentice in Bo, while living with his paternal aunt. The latter was now also looking after Gbesse's second daughter, whom Mama Kɔɔ had been nursing in the big house five years earlier. Eddie "Bo-Pujehun" had moved away in 1985, and no resident extension agent had taken his place. No other strangers were currently part of the Kamara *mawɛɛ*.

Kema was back in the Kamara big house, as were *kaamɔ* Jussu's two widows, Mariama and Sao (Fig. 1, C). Mariama's grandson still shared her bed (Fig. 1, C7). The tension between Mariama and her sister-in-law Kema—suppressed while the man who was brother to one and married to the other was alive—was now palpable. Monjama Wulo, Sao's daughter, was again living in the big house with a different suckling infant (Fig. 1, C6). Mamì "Fassia," another one of the dead chief's daughters-in-law, was pregnant and sleeping in the big house. Fataba, who five years earlier, when I first visited this big house, had been a small girl sharing her bed with her father's sister's daughter, was now living there as a young married woman nursing her first child. She was sharing a veranda room in the house with her own mother and the latter's youngest baby. As with Mama Kɔɔ and Kadì during that first Kamara big house census—and others elsewhere—here again was a mother-daughter pair going through childbirth and nursing at the same time.

Of the other women who in August 1985 had been nursing infants in the Kamara big house, three had taken apart their nursing mother's beds and moved with them to other locations. Mbeindu had returned to her husband, as had Mama Kɔɔ. Mamì never returned to Lamin, the husband who had fathered six of her children. She filed for divorce in the chiefdom headquarters, borrowing money from her mother and from women in the Kamara big house. Mamì was also supported by others, because her husband had been disliked among various Kpuawala groups for the high prices he commanded as a trader, and his gambling and drinking had resulted in his being ostracized among the elders who otherwise would have been his natural allies, given his age and status.[16]

Other women in the big house had made permanent moves as well, albeit less formally. Like Kadì, who was still in the Liberian border region with her father—an area that by 1990 had become unsafe with the onset of civil war just over the border—Hawa, Abdulai's young second wife, was now gone. Hawa's relationship with Abdulai had been troubled from the beginning. Soon after her Sande initiation and marriage in the summer of 1985, neighbors often woke up in the middle of the night to the sound of loud arguments between the newlyweds. During the day, women in the *pɛɛ wai* would talk amid laughter, whispers, and innuendoes about the cause of these marital arguments, which in the absence of ceilings and soundproofing could be followed in their entirety by anyone living in the next room. Apparently the rows were caused by Hawa's refusal to have sex with her husband.

On several occasions, Hawa tried to leave Abdulai and return to her mother's big house at the opposite end of town. However, these attempts were thwarted by her father, who did not want to return her dowry and therefore sent her back. As soon as the dry season arrived, she and her mother left to visit her maternal grandmother in a distant community. During all this, Hawa's co-wife, Massa, was living next door in the big house and working with her during the day. Massa never said much about either her husband or her younger co-wife when conversations in the big house turned to their marital squabbles, but she laughed when someone repeated Hawa's words about Abdulai's sexual advances. When the latter accused Hawa of having an extramarital affair with a young Kpuawala man, Massa came to her defense and kept on working amiably with her.[17] There was a marked distinction between Hawa's nighttime arguments with Abdulai and her cheerful involvement in the daytime with his senior wife and children—one of whom, Fataba, was almost her own age.

Disagreements among the Kamara brothers did not appear to bode well for the future of this *mawɛɛ* or for the big house, which had not regained its 1985 levels of population in the intervening years. However, a new *pɛɛ wai* was being built in the only compound that had been without one. This project came to fruition after years of pressure on the Kpuawala leadership by women of the Sande society, who were particularly concerned about not having a *pɛɛ wai* in the compound occupied by the owners of their secret society's ritual paraphernalia. Five years earlier I had heard the issue intermittently brought up during public meetings held in town on "development" and community matters. This was the favorite topic of the highest-ranking Sande woman in the compound in question, who with the backing of the other female elders would remind the assembled authorities that Kpuawala needed a *Sowo wɛɛla*, a "Sowei" or Sande house.[18] In addition to serving as a *pɛɛ wai* during normal times, this house was also to be a repository of Kpuawala's Sande society ritual objects and would be the center of initiation activities. The new construction of the Kpuawala *pɛɛ wai* underscores the continuing importance of big houses in the physical and social geography of the community, particularly for women.

The picture emerging from this chronicle of changes in the Kamara big house and in its occupation is one of flexible, often temporary arrangements and one of friendships and resentments among sometimes unlikely partners. Kema inspires friendship in one sister-in-law and enmity in another, who moves out when she moves in. Mothers and daughters live side by side nursing their babies. Some senior co-wives virtually ignore their juniors; others become their allies against a common husband.[19] The period spent in the big house can be an interval between other times when women live with their husbands, or it may mark a change in their relationship—a permanent separation or the end of their cohabitation with the onset of old age. As a place, then, the big house may be the ideal *mawɛɛ* residence, its physical anchor in a settlement's landscape, but in practice it is a place of impermanence, with no stable dwellers over time—and even without fixed physical features, as beds multiply or shrink in number and things get moved around.

Despite the complexity of relations among big house members, there is a tendency for those who do not inhabit this space to exaggerate the cohesiveness linking its residents. My own impression of big house camaraderie is a case in point, but others—married men in Kpuawala, for example—also emphasize how big house living fosters the creation of strong bonds among women. Thus the very men who, though physically absent from this space, bring about through it the proximity among their female kin, wives, and children—these very men feel they might lose from this situation because they are aware that, despite potential internal conflicts, women in the big house prefer to present a united front to the outside world. Mama Kɔɔ's and Mamì's refusal to admit to the tension between them in front of me or their male elders may be an example of this solidarity.[20]

Some Kpuawala men even argued against having more than one or two wives on the grounds that it was difficult to know what the others were up to when they were in the big house on nights when they were not sleeping with their common husband. They held a suspicious view of possibly conspiratorial relations among women in the big house, alleging that *mbaa nyahanga*, women friends or co-wives, covered up each others' affairs. Indeed, given the lack of privacy in the big house, and the need to leave the door unlocked either to creep out and meet a lover or to allow the latter to come in, it was impossible for other residents to be unaware of such affairs.[21] During a court hearing involving an adultery case in Kpuawala, a woman who was watching the proceedings next to me confided that she *knew* the adultery allegations to be true, although she would never admit it in public. "Today," she said, "she is having an affair, but tomorrow it might be me, and I would not want her to tell!" For this reason, she thought the young woman involved in this case was stupid to eventually confess to having a lover. It soon became clear that the woman who confessed to the affair meant to leave her husband and thus had no interest in resolving the conflict.

The gender dynamics of sleeping arrangements should not be overemphasized. The big house is a space for women and children, and men past their boyhood never sleep there. However, women and children do sleep in other, smaller rooms, and during their reproductive years, women share for varying lengths of time their husbands' living quarters and store some of their possessions there. Women's beds in the big house share, to some extent, their owners' fortunes and mobility. And although the big house's collective, dormitory-like atmosphere restricts women's ability to conceal things from each other, it creates a degree of cohesion that seals off this space as a whole from the outside world. Hence men's perception that women in the big house conspire to conceal information about each other from their husbands and from male kin.

Some of the same principles that are at work in women's big houses apply more generally to houses, though on a different scale. These are places where individuals can conceal their possessions from others, and they are places that often reveal very different dimensions of these individuals' lives from what is apparent to the outside world. Sellu's bedroom enclosed a world that was not only in stark contrast to the external appearance of his rural house: with its wealth of commodities, it also evoked his former participation in a much more cosmopolitan, urban-based lifestyle—a life to which, given the right circumstances, he could easily return in the future. The historical evidence points even more strongly to this contrast between the world of daytime activities and appearances on the one hand and, and on the other, the role of houses as places occupied at night and in sleep, sanctuaries kept shut to contain and conceal individual possessions and knowledge. Only two of Kpuawala's ten *mawɛɛ* heads occupied individual, single-room houses, but they often emphasized that rooms in shared houses were a relatively recent historical introduction. In the past, dependents—women and children, but also slaves and junior men—lived in various forms of collective housing, whereas heads of households had their own one-room houses.[22] This suggests a link between residential arrangements and hierarchical status, with high-ranking people having more individualized living spaces.[23] As we shall see, this correlation agrees with Mende ideas about the capacities that lead to positions of power, among them the ability to contain knowledge—to keep secrets—and protect bodily and spatial thresholds. Here one begins to see a gendered differential in the formation of these capacities, or in the level at which they can be exercised. Women in the big house could hardly conceal from each other the kinds of things Sellu kept locked away in his bedroom, for example, but their own boxes served the same purposes. The size of these boxes was indeed more appropriate to their owners' more limited means, and to their greater physical mobility, compared to men who had much more vested in a single place. This disparity leads to the question of what social factors give women more apparent mobility and residential options, or give men more permanence, within the domestic group.

IMAGINARY HOUSES

The big house is said to be *the* core building in a *mawɛɛ*'s spatial location in a settlement. The etymology of *mawɛɛ* itself links this social unit to residence in that it is a contraction of *mu*, "our," and *p/wɛɛ*, "house." Given the interchangeability of *mawɛɛ* with terms such as *mbonda* ("family") in peoples' everyday parlance, we can think of it as a kind of extended family or household. And yet, as we have seen, the residential arrangements of *mawɛɛsia* (pl.) differ considerably. The lack of fit between the ideal and what exists in practice leads us back to Certeau's contention that efforts to read spaces as texts—to make them intelligible as forms of cultural inscriptions—make us miss practices that unfold in a temporal register. To understand this discrepancy, one needs to address the practices in relation to which the *mawɛɛ* is a relevant social unit—that is, the particular activities organized around this group's membership.

I noted in the biography of the Kamara big house that *mawɛɛ* members collectively work on a "big" rice farm (*kpaa wai*) every year. This social unit is also the basis for recruiting labor for communal village projects, for tax collection (each *mawɛɛ* head had to collect the yearly head tax from adult farmers or traders under his protection), and for distributing gifts that visitors brought to the community. (Rice, money, and any other gift commodities were divided "by *mawɛɛ*" and later partitioned among adults *within* this group.) Together, *mawɛɛgulɔbla*—those "in front" of *mawɛɛsia*, their heads—were called upon by the village chief and his speaker to preside over court cases and to make decisions affecting the community's governance. Thus heads of *mawɛɛ* not only were engaged in the organization of domestic and farming units but were also links between these and the encompassing system of governance, with its political institutions and administrative structures. This articulation between different social and organizational levels suggests one reason why the "house" terminology embedded in the category *mawɛɛ* does not—or at least does not *always*—imply only domestic co-residence.

This point is brought home by the range of residential patterns of the ten *mawɛɛsia* in Kpuawala. Some Kpuawala *mawɛɛsia* occupied contiguous buildings in a compound, but the fact that there were only five compounds for ten *mawɛɛsia* implies that this was not the main organizational principle behind house groupings. When Kpuawala people referred to "their place," their compound,[24] this place tended to be defined by a clearing with an open-sided shelter where people gathered for public, community events—the *sɛmɛ*—around which residential and other structures were built. There were five of these clearings and meeting houses in Kpuawala (Fig. 3). A further problem in mapping *mawɛɛsia* onto the settlement's physical space was that although some were closely identified with a set of buildings—and in one case, even with a whole compound— others were scattered across the village's houses and wards, with no identifiable residential "center." Indeed, the location and number of big houses in Kpuawala made the residential picture even more complicated, as I noted earlier, given that their location could be mapped onto specific compounds or *mawɛɛsia* (Fig. 3).

Thus, even though connotations of *both* domesticity and co-residence were embedded in the daily use of the term *mawɛ* and its equivalents in Kpuawala, neither sufficed to describe all the different social and residential arrangements that fell under this label. Such discrepancy between cultural definitions and the historically situated, strategic practices of social actors has made for contradictory assessments in the anthropological literature. In Kenneth Little's classic monograph, the *mawɛ* was a social unit that "worked strictly on patriarchal lines. Individual *mawɛisia* [sic], controlled by a group of younger brothers or sons, provided the head of the family with produce and any labor he required. He, in turn, upheld the interests and prestige of those junior to himself" (Little 1948: 39). By contrast, Paul Richards focused on the labor question and pointed out that despite an ideology that saw the *mawɛ* as coterminous with the group responsible for a big rice farm, the latter "[was] a seasonal, 'economic' subdivision" (Richards 1986: 49), for which

> The appearance of "domesticity" can be misleading, . . . since the farm group is not necessarily a regular and permanent "family" unit. Whereas some household units are stable for season after season, other farming households are short-term arrangements, perhaps for a single season only. . . . Any appearance of domesticity in these cases is limited to the farm hut, and the individuals concerned go their separate ways upon reaching the town in the evening.
>
> *(Richards 1986: 67)*

Many anthropologists have noted how difficult it is to study houses and households, given that these are both places and social units, which encompass people with a multitude of—sometimes conflicting—allegiances to kinship, marriage, generational, and other groups (see Carsten and Hugh-Jones 1995: 39; Guyer 1981: 97; Lévi-Strauss 1982: 184; Yanagisako 1979: 162–166). Others have shown how, over time, this

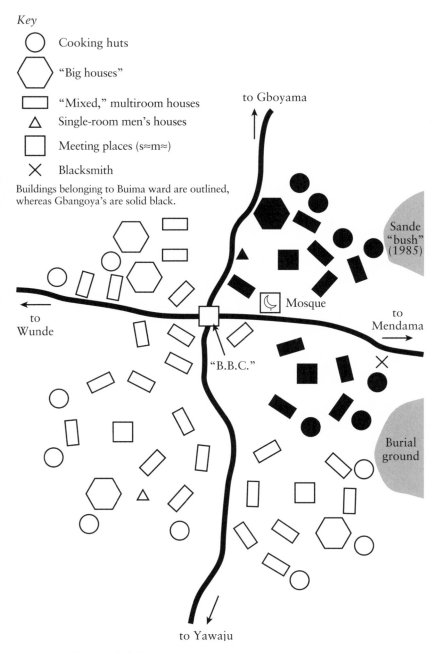

Key

◯ Cooking huts

⬡ "Big houses"

▭ "Mixed," multiroom houses

△ Single-room men's houses

▢ Meeting places (s≈m≈)

✕ Blacksmith

Buildings belonging to Buima ward are outlined,
whereas Gbangoya's are solid black.

to Gboyama

Sande
"bush"
(1985)

to
Wunde

☾ Mosque

to
Mendama

"B.B.C."

✕

Burial
ground

to Yawaju

Figure 3.   Kpuawala Map

heterogeneity can account for dramatic changes in a group's composition and in the appearance of the physical space it occupies (Bohannan 1954:4; Goody 1958). In a manner similar to my earlier analysis of changes over time in the Kamara big house population, such studies document what has come to be known as the developmental cycle of domestic groups—their formation, expansion, and fission. As the term *cycle* implies, however, these processes have been described primarily in the context of cyclical phases that parallel the human process of growth and aging, rather than, as in my own analysis, as a result of strategic choices by social actors who have different stakes in the reproduction of such units and who ultimately can cause them to disappear through conflict.

What my own analysis adds to this debate on the *mawεε* is the fact that only a perspective on this unit that is mindful of the different social investments in it of men and women of different age, reproductive status, and marital status can begin to address some of these discrepancies. Gendered residential, mobility, and labor patterns impart different dynamics to this social unit and inscribe it differently in their respective domains. These differences are also due to the fact that, compared with the jural rights at stake in patrilineage membership and politics, the principles of *mawεε* affiliation are more heterogeneous and contingent. At the same time, this heterogeneity accounts for the fundamental instability and impermanence of the *mawεε* as a social unit.

Little's definition also points to an added dimension of the *mawεε*. In addition to having residential connotations, it encompasses putative kinship aspects. In Kpuawala, kinship was a fundamental element in *mawεεsia*, at least in principle, for these were said to "belong" to one or more related members of a named, land-holding, and male-controlled patrilineage, or "those within a birth/talking [group]" (*ndehu*, from *nde*, "to talk, to give birth," and *hu*, "inside").[25] The *ndehu*'s very name reflects its identity as a group characterized by common descent, wherein consensus is reached through a shared discourse. The notion that kinship and consensus are both manifested and shaped through shared talk is fundamental in Mende, where the concept of unity is expressed as one word, or voice (*ngo yila*)—as speaking in unison. Thus the *ndehu* is a social unit whose cohesion is founded in a common ancestry articulated through male links, as well as being grounded in inherited land and reproduced through continuing, consensus-building communication among its members. Membership in a *ndehu* becomes relevant primarily in the context of issues related to the ownership of land, such as disputes over boundaries and requests for farming rights in a given year. Another example is requests made of the *ndehu* for occasional access to its waters and forested areas by junior members or strangers—guests who are temporarily residing in the community as dependents of particular *mawɛɛsia* and who want to fish, hunt, or harvest palm fruits on its land. On such occasions, the patrilineage's senior and junior members, both male and female, come together for consultations before publicly debating ownership matters or granting farming and harvesting rights.

In Kpuawala, female kin had important roles in the *ndehu* as well. Indeed, female *and* male kin within a particular Kpuawala *mawɛɛ* would talk about owning it (*mu womia*), along with the wives who had married into it and their offspring, its resources, and its dependents. Such claims were often backed by a restatement of common descent from a landowning, local lineage. Thus there were occasions on which, in spite of the *mawɛɛ*'s flexible and heterogeneous composition, which often included short- or long-term guests as well as affines, it was important to differentiate between the lineage members who owned the group and the larger, technically dependent membership of the unit as a whole. Although in certain circumstances gender or age was the critical factor in separating patrons from dependents within the *mawɛɛ*, in other circumstances it was membership in the *mawee*'s core lineage. However, the same mobility patterns that often made female kin more marginal than their male counterparts in controlling the *mawɛɛ*'s resources, and in exercising authority at the lineage level, also gave them *and* female affines unusual opportunities for playing prominent roles in certain domains of *mawɛɛ* life. This happened both through the creation of segregated spaces, such as the big house, and through the acquisition of specialized knowledge and skills that could make anyone, including women, indispensable and hence powerful in some way.

By contrast with the *ndehu*'s relatively restricted membership, the *mawɛɛ* is, then, a more inclusive, expansive social unit. It grows up around the *ndehu*, takes its name from the *ndehu* (as with the "Kamara" big house and *mawɛɛ*), and is crucial to the *ndehu*'s reproduction over time by including wives, foster children, and unrelated male dependents. In addition to locating the *ndehu* in an inhabited space, in "our house"— if only ideally—the *mawɛɛ* shifts the emphasis from jural rights to everyday practices, which is why it has much more currency as a unit for social affiliation. Whereas the *ndehu* is vested with jural rights in land and with authority over its stewardship, the *mawɛɛ* is primarily concerned with the processes that shape this land into a mosaic of farms and fallow plots, cull the resources its forests and waters yield, transform them into food, and consume them.

KINSHIP, MARRIAGE, AND RESIDENCE: MAWƐƐ IN PRACTICE AND HISTORY

The preceding analysis must be seen in the context of actual lineage and *mawɛɛ* composition in a particular place, time, and historical context. In the 1980s, Kpuawala's some 250 inhabitants were divided among 10 *mawɛɛsia*, grouped in 2 named town wards, Buima and Gbangoya. The *mawɛɛsia* ranged in size between 5 and 36 people, but only 3 had fewer than 26 members. The Buima ward had larger *mawɛɛsia* than Gbangoya, and it had a considerably larger population, which occupied a greater share of the community's 38 residential buildings.[26] Furthermore, four of the five Kpuawala big houses were in Buima compounds, which also tended to have stronger identifications with their three constitutive lineages. Thus *kene* Vandi, the ward head, who was also head of a *mawɛɛ*, lived in a compound shared by the *mawɛɛ* that was headed by his brother and was named after both of them. The compound included a single patrilineage, name, and meeting place, but it was home to two *mawɛɛsia* and their respective big houses. There was, in other words, a correlation among a *mawɛɛ*'s size, its ownership of a big house, and its location in an identifiable, named village compound.

Each of the larger Kuawala *mawɛɛsia* was located spatially in its own compound, the members living in houses surrounding a *sɛmɛ*, or meeting place. However, this was not the case with some of the others, particularly the smallest *mawɛɛ* in town, headed by Diboh Koroma. Diboh, a dwarf, lived in a male relative's house, and his own *mawɛɛ* included only five people. In 1984–1986 he was still unmarried in his early forties, although the presence in town of a teenage girl who bore a striking resemblance to him—and who also was the only other dwarf in Kpuawala—suggested that he already had at least one offspring. The girl's mother, Tɛnɛ, was then married to a stranger, a Kpaa Mende man from western Mendeland. Diboh's elderly widowed mother, Hawa, shared a house with a widower in the same Gbangoya section. Diboh's sister and her co-wife, along with their husband and a son, were all considered his dependents, but they lived across town from him in a Buima ward house. The old widower with whom Hawa had been living later died, and she too moved in with some relatives in another Buima house, leaving only her son in the Gbangoya section, where their *mawεε* had originated.

In Kpuawala Diboh's *mawεε* was scattered, had no residential center, and was not even identified separately in the funeral thrift association rosters. The one way in which its members still acted as members of a same *mawεε* was that they gathered together to work a common big farm on land to which Diboh had inherited rights, as well as having smaller plots nearby. Though Diboh's *mawεε* was recognized as a separate group in political and social events, it seemed to be approaching a stage where it would no longer be a viable unit and would be incorporated elsewhere. Diboh had no wife or potential children who could offer the prospect of future growth, and he had no living brothers who might contribute to his *mawεε*'s expansion. More tellingly, there was no big house to anchor this group in a particular place. By 1990, however, Diboh had finally married Tεnε—his daughter's mother—after the death of her husband. The latter's children were now part of Diboh's *mawεε*, and though this new family unit still lived as guests in a different *mawεε*'s compound, their separate identity seemed stronger. With the addition of a young male stranger who helped on the farm, Diboh's *mawεε* now seemed a potentially viable, expanding unit.

Though *mawεε* composition varied seasonally and over time, the asymmetry between Buima and Gbangoya pointed to more fundamental differences. Success in farming and wealth were interdependent factors said to be key to the larger size of some Kpuawala *mawεεsia*, and this in turn meant that these households were likely to have many wives and children to occupy big houses. But genealogical depth was claimed by others to be equally important, shifting the focus of *mawεε* life and fortunes into a historical domain. The head of the largest Kpuawala *mawεε*, who was also the oldest man in town and the chief's speaker, claimed that his household and the Buima section in which it was located were more populous because they "arrived first." He linked the size of his kin group to the depth of its historical presence in the area, claiming direct descent from one of Kpuawala's founding heroes. As evidence for this claim, he pointed to the fact that the only two ancestral graves within the settlement boundaries, as well as Kpuawala's foundation shrine, were behind his house in his own compound. The speaker's claim about the whole ward descending from the same founding warrior also suggested that *mawεεsia* themselves were the result of processes of fission from core descent groups as these expanded by incorporating wives, descendants, and dependents. This process was illustrated by the earlier example of *kene* Vandi and his brother occupying the same compound but each heading a separate *mawεε*.

In addition to the preceding factors—which are related to the developmental cycle of domestic groups mentioned earlier—more permanent changes in the historical relationship between landowning patrilineages and the organization of farm labor must also be analyzed. This is necessary if we are to understand the problematic relationship between units of Mende social organization and institutions or places that are considered crucial to their existence but are in fact impermanent and highly variable. Among the factors that account for changes in agrarian production in this region within the living memory of many Kpuawala elders was the 1928 outlawing of domestic slavery by the British Protectorate government (Grace 1977). The *mawεε* had a key role in organizing this labor (Little 1951: 96–97), a fact that lends strength to the claim that shared activities, rather than kinship or residence, have long been this institution's crucial membership criterion. The historical centrality of slave labor to the *mawεε*'s existence also sheds light on the more inclusive criteria for membership in this unit, in relation to the "birth group." But it also provides a clue to the dramatic range in size, configuration, and residential patterns of contemporary *mawεεsia*, given the demise of the institution of slavery that provided their core membership and labor, along with wives and children. One would be hard pressed to find today in Sierra Leone a *mawεε* such as the one described by Little as fairly typical of the days of slavery, with "some 120 people" making up a whole village (Little 1951: 97).

Slaves were assigned to particular big houses and were subject to the latters' senior women, under whose supervision the *mawεε*'s big farm was cultivated, providing the group's main sustenance (Little, ibid.). Thus the evidence suggests that historically, there may have been a stronger correlation among the *mawεε* as a social unit, a common residential pattern oriented around the women's big house, and agrarian labor on the big (rice) farm. Linking these different entities and levels was a common dynamic of enlargement—marked by the adjective "big" preceding them—that was, and continues to be, central to Mende ideas of power and hierarchy.

Seen in historical perspective, then, the shifting meanings of the term *mawεε* can be understood as reflecting changing features of Mende society and landscape. Where once large *mawεεsia* with dozens of dependents had been more clearly associated with an inhabited space and a farm—a big house and its contiguous buildings, often even forming autonomous hamlets amid the cultivated terrain—the demise of slavery brought about a reduction in size. More generally, comparison with nineteenth-century colonial literature suggests that once people no longer needed to congregate in larger, fortified settlements for protection during warfare, villages themselves became smaller and more numerous. As residential patterns diversified and some *mawɛɛ* members became more mobile, Mende settlements overall grew more stable and less susceptible to destruction or relocation.

The "bigness" of *mawɛɛ* houses and farms depended on a multiplication of dependents—women, children, and slaves—where the roles the women played as wives and potential mothers, as well as laborers and supervisors of the labor of others, were crucial. In oral histories, accounts of how the Mende came to populate their current home, in a West African forest belt that was sparsely inhabited just two centuries ago, focus on marriage as a key expansionist strategy. A common theme in these stories is that of local, landowning *ndehu*s acquiring more dependents by giving wives to foreign warriors and hunters new to the area, thus transforming them from mobile exploiters of forest resources (hunters) or of captive labor (warriors) into settled agriculturalists.[27] This theme also appears in the foundation myths and histories of settlements throughout the Sierra Leone–Liberian region (Murphy and Bledsoe 1987; Rodney 1970). But only a thin line separated heroic warriors from slaves, given that enslavement was the common fate of captured enemies in precolonial warfare. Thus over time, the marriages that had cemented relations of dependence also helped subvert them: slave descendants became assimilated as free persons, were incorporated into *mawɛɛsia* through the mediation of women, and eventually split off into new ones.[28]

In more recent times, *mawɛɛ* "shrinkage" has also been the result of out-migration of men to urban areas or to other rural areas where cash crops or alluvial diamond mining offered better economic prospects. Another factor in *mawɛɛ* "shrinkage"—albeit one whose impact on rural Mende practices is questionable—is the classificatory discourse of government administration. In this context, the *mawɛɛ* has been condensed down to its constitutive of women and children units. During the 1985 national census, enumerators in Kpuawala counted residents by *mawɛɛ*, describing a *mawɛɛ* as being made up of "those who eat together, from the same pot" (in English, on their forms, they referred to this unit as a household). This definition included only a woman and her young children, given that this was the only group of people who consistently ate out of the same pot. In a polygynous marriage, a husband would be part of only one such group at any given time, because his wives took turns cooking for him, as well as his dependents and guests. Though none of the Kpuawala people would have recognized the census workers' definition of *mawɛɛ* with its exclusive, minimalist emphasis, it reproduced at another level a familiar cultural pattern by placing women and children at the core of this institution, if only to isolate it from the accretions and multiple social ties normally included in local understandings of this social unit.

Furthermore, the census definition of *mawɛɛ* reverses the structures of authority in rural Mende understandings of this institution, shifting attention from the male relatives who control it to their sisters and wives and these women's children. Ironically, this tendency parallels the greater reliance on female labor in farming in the modern context in which male out-migration and the absence of coercive strategies for acquiring male labor have brought about a reduction in the numbers of men available. This miniaturization of the *mawɛɛ*—its condensation into cookers of food and those they feed on a daily basis—is also consistent with the historical trajectory of this institution, which does appear to be shrinking. But by the same token, the census definition of *mawɛɛ* undermines the big house's central place in this institution by reversing the logic of enlargement it articulates. The cooking pot referred to in census documents is clearly the smaller one for daily meals, not the big one brought out for large, collective events. This perspective severs the lateral links among female affines and kin, and their children, whose shared life and work in the big house finds expression in collective meals prepared in the big pot.

CONCLUSION

In his analysis of societies where the house was a major organizational feature, Lévi-Strauss remarked on this institution's ability to "compound" forces that "seem destined to mutual exclusion because of their contradictory bend," at levels ranging from the family to the state (1982: 184). The house, he argued, "expressed an effort to transcend, in all spheres of collective life, theoretically incompatible principles" (Lévi-Strauss, ibid.), such as the contrasting pulls of descent, residence, marriage, choice, and heredity. But the house can be seen as transcending these incompatibilities only if it is presumed to outlast changes in its composition, which from this perspective would appear to be only cyclical variations (e.g., Goody 1958). Kpuawala *mawɛɛsia* fit this model in some respects. The difference between larger Kpuawala *mawɛɛsia*'s strong identification with a particular big house and compound, and the absence of any such overlap in the case of Diboh's small household, may be an indication that they are simply at different stages of their development and histories. This perspective would also seem to be supported by the fact that Diboh's household belonged to the Gbangoya section, which, as we have seen, had about a third fewer members than Buima and whose foundation followed that of the latter.

However, the analysis of Kpuawala big houses and of their role within the *mawɛɛsia* suggest that it might be more productive to think of these heterogeneous institutions as *points of articulation,* whose biographies are shaped by an "interplay between permanence and impermanence" as a result of different, intersecting principles of social identity (Carsten and Hugh-Jones 1995:39). This interplay is due in part to the fact that gender tensions are at the core of big house and *mawɛ* sociality, wherein feminine domains and activities are essential to an institution whose ownership and main authority are male. These, along with changing alliances reflecting kinship, marriage, age-group, and co-wife relations, can turn the big house—this core of *mawɛ* identity and location—into a hollow, empty, and sometimes even nonexistent place. The gap between cultural ideal and the history of particular *mawɛɛsia* is marked by the latters' dislocation and shrinking—a process that, as I have suggested, is inscribed within the historical trajectory of changing demographic and hierarchical relations in rural Sierra Leone. During my stay in Kpuawala, one *mawɛ* became part of another, larger *mawɛ* when, at the death of its head, it lacked a surviving male of the right age to take on its leadership. The *mawɛ* joined that of a half-brother's son. But the government's use of the *mawɛ* as a census category suggests how this entity might continue to be reproduced, albeit in different forms, despite changes in rural living and labor practices. And it may be in connection with the classificatory practices of the state (which, though changing its content and reducing it to "people eating out of the same pot," still uses the category) that we can best understand the transitory nature of *mawɛɛsia.*

And yet we must deal with the enduring nature of the *mawɛ* and big house as institutions even in the face of historical changes that in some cases leave the former with no traces of kinship, marriage, or co-residence links between its members and have reduced the latter to a name applied to a variety of residential arrangements. In Kpuawala, in the absence of a separate physical structure or large room, even an ordinary bedroom at the back of a house could be referred to as a big house and used in very much the same way as the Kamara one.[29] This suggests that despite formal and demographic changes in the big house, the institution has enduring value. This is because women—as Lévi-Strauss noted too—"are the sensitive point" of houses. But unlike Lévi-Strauss, one must also take women seriously as social actors to understand how their strategies reproduce or permanently undermine *mawɛɛ* viability.

I have shown that these strategies often revolve around sites and objects that are smaller than the big house with which they are associated. And yet the use that women make of these objects is key to the dynamics of *mawɛɛ* enlargement related to the productive and reproductive efforts of big house members. Thus through these small things—the "narrow gate" of a bed, or the paths taken by a cooking pot—one can more easily follow the intersection between women's social roles in the context of kinship, marriage, age, and other identifications, and their actual choices and strategies. In this sense, as Bachelard suggests (see the opening of this chapter), the detail opens up a whole world. Size is relative too: although small in relation to other things, the big pot is much larger than those ordinarily used by individual women to cook for themselves, their children, and their husbands. If big houses stand in metonymic relation to the *mawɛɛ*, then big cooking pots map this relationship onto an even larger scale. They underscore the social and economic importance of women's labor as food preparers (for what women prepare in them are not ordinary meals for "domestic consumption"), not only for the big house and the *mawɛɛ* for which it stands, but also for recruiting labor on the big farm and for the community as a whole.

By contrast, the metaphorical relationship between beds and their owners' position in the big house is marked by their centrality to the language of sexuality and adultery. Big house beds are dismantled or only intermittently occupied when women resume sleeping with their husbands after weaning a child, and anyone "jumping between" their occupants before then is a source of dangerous distractions. Thus these beds are interfaces between women (as individuals or as nursing mothers forming an indivisible unit with their babies) and the larger collectivity encompassing them. Beds in the Kamara big house flagged particular stages in their owners' reproductive life—pregnant, giving birth, nursing a baby, postmenopausal—as well as displaying, through their condition and accoutrements, their owners' relative wealth or the degree of cooperation among big house inhabitants at a particular point in time. The changing configuration of beds in the Kamara big house underscored women's residential mobility, which derived from their ability to play kin against affines, mothers or friendly co-wives against husbands, and so on. These are the tactics—the "gestures"—that would have been lost in a synchronic picture of residential arrangements in Kpuawala.

But women's mobility in relation to the big house also exposed how relatively restricted their movements were in relation to other levels. As Mamphela Ramphele has pointed out in her study of South African migrant workers and their status as "bedholders" in crowded, shared hostel rooms, there is a whole political economy to inhabiting such small spaces: one has to "either 'shrink' to fit this space or expand the space to accommodate [one's] needs" (Ramphele 1993: 22). The fact that in Kpuawala, Sellu could conceal his possessions in a locked room to himself, whereas Mamì had no way of hiding her new mosquito net from envious big house neighbors, suggests that there are limits to the expansion of spaces when one does not also have a choice about who and what occupies them. However, Mamì's ability to choose among different housing options—even if only to distance herself from her uncle's jealous wife—was important for the avenues it eventually opened. In 1993, the last time I saw Mamì in Kpuawala, she was married to Braima, a longtime lover, who in order to marry her had separated from his jealous first wife. Mamì had a room to herself and her youngest nursing child at the back of Braima's house. Her mosquito net was made from lace curtains—as light and gauzy as the one I had given her eight years earlier, but decorated with cream-colored flowers.

Gani Ceremony, Sande Initiation, Wunde Chiefdom (1985)

CHAPTER 5

Becoming a *Kpako*

The Body and the Aesthetics of Power

In this chapter, I examine the social construction of Mende "big people" (*nu wai*, or *kpako*, sing.). I argue that discursive and spatial expansion of a person's status, a kind of aura, is central to local power dynamics. However, the same dynamic movement in the opposite sense—leading to a diminishment of one's aura—makes power vulnerable to dialectical reversals. The category of big people is gender-inclusive, and much has been made in the regional literature of the manifestation of this principle in women's access to political office.[1] Here I put this principle in the context of a broader discussion of the overall cultural logic that produces big persons, both within and outside the political domain. This is a logic informed by an aesthetics of concealment, through the production of specific cultural forms and social transactions that shape relations of inequality.

Paradoxically, the dynamic of concealment is visibly expressed through an expansive aesthetics of power. In many societies, powerful people are represented as extraordinary beings larger than life—or at least larger than ordinary people.[2] The image of the big person often translates into a political discourse where the sanctioned accumulation of power is expressed through the language of consumption: one becomes a big politician by consuming state resources, as well as those of one's adversaries (e.g., Bayart 1993: 275).[3] This idiom of consumption is also a feature of the logic of witchcraft in many parts of West Africa. Though in some cases the status of big people is conveyed by their large, well-fed bodies, in Mende there is no stable correlation between physical size and the visible order of power. Becoming a big person has to do with bodily states and processes, but of a different order. These are processes of bodily and social enlargement of the self, which are linked to the control of secrecy and the incorporation of esoteric substances (medicines) in the body. However, there are limits to these processes of expansion, given the close relationship among secrecy, silence, and power: "Silence inhibits self-transformation. A man who will not speak can dissemble, but only in a rigid way; he can wear a mask, but he has to keep a firm hold of it. The fluidity of transformation is denied him; its result is too uncertain; . . . People become silent when they fear transformation. . . . All men's movements are played out in speech; silence is motionless." (Canetti 1984: 294). Thus the silencing power of secrecy already carries within it the seeds of its destruction, for it is precisely when secrecy is most successful in imposing its rigid constraints that it undermines the flexibility required for power to constantly adapt itself to changing contexts.

The status of the big person depends on an inner topography of the body, which in turn displays itself on the surface just enough to elicit an excess of respect and fear in others. A visible expression of wonder is triggered by the concealment of the political nature of (often authoritarian) strategies of aggrandizement. These strategies are as much a product of the practices of the big person as they are the result of the exaggerated forms of deference toward them demonstrated by other social actors. A dialectic is at work between the visible expression/wonder, and the hidden contructs of power. This has led William Murphy to speak of Mende political power as an analogue of the Kantian sublime and of Weberian political charisma:

> Both charisma and the sublime represent a semiotics of transcendence, a sensibility associating certain objects and events in the world with obscure powers and forces beyond normal everyday life and understanding. In Mende political culture, the language of *kabande* expresses similar meanings. This cultural semantics is summarized in Innes's Mende-English Dictionary translation of *kabande* as "magic, mystery, marvel, wonder, the marvelous, wonderful, mysterious" (Innes 1969: 37). It is also exemplified in the usage which praises God as possessing *kabande*. . . . *Kabande* shares the connotations of awe as in Otto's sense of the *mysterium tremendum* at the root of the human experience of the sacred.
>
> *(Murphy 1998: 566)*

For the purposes of my own analysis, the focus on the lexicon of wonder implicit in the sublime has to be problematized from the perspective of the potential loss of power. In other words, the same semiotics of transcendence that generates this infinite sense of respect for powerful leaders—as quasi-mythical, sacred figures—may also be their downfall. Power may undermine itself by inspiring its awestruck witness to match it—that is, by elevating the witness's *own* sense of power (see Kant 1978 [1798]: 146). This is even more true of contexts in which secrecy is a constitutive feature of power and of the wonder it inspires, for secrets add a greater element of unpredictability and hence a greater risk of disastrous outcomes. Both the exercise of power and the subjection to that power are more unstable in the presence of pervasive strategies of concealment (see Canetti 1984: 295). Thus although the sublime may be a dimension of power in Mende, one must consider how its constitutive elements—surprise, excess, and even catastrophe—also make power intrinsically unstable and therefore contingent.[4] As I have discussed elsewhere, the fact that political discourse is always pervaded by the possibility of deception can be used *against* those in power. This occurs, for example, when they are accused of having used covert, illicit means to attain their position (Ferme 1999).

Secret knowledge and practice are necessary for enhancing a big person's aura. Secrecy and power share a sociological dynamic—they are both predicated on the relationship between the subject's concealed aims and their visible manifestations in the external world (Simmel 1950: 337–340). Furthermore, they are both strategies for magnifying reality through the aesthetic display of the body and through the expansion of its boundaries. Mende discursive practices stress the location of potent substances inside the body, but the power of big people is punctuated by the extension of personal attributes and possessions beyond bodily boundaries, by making visible on the surface the hidden dimensions of power. This visibility, however, may itself be a form of concealment. Indeed, in much of the Mande-speaking region, the relationship between power and its aesthetics is often construed through the appearance of an ugly mask. Among the Bamana (Bambara) of Mali, the most powerful ritual object of the Komo secret society is the *boliw*, which is generally thought to be ugly, in contrast to the beautiful masks that appear in public in connection with this society's activities. Whereas the Komo's wooden "animal" masks have detailed, sculpted features thought attractive and pleasing by the Bamana audiences at these events, the *boliw* is an almost shapeless, solid form—a heterogeneous assemblage of unknown materials encrusted with layers of sacrificial substances. The object's "full symbolic significance is not visually accessible, nor is it information to which the non-initiate are privy" (McNaughton 1979: 26). Here an aesthetics of the ugly protects the incommensurability of the ritual object and enhances its efficacy. Hence nothing becomes visible for the one who does not know how to recognize disguised power.

McNaughton argues that this object's importance derives from the secret contents of an unattractive and nondecipherable exterior and, further, that this is a more general feature of Mande notions of power—applicable to sorcerers and other persons with extraordinary capacities. But the dynamic relationship between the *boliw*'s secret core and its effective manifestation in the world is suggested by the fact that its potency increases in proportion to the evolution of its appearance through the smearing on its surface of layers upon layers of animal fat, blood, and vegetable matter that made up the sacrificial offerings. Thus the key to the *boliw*'s power is the efficacious relationship between a secret core and the surface expansion it activates. However, there is more than a dynamic of visible expansion at work on this sacrificial object, for smearing substances on a surface is also an act of dissimulation. It conceals the existing surface in the very act of creating a new one. Furthermore, though it is not in itself considered attractive, the *boliw* is the concealed agent behind the beautiful public appearances of the Komo, such as its wooden masquerades and dance performances. What is central to its power is a dynamic of expansion that goes hand in hand with the dissimulation not only of a hidden source but of the outer surface as well.

There is a parallel stress on the ugly in a Mende masking practices—for example, in the paired appearance of the beautiful *Sowɛi* and the unattractive *Gonde* in Sande public performances. The *Gonde* is usually an old, damaged *Sowɛi* mask, and thus it is visibly similar to the latter in form and yet unmistakably ugly. It is a caricature of its beautiful counterpart, and this ironic dimension is expressed in the humorous performance of this mask, which contrasts sharply with the seriousness of the *Sowɛi*'s demeanor. Scholars of masking in this region have seen in this juxtaposition of the *Gonde* with its beautiful counterpart a "balance of opposites" that expresses the ironic continuum between beauty and ugliness (see Boone 1986; Hommel 1981: 86–110). The paradox of the simultaneous display of beauty and ugliness has moved some to claim that an anti-aesthetic is central to Mende ideas of (female) powers (see Phillips 1995: 90–92), because the ugly member of the pair ultimately "serves to reinforce the dignity and transcendent power of the *ndoli jowei* [sic]" (Phillips 1995: 92). Similarly to Murphy's argument about the sublime, the point here is that the aesthetic emphasis on something that appears absurd and grotesque produces a sense of awe for the transcendent.

However, these interpretations see an aesthetic expression of (balanced) order in these manifestations, whereas Murphy rightly leaves the dialectical movement unresolved by emphasizing the eruptions that break through predictable structures. Like Murphy, I also take the idea of the rupture of order not merely with reference to the mask's performance but also as a more general manifestation of a Mende aesthetics of power.

The issues raised here by the reversibility of the beautiful into an aesthetics of the ugly, or vice versa, lead to the question of containment. The greater appeal of the contained source over the visible manifestations of power is in part due to the asymmetry of processes of enlargement compared with shrinkage, as we saw in the discussion of the relationship between small and large in Chapter 4. One might add that the dynemic enlargement and shrinkage is more important than the fetishistic stress on the hiddenness of power per se. The process of dislocation entailed by expansion gives the illusion of both immobility (power claims to be the same everywhere) and mobility (it appears through others). Thus although power requires mobility to reproduce itself, in the process it runs the risk of leaving a fragile center. I take the paired appearance of *Sowɛi* and *Gonde* as an ironic index of power's decay, which is always present in the Mende collective imaginary. This points to the fact that the augmentation of power through its manifestations of enlargement and shrinkage is not sufficient to guarantee its stability and success. Rather, it requires the renewed negotiation of the sources of its legitimacy, because it constantly depends on the recognition of power's disguises. Hence, the value of a sociopolitical rhetoric that makes possible the manifestation of individual or collective forms of consensus. Conversely, the same mechanisms open the way to dissent, thus making the status of political office holders, and of big people in general, more fragile.

Furthermore, the expansion of power entails fragmentation in that in this region, political and ritual leaders are usually paired with speakers. This practice of fragmentation is also a recognition of the limits of legitimacy and of the need to produce it at multiple levels. For example, the Wunde Paramount Chief had an official speaker, but he also had an informal, trusted one in his brother, who was also known as his "eyes" (*ngi yamɛi*). The brother traveled around the chiefdom on the chief's behalf and attended events about which he brought back reports, while also acting and speaking for the chief. By contrast, on some occasions the chief sent a trusted person to attend a gathering to understand the issues discussed (*humɛni*, "to hear inside") and report on them, but without authorizing this person to speak on his behalf. Here, then, the process of fragmentation of chiefly power and office went beyond its separation from speech to sight and hearing. The chief's senses—his vision, hearing, and speech—were a metonymical token of his powerful presence. In a similar manner, multiple "eyes" were thought to permit witches to see more than ordinary people saw.[5] This reference to witchcraft is not accidental. As we shall discover below, it shapes the darker side of power and its potential downfall.

The figure of an intermediary speaker is also rooted in the Mende experience of the (English) language of state rule as foreign and thus always "interpreted." In postcolonial as well as colonial Sierra Leone, whenever the District Commissioner came to Wunde, he spoke in English, and an interpreter translated his words into Mende. British colonial rule in Sierra Leone set the historical precedent for translating the language of state rule in this area, where there were no significant precolonial state structures.[6] But this interpretative skill has spread beyond the realm of national politics into all practices of communication involving dangerous transactions. Thus in the rituals associated with the women's Sande and the men's Poro societies, the *Sowɛi* and *Gɔbɔ* masquerades that embody these sodalities' powerful attributes and values are silent, while "interpreters" who accompany them translate the performers' gestures for the audience (see Jedrej 1980: 139), spelling out the meaning of the performance. Other, less important masquerades without significant ritual associations, such as the *Falui*, speak a nonsense language made up of a mixture of Sierra Leonean and European words, which their interpreters translate into Mende. The person speaking for these masquerades is referred to as *tapretei*, from the word used for the English government interpreter. Often the interpretation did not concern only the discourse, gestures, and performance of the mask. Instead, it represented a form of containment— a means of control over potential dangers erupting from the performance.

Thus there are different modalities for mediating the rituals of power. In some cases, intermediaries such as government or ritual interpreters simply "turn" words and gestures of authority figures who are present into intelligible Mende (*i njɛpɛ potea Mɛnde yiei hu*, "she [or he] turned the talk into Mende"). In other contexts, speakers act as representatives for those who are either absent or silent, as in the case of the mouthpieces for chiefs and the Sande and Poro masquerades. In the case of the *Falui* and storytellers, the creation of a language—a *bricolage* of European and African idioms, which must be "turned," or translated, into Mende— suggests a mimicry of the very process of communication. Translation, as

Mbembe pointed out, already involves the mockery of the very forms of political and state rule that permeate everyday life in the postcolony (see Mbembe 1992). In this case, the particular form of invented language is a grotesque parody of Krio, the national *lingua franca*, because it is made up of the same elements (African and English languages) but with unintelligible, absurd results. This discursive practice, then, points to the politics of translation, and to language as the terrain for elaborating concrete political practices. As we have seen for the idiom of slavery in kinship relations (see Chapter 3), language offers a crucial key to understanding the specific forms of the political in any given context.

The multiplication of the powerful person through the speech of others is predicated on the rituals that separate extraordinary people from ordinary. The most immediate marker of such a separation is bodily posture, which tends to produce a discursive and symbolic space that entails specific configurations of meaning and power. An emphasis on bodily postures signifies, therefore, the extension of powerful persons' aura to the surrounding space. For example, in Kpuawala, when working and resting, women and children sat close to the ground, on low stools or mats. By contrast, senior men usually occupied hammocks, which were also offered to honored guests in the absence of other forms of off-ground seating, such as chairs. As we have seen, these symbolic postures were the performative indices of rank within a given social hierarchy. Linked to these postures, too, was a cultural model of autonomous self within the constraints of interdependence, where attributes like bravery and quick judgment (associated with warfare) were valued. There was a correlation among rank, elevation off the ground, and postures indicating visible retreat from one's immediate surroundings. For one thing, the presence around high-ranking persons of attendants, followers, and advisors created a visible barrier between them and ordinary people. The separation among people of different ranks was also conveyed through practices such as persons of lower status bowing close to the ground while the object of deference looked aloof from a standing or sitting posture. All these gestures created a space of distinction, within a symbolic framework that has analogues elsewhere (see Bourdieu 1979).

Furthermore, these postures were congealed into specific insignia of power, with a long history in the colonial and precolonial imaginary (the use by chiefs of umbrellas, staffs, thrones, head covers, and different strategies for elevating big people off the ground, from carrying them in hammocks to vehicles).[7] When conducting official business, Wunde's Paramount Chief sat in the wooden throne given by the departing British

Protectorate administration to his father and predecessor in the post. The throne was an apt symbol of the colonial process that was instrumental in institutionalizing the office of this and other chiefs, who replaced the historically and locally variable figures of Mende political rule—"war chiefs" and "land chiefs" (*kɔ mahanga* and *ndɔlɔ mahanga*, pl.). Indeed, the formalization of the office of "Paramount Chief" occurred in the same period as the 1896 declaration of a British Protectorate in the Sierra Leonean hinterland (Fyfe 1962: 542). Thus signs of authority such as the throne mark a spatiotemporal separation, as they transmit a historical memory of political domination. The throne bears the inscription "EIIR," to commemorate Queen Elizabeth's visit to Sierra Leone in 1961—the occasion of the country's independence celebrations—when an examplar was given to each Paramount Chief. It complements the brass-topped cane staff that the British administration bestowed on Paramount Chiefs in the early years of the Protectorate, which is still the main insignia of office in contemporary Sierra Leone.[8]

In the throne, the departing colonial administration left behind an icon of its own sovereignty—one that contributed to immobilizing Mende rulership, as well as isolating it spatially. The dynamic polities linked by clientship to hegemonic towns ruled by warlords, wealthy traders, and/or religious leaders gave way to chiefdoms with relatively fixed boundaries and administrator-rulers. Rather than being endowed with the charismatic attributes of their ancestors, these contemporary chiefs were the last links in an administrative bureaucracy based in relatively distant urban centers. This contrast in bodily, spatial, and political dimensions of power is aptly conveyed by the differences between contemporary and past images and postures of Mende Paramount Chiefs. Whereas early representations of chiefs in the Sierra Leone hinterland still reflected the dynamic stance of warriors, with the consolidation in the twentieth century of a colonial and postcolonial state, holders of political office were represented in immobile stances, usually sitting on thrones. These very objects, and their immobilizing effects, were the visible signs of the state's disciplinary practices in molding vernacular idioms and figures of power.

THE AESTHETICS OF BODY SURFACES

In 1890, T. J. Alldridge went on trek across Sherbro and Mende territory. He was charged by the British administration of the Colony of Sierra Leone to sign peace treaties with the chiefs of the hinterland.[9] When he reached the upper Mende territory of Luawa, which overlaps with the Liberian border region, he encountered for the first time the legendary warrior Kai Londo, whom he photographed and described thus:

> The beautiful gown which [Kai Lundu] is wearing is entirely of country make. *It will be observed in this photograph that he has put on no ornaments.* He had a very great objection to any ostentatious display either on himself or on any of his numerous wives, and at a great meeting which I held a long time afterwards at Kangama, in which the principal chiefs in the adjacent country were present, some of them with their wives being covered with a mass of country-made silver chains and plaques, Kai Lundu drew my attention to it, saying that, although he possessed a great quantity of such things, he had not only appeared without any himself, but had also prevented his wives from so adorning themselves.
>
> *(Alldridge 1901: 191, emphasis added)*

Alldridge was surprised: here was a man who, though "of small stature," was of "large intelligence. . . .[and] immense power" (Alldridge 1901: 190), and yet he wore none of the adornments visible on others of his rank, and which by his own admission he too owned. In the picture, Kai Londo is shown standing alone in a clearing, looking straight toward the camera. His feet are slightly apart, hands planted on his hips. By contrast, most of the other chiefs photographed by Alldridge are portrayed sitting and surrounded by their wives and retainers (see Alldridge 1910: 160, 180, 188, 194). Around Kai Londo's ankles and neck hang medicinal bundles, a kind of adornment that does not attract Alldridge's attention because it is not so radiant as the precious metal jewelry worn by the other chiefs and their wives. And yet these amulets point to a concealed aesthetic associated with Kai Londo's "immense power," one linked to dynamics of consumption.

Medicinal amulets, Qur'anic inscriptions, or special substances processed and mixed to confer particular protections and powers are always enclosed in a case or container, which is then either hung around the body or carried inside a pocket, concealed in one's clothes. The effects of these medicinal amulets mimic their manufacture: the words and substances that must protect the wearer or make things happen are potent when they are concealed within containers. In an analogous manner, liquid medicines that are made from the washing off of Qur'anic inscriptions on wooden boards consist of words first dissolved in water, which become effective only in this form—as a drink contained inside the consumer's body.[10] Kai Londo's amulets were a potent form of adornment, and so too was the gown that concealed much of his body's surface and shape. Other aesthetic objects could be concealed under the gown. Something other than shiny metal radiated from these adornments.

Alldridge's expectation was that, like other chiefs, Kai Londo and his wives would wear precious ornaments to make visible the power of their rank. The fact that others did so suggests that this was an unquestioned feature in the Mende aesthetics of power, too. But Kai Londo's appearance, the appearance of *the* most powerful warrior-chief that Alldridge encountered on this particular occasion, signaled a more subtle understanding of the interwovenness of aesthetics and power. One clue is offered by the name of this powerful warrior, *Londo*, which in Mende means "silent." His name already highlights a relation between the seat of power and the power to silence. Though the name did not necessarily make Londo silent—Alldridge's account suggests he knew how to speak persuasively—it pointed to the ability to be silent, or make somebody silent, as a fundamental feature of power. Indeed, Londo continues to be a popular name for people of high rank in Mende.[11] But so are names that suggest rhetorical virtuosity and persuasiveness. Another warrior contemporary of Kai Londo was Ndawa, "big mouth,"of Wunde, whose name played on the polysemy of the word for mouth, name, and opening to suggest that his fame was linked to expansive speech.[12] The dynamic between an expansive aesthetics of power that shows itself visibly—through adornment, rich clothes, and persuasive speech—and a secretive one in which smallness, an unadorned exterior, and a quiet demeanor produce an even more potent aura, continued to be at work in Mende chiefship.

However, even an expansive exterior (for example, in the semiotics of clothing) entails a component of concealment. All the cotton clothes worn in Mende, which range from those made with locally grown and woven cotton to imported, lighter fabrics, tend to be starched and pressed when worn by a big person, or even by more ordinary persons on special occasions. The stiffness of starched clothes, marking special people and special occasions, conveys an aura of distinctiveness, for it helps shape

> a more general, stylized, almost abstract sphere around man. . . . That new clothes are particularly elegant is due to their being still "stiff," they have not yet adjusted to the modifications of the individual body as fully as older clothes have, which have been worn, and are pulled and pinched by the peculiar movements of their wearer—thus completely revealing his particularity.
>
> *(Simmel 1950: 341)*

Thus, in addition to other ways in which clothes reflect the wealth and status of their wearers, such as through their styling, their cut, and the abundance and texture of their fabric (see Barthes 1967; Bourdieu 1979; Veblen 1967 [1908]), when they are relatively stiff, new-looking, clean, and starched, they also do so by concealing a body's individuality in favor of a more "abstract" appearance. This abstractness can also be attained by wearing many layers of cloth, as Mende big people often do. Abundant cloth and starched cloth, then, enhance the powerful body at a different level.[13] The big person can conceal more about herself than the ordinary one, and special occasions tend to erase everyone's individual particularities in favor of collective traits. Starched clothes, by standing out from the body instead of following its shapes—by concealing instead of revealing it—partake in the concealment of power.

Another dimension of the power of big persons is that they are able, through clothes, to create new styles that embody valued social principles of unity and consensus. During major social and political events, such as a national party convention or a wedding in an important family, followers of a chief, members of parliament, or relatives of the groom and bride would attend dressed uniformly in matching clothes, or *ashɔbi*s, commissioned especially for the occasion.[14] *Ashɔbi*s were said to be a way for outsiders to easily identify people from a particular chiefdom, association, or political constituency at large gatherings. But they also conveyed a rhetoric of "unity" among those wearing the same fabric. As one participant in a chiefdom celebration told me, *ashɔbi*s are worn "so that people will know that we are one" (*kɔɔ nunga ti kɔlɔ kɛ mu yakpe*).

The visual impact of *ashɔbi*s at large gatherings is striking. For example, the yearly national party conventions held until the 1992 military coup that overthrew the *All People's Congress* were attended by Paramount Chiefs and their followers in matching clothes, so that each chiefdom delegation formed a clearly distinguishable color block in the crowd. Notwithstanding the uniform fabric pattern, there was an extraordinary variety in cut, in style of dress (which ranged from clothes modeled after European urban fashions to regional West African models), in finishing details, and in tailoring of *ashɔbi*s. Thus within the general uniformity, wealthy people added expensive embroidery and extra layers of cloth, whereas others, who could not afford a whole outfit, added only matching tops and head coverings. For big persons (Paramount Chiefs, Ministers, and patrons) who chose the *ashɔbi*'s pattern and organized the acquisition and distribution of fabric for their follower's clothes, these "uniforms" were another way of visibly extending themselves beyond their bodily boundaries. They gave an aesthetic value to a sartorial expression of common purpose, for people's comments at large ceremonial gatherings suggested that such uniformity was attractive.

There is also a temporal dimension to this process: expensive clothes remain well after the event or person that occasioned their making, and thus they act as a lasting mnemonic marker. On very important occasions, such as a presidential election or a visit of foreign dignitaries, special cloth patterns were commissioned to commemorate the event. These usually incorporated a silk-screened photographic portrait of the prominent person, or a logo and symbol related to the event, as well as the date and nature of the occurrence. Thus years later, one still came across clothes commemorating the 1980 Organization of African Unity summit in Sierra Leone; the 1985 election of the country's new president, J.S. Momoh; and the installation of Lansana Conteh as president of neighboring Guinea after the death of Sekou Toure.

Indeed, as an event became increasingly distanced in time—and its direct memory in conversations, songs, and other forms dwindled—its remembrance through *ashɔbi*s that were produced for the occasion increased. Clothes that were initially worn by people only in special circumstances were gradually seen more often and circulated more broadly as they became everyday dress, clothes for children cut out from worn adult garments, and eventually rags. They were also worn by people who were not associated with the original event or person, because leftover fabric continued to be sold beyond the geographic and temporal context of its production. Thus the Kpuawala woman I saw wearing a "Lansana Conteh" *ashɔbi* had never been as far as Freetown, let alone neighboring Guinea. As the *ashɔbi* circulated ever more widely, it lost its specific links to particular people, events, and places. Thus a different form of abstraction from that linked to the elegance of stiff clothes is generated by clothes associated with powerful persons or important events. Here the powerful person and the important event project their fame and imagery across spatiotemporal distances. Ultimately, the iconic images on the textile's surface lose any specific connection with the original model.[15] This suggests that there is an optimal spatiotemporal range over which a person's fame, reputation, and power should expand—and beyond which they cease to have any specific value for a particular individual or community.

The circulation in space and time of the icons of prominent personalities represents in a larger sense the dynamics of detachment and circulation of powerful persons' charisma, even beyond the confines of their actual control. These images also incorporate political events within a West African and local aesthetics of power. In the process, power is extended by detaching and circulating personal attributes, images, clothes, and objects from persons or institutions, to deploy them elsewhere on other bodies. The latter in turn assume a kind of uniformity that bespeaks their common identification with potent and dangerous agencies, either for the purpose of aggression and discipline or as a tangible record of historical events. Both aspects are evident in uniform clothing. Military and school uniforms evoke the historical legacy of colonialism and European education, as well as representing certain forms of discipline and force. So, too, *ashɔbi*-wearing crowds sometimes turn political celebrations into violent confrontations, in which having opposing sides clearly demarcated and recognizable by their clothes becomes a liability rather than a fearsome show of unity.[16]

THE PARADOX OF AUTONOMY

According to a Mende proverb, "the snake that walks alone loses respect" (*njia ngila-ngila a baa gbua kalima*). It is not the appearance of the solitary snake that loses it the respect and power appropriate to one of the most feared animals in the Mende universe. Rather, the proverb expresses the paradox of power: the big person is somebody who is relatively autonomous and in control of others but also depends on them to remain in power. Here I look at how local power may be both gained and lost in the interstices of this paradoxical dynamic.

The aura surrounds the big person, extending the extraordinary body further in space. An excess of followers denotes superfluousness, gratuitous expenditure, which allows "the mere *having* of a person to become a visible quality of its *being* . . . [a]round the precinct of mere necessity, it lays a vaster precinct which, in principle, is limitless" (Simmel 1950: 340; original italics). This process of surrounding the powerful person with others signals a politics of superfluousness, not only in the physical presence of dependents but also in the assumption that the big person will support them. At the same time, those who accompany a respected and feared being extend his or her presence in space.

In particular, both chiefs and big men tend to expand their networks by being offered women in marriage, or children in fosterage, by families eager to become connected with them. For both male and female patrons of multiple wives, children, or other dependents, the significance of this kind of extension through the strategic acquisition of dependents is that it produces wealth in the form of labor (farming, mining, and the like). When talking about the area's big persons, Wunde men and women would comment first on the crowds of people around them (wives, children, or other relatives and dependents) and then on the enormous size of the rice farms that such crowds made possible through their labor. In turn, large numbers of dependents also consumed many resources for their sustenance. Thus the transformation of ordinary persons into extraordinary ones through multiplication was linked to technologies of food production or of mineral extraction, especially diamonds (which, however did not exist in the immediate vicinity), and this ensured the continuity of such a large group, and of the big person.

The first indication of a rural Mende's wealth, be he chief or commoner, was the number of his wives, children, and other dependents. This principle extended to the realm of kinship and marriage the notion that a politician's or chief's wealth and political influence could be gauged by the size of the crowds surrounding him. For example, during the farm-burning season in April, Kpuawala people could easily identify the owner and size of a plot that was on fire from the quantity and location of smoke appearing on the horizon. One day, at the sight of a particularly large smoke cloud, several Kpuawala farmers guessed by the fire's size that Alhaji Momoh, the section chief, was burning his farm. They exclaimed in wonder at the enormous size of his rice farm—which in that year, 1990, happened to be visibly accessible, right by a heavily traveled secondary road. Their comment concerned the crowds of wives and children who through their labor made it possible and necessary to have such a large farm (*ngi nyahanga, kɛɛ ngi leenga, ti vahangɔ!*).

The display of wealth in people and that of wealth in resources are interrelated aspects of becoming a Mende *kpako*, and marriage was a key to this process, for it facilitated the "finding" of people (*numui kɔkɔ*)—in other words, obtaining dependents. These interrelated processes were in turn necessary to move forth, to develop (*lee kulɔma*) oneself and one's dependents. Women were indispensable to both processes, and men had to work hard to secure their assistance.

This notion was reiterated by Bockari, a man who some considered Kpuawala's most wealthy and successful farmer. In Kpuawala, many spoke of him as a big man. He was the head of a *mawɛɛ*, a fact that gave him the age seniority that would automatically make one a *kpako*. Also, he was wealthy: every year he laid a large farm, a task in which he was assisted by his five wives, several children, and other dependents. He claimed that any amount of food or cash surplus he might generate would be rapidly consumed by his dependents. Then he pointed proudly

to the 15–20 people working around the forest clearing where we spoke—
a selection of his wives, children, mothers-in-law, and strangers—and
said, "These are my wealth!" (*tiaa mia a nya gbatɛ lɛi*). He added that he
could easily indebt himself beyond his means if only two or three of his
in-laws should die, leaving him to shoulder heavy funeral expenses.[17]
Thus the same visible marks of power—wealth and dependents—could
also lead to his downfall.

There was also a more ambivalent side to people's perceptions of
Bockari. One young man once told me that while traveling on a path that
ran by Bockari's farm, he saw him bent over in the distance performing
ambiguous gestures. The man's immediate assumption was that Bockari
was burying secret medicine under his fields to ensure a good harvest but
that this medicine must have come at a high cost. He suspected that
Bockari had a deal with *ndile*, the dangerous python spirit, and that in
exchange for the medicine that gave him such wonderful luck in farming,
he must have sacrificed a human being (a child or other kin). The man
suspected that this was the reason behind the sudden death of one of
Bockari's children. This suspicion suggests that to acquire power through
wealth and dependents, some people are willing to sacrifice their children
and dependents—that is, the only really lasting source of wealth. This is
because there is a link between becoming a big person and having many
children. By contrast, infertility can be either a sign of illicit, excessive
accumulation of wealth—involving secret transactions with evil forces—
or a harbinger of imminent disaster.

The fact that Mende women[18] can be visible signs of, and vehicles for,
the extension of big persons points to the location at different levels of
their own agency, and of their specific modalities of expansion, in a
world that conceives the big person as a gender-inclusive category. I suggested earlier that having many wives and children is an important attribute of the male *kpako*, as well as being the chief means for ensuring his
wealth. By contrast, a female *kpako* is defined precisely by her *independence* from domestic ties, which in Mende means the supervision of male
relatives or a husband. Like all prominent Mende people, big women
must also attract and cultivate dependents, but these are not necessarily
seen as extensions of their own family and relatives. The figure of the
kpako nyaha, the important woman, underscores both the differences
between male and female powers and the ambigous status of all big people. In particular, a big woman highlights the paradox of autonomy or its
counterpart, interdependence.

A Mende Sande song warns,

> Take my oath, take my oath on the (Sande) medicine, oh Sande! A big woman
> is Satan, she goes after your husband, to take him away from you (lit: get him
> out of your hand); but pay no attention, or they will say that it is jealousy. A
> big woman is dangerous. . . .
> *(A nya ma jondu wua, a nya ma jondu wua hale ma, Sande-ande oh! Kpako*
> *nyaha Setanɛi mia, i wɛɛga bi hini ma, a kpua bi yeya; bɛɛ lali ma, tɛ toloi mia.*
> *Kpako nyahɛi masubɛi mia. . . .)*

As a single person, a big woman is seen as a potential sexual threat to
other women's husbands, with whom she might have affairs. The notion
that a single woman might be celibate was scarcely entertained by Wunde
people confronted with the question, for (among other reasons) regular
sexual intercourse upon reaching adulthood was considered essential to
maintaining a healthy body replenished of "filling" fluids, and one would
unnecessarily endanger one's life without it. However, the big woman's
attributes go well beyond those of a sexually predatory person. When I
returned to Kpuawala on my second visit, still unmarried and childless in
my thirties, people jokingly remarked that I was truly becoming a *kpako
nyaha.* Indeed, a woman is called *kpako nyaha* precisely because she has
no husband or male patron taking care of her, and this demonstrates her
ability to look after herself—to be "for herself" rather than someone else
(*ta ngi yakpe va, ii yɛ numu wɛka lɔ va*). However, she usually fulfills
other criteria common to her male counterparts as well, such as supporting related and unrelated dependents of her own.

The connotations of being a *kpako nyaha* are rather more ambiguous
than those of a "big man," as is illustrated by Jina's case. Jina was a *sowɛi*
—she belonged to the highest ranks within the women's Sande society.
And yet she chose *ndopo jowo*, "child *sowɛi*," as her society name,
whereas most other high-ranking women preferred names, such as
"silence," "money," or "I see everything," that enhanced the mystique of
their position. Jina was from outside Kpuawala and had married a
younger man. She was a gifted dancer and had a reputation as a musical
performer at Sande events, for which she was sometimes called from considerable distances to perform. Unlike her husband, Jina had gone to
school and could write and speak English. She looked different from
other women of her age in the community, wearing a large sports wrist-
watch, stylish hairdos with artificial implants and beads woven into
them, and expensive clothes often tailored in the latest fashion. All these
items advertised her relative wealth, as well as associating her with the
cosmopolitan world beyond Kpuawala, something she occasionally

referred to by stating that she was not a "bush person" (*ndɔgbɔ mɔ*) like most of her neighbors and that she "knew the world" (*ngi ndunyɛi gɔlɔ*).

On several different evening visits to Jina at her house, I found her entertaining her own and her husband's friends with palm wine she had ordered and paid for herself. Drinking—particularly by a woman—was looked down on in this Muslim community. I first heard her defined sarcastically as a *kpako nyaha* by a couple of older Kpuawala women, who were discussing the hardship her absence caused her husband during the height of the rainy-season farming activities. He had been complaining about the fact that she had gone back to her hometown for a visit when he most needed her help, and the women were commenting in his absence that he could not expect anything else from a wife who was a *kpako nyaha*, a "big woman." They explained that it was not appropriate for a man to marry a woman who was older and better educated than himself or someone with Jina's assertive, even abrasive manner. It was obvious to these elderly women that Jina was wealthier than her husband—that she made more money than he did through performing as a skilled singer and dancer, and through business ventures. According to the women, this disparity in wealth should be embarrassing to him (*mawufengɔ*) and explained why he was in no position to impose his authority on her.

By contrast, in the same period Jina's mother-in-law Tene lamented her absence, confiding to me that Jina always took good care of her, whereas her son did not feed her and treat her with respect. Tene claimed that Jina always returned from her trips with gifts of cloth and food for her, whereas her own son had not supported her in many years. She added that Jina had played a key role in helping her husband pay for a second wife's Sande initiation, although he later claimed that she had simply lent him money to cover the expenses. Jina was childless, and this was a matter of some concern to her. On more than one occasion she came to ask me in private whether I knew of any medicine that could help "cure her belly" (*i nya gohu hale*)—to eliminate the pains and menstrual irregularities that she sometimes experienced and that she considered responsible for her infertility. Local rumors suggested that witchcraft may have been another factor in Jina's infertility. Wealth and infertility were not the only factors that made people suspect the presence of "witch spirits" in a person. Among other reasons, in Jina's case, was the fact that she was a twin—a category of people with extraordinary powers. As we will see in Chapter 6, Jina, the second-born twin, was thought to have the power of divination and ability to mediate between humans and spirits, both good and bad (Gittins 1987: 170–178).

Other big women were older than Jina and held prominent positions in the community as ritual specialists (such as Sande society leaders), representatives to the town council, or senior wives and sisters of household heads, in charge of the big houses where women and children lived. Particularly important ones were admired and depended on by both men and women, but they were also envied and criticized if they were too open about their autonomy. In Jina's case, her relative youth, education, ritual expertise, and worldliness, as well as her childlessness and outsider status, contributed to the ambiguity of her position and to people's ambivalence toward her. As in the case of the wealthy farmer Bockari—whose success was assumed to be linked to the premature deaths of several of his babies—Jina's status as a big woman was deemed to have resulted from acts of witchcraft and the sacrifice of her reproductive potential. Jina was suspected by some to have taken a socially destructive path to the accumulation of power, in which her bodily capacity for secrecy was instead used to harbor a witch spirit whose hunger could be satisfied only by consuming the fetuses she never carried to term.

Certain states of consciousness make people—and especially women, children, and those weakened by illness—more vulnerable to the invasion of witch spirits over which one has no control. These spirits tend to work at night, entering people during their sleep and visiting dreams. Miscarriages are thought to be one of the possible consequences of witch spirits having sexual relations with a pregnant woman in her dreams. The object of the witch's activity is not the host but the creature she carries in her belly. For example, Hawa, a woman who was ill for several months with pain in her abdomen, said that she had been visited one night in dreams by a spirit, who after having sex with her, reached inside her to "spoil her belly"—to cause a miscarriage. Since that miscarriage, she had never fully regained her health. She died later on during my stay in Kpuawala. The idiom of Hawa's own account of her illness, and of those speaking about her, described the process she was undergoing as one of "drying out" because of an insufficiency of bodily fluids and healthful substances inside her. Witches were said to eat people from the inside out, thus reversing through negative consumption the process at work in the aesthetic display of powerful bodies.

This negative aesthetics is linked to Mende views of the body, and of the belly in particular. The salient feature of a pregnant woman is her "full" abdomen, a fact highlighted by her being called "belly woman" (*ko nyaha*). The capacity for giving birth (*nde*) is a powerful one, but it also makes a woman particularly vulnerable to possession by a witch spirit, who might endanger her own or her child's life by entering her body while it is opened in childbirth. Thus childbirth is seen as a form of translation—of movement across bodily and virtual boundaries that must take place under the supervision of the Sande leaders. Their ritual mediation has parallels with that of speakers and interpreters for powerful people, who make manifest and intelligible the latters' speech (*nde*, the same word as for childbirth). In Mende, then, childbirth (*nde*) is linked semantically to speech, but also to lineage (*ndehu*, "born inside [a group]"), which, as I pointed out earlier (see Chapter 4), anchors kinship to shared speech and points to an inner circle of communicative exchange. Speech and birth unfold over bodily thresholds (*nd/la*), which are themselves part of a rich semantic cluster encompassing name (*nda*), door (*nda*), mouth (*nda*), anus (*tokpula*), and vagina, the "mouth below" (*ndabu*, cf. Boone 1986:99). However, the dialectic implicit in giving birth and speaking, and in opening doors and naming, cannot be exhausted merely by paying static attention to these sites. Rather, it shifts our attention to the larger dynamic processes that unfold there, such as incorporation and expulsion. Thus, as we saw with Kai Londo, knowledge of names provides an entry not only into the intimate history of individuals but also into an encompassing social and political history.

An essential attribute of powerful people is the ability to control bodily processes, which have their symbolic figuration in thresholds that cannot be trespassed illicitly. This linkage (between spatial and bodily thresholds) is made explicit in childbirth. In one instance in Kpuawala, a midwife attending the delivery stopped a pregnant woman from standing in a doorway left open to let in some light. The woman was peeking in to see how labor was progressing, but Mama Kema told her to move in or out. She explained that "if a pregnant woman stands in a doorway, the child will not come quickly."[19] Later, she speculated with other midwives about whether "witchcraft business" (*hɔna hinda*) connected with a similar mistake might account for Morigwa's protracted labor, and she washed the same open door with a special medicine. The liquid was *nɛsi* (water used to wash Qur'anic verses off from the wooden slates where they were copied down and learned), which she had obtained from *kaamɔ* Jussu (see Bledsoe and Robey 1986:26).[20] After collecting in a dish the *nɛsi* used to wash the door, Mama Kema gave the women in labor some to drink and poured the rest on her belly and in her vagina. These ministrations, she said, would speed up childbirth while keeping away "bad things." In her parallel ministrations of *nɛsi* to door and bodily orifices, Mama Kema appeared to be treating it as a lubricant—in one case to speed up the exit of the baby, in the other to facilitate the exit of any witch spirits who might have entered the space where the delivery was taking place, as well as the woman's body. The *nɛsi* took on these lubricating properties by partaking in the aesthetics of secrecy: potent words were concealed through a process of dilution in water, only to be made manifest again through their healing effects. Once more, the strength of this aesthetic display lies in the dialectic of hidden source and manifest effects of healing.

Other *nɛsi* formulas are applied analogously to body and space to *close* them, rather than to facilitate movement across their thresholds.[21] This ability *both* to control and speed up movements over thresholds *and* to put a stop to them by closing the thresholds off was central to the status of senior Sande elders as big women. Women in childbirth were at greater risk of losing control over these very processes—and over the speech that could reveal secrets—but as powerful midwives and in other ritual roles, they were also the only ones with the skills to mediate these transitions. These were dangerous, violent moments, in which dramas of life and death were played out. They were situations in which life-giving and life-taking practices could overlap instead of occupying distinct spaces. Women with the power to control these processes called themselves warriors, bringing potent symbols of warfare and death right into the midst of fertility and reproduction. It was by virtue of their skills in administering various forms of death—to girls whose clitorises they cut in order to initiate them into womanhood, to witches harbored in mothers or babies at childbirth—that Sande big women could ensure future life. The fact that a parallel ritual role was reserved to the most male of women, the *mabɔle*, suggests that certain mediations between the living and the dead, between the visible and the invisible, were central to the powers of big women. Among the *mabɔle*'s ritual roles is that of mediator in the final stage of Poro initiation, when she helps new members go out into the world by placing each of the initiates' feet alternately on top of hers, to lift it and carry it over the threshold of the meeting place. Thus a mediating (feminine) element is necessary to facilitate the symbolic transition to a new stage of life. These powerful mediations must be kept in mind when we note that, at war, men appropriate transgressively feminine symbolic elements—from dress to wigs and makeup—that may appear grotesque. Indeed, a feature of the grotesque is that it plays out the dramaturgy of power at the lowest bodily levels, the sites of sexuality and reproduction. These are sites where female bodies are construed as being weak but over which big women had the most extraordinary—if ambivalently valued—powers.

Like the *mabɔle* and big people in the political domain, big (Sande) women are skilled in bringing forth speech that might endanger life if it were to remain concealed. However, their skills are not always matched by a symmetrical ability to silence potentially dangerous words. During an interval in another Kpuawala child delivery, the midwives who were assembled in the room gossiped about how the town *imam* had approached one of them during the previous spring's Sande initiation and told her that the women under their control were making too much noise (*sɔlɛ*). He said that people could overhear their conversations about women's secret matters and implied that it was the role of a Sande big woman to silence her subordinates. He contrasted the women's behavior with that of men engaged in their own initiation, when even gatherings of a hundred or more men could maintain absolute silence. By contrast, he implied that Sande women would spoil their secret medicine through their excessive speech.[22] Thus the process of birthing, and the parallel speech disclosing previously concealed acts and feelings, which was necessary to speed up that birthing, may also have made women more prone to leak secrets in situations when this had damaging consequences.

The practice and idiom of clitoridectomy underscored the ambivalence surrounding women's discursive and bodily "openness."[23] Clitoridectomy was an act of violence and bloodletting, performed with a knife, by elders of the Sande society on the bodies of initiates in their care. It was seen as an act of opening up the body, referred to as "cutting the rope, or string" (*ngeyɛi tee*)—cutting the protruding lips that were supposed to "itch" (*a yange*) if a woman engaged in sexual intercourse without having had them excised. This act of cutting may have opened up the female body to intercourse and childbirth, but it also exposed it to the risk of uncontrolled loss.[24] Whether operations were successful depended on the medicinal knowledge of the particular Sande official who performed them, and especially on the extent to which her potions and the words with which she deployed them were potent. In this situation, a rival Sande leader or an enemy of an initiate's family might do witchcraft work to render her medicine ineffective. As a result, Kpuawala Sande elders said that in the past the initiate was said sometimes suffered complications like bleeding to death or infections following the operation. It is important to keep in mind, then, that for both men (who are scared and put through ordeals, as well as being scarified) and women (who undergo clitoridectomies), initiation is a violent, painful experience, one in which big women as much as big men wield the knife and in which the urgency of protecting secrets and bodily boundaries is inscribed in the initiate's flesh.[25] At the same time, the ultimate betrayal evoked by these scars, which are produced with the collusion of mothers, fathers, and other close kin, creates the potential for challenging the ambition of power to aestheticize itself in new, ever more excessive forms.

The *imam*'s concern with controlling female discursive practices resonates with the containment of female fertile sexuality through Sande initiation, making big women such a problematic category. Indeed, on a daily basis in Kpuawala, one had the impression that the affairs of the men's Poro society were shrouded in secrecy to a greater extent than Sande affairs. Sande songs were often sung in everyday contexts, and women encouraged children to stage mock initiations complete with bodily decoration and dances, but no such behavior characterized the Poro. I was rebuked for simply asking when men would hold their "coming out" ceremony in a nearby community, a public event that was going to be attended by everyone. And whereas most evenings during Sande initiations were characterized by festive dancing and singing throughout the community, Poro men came to town at various stages in their initiation rituals and silenced noninitiates, who had to stay quietly inside their homes, behind closed doors and shutters. Thus the different levels of containment of the sexual body are inscribed in the institutional settings of the secret societies. Ultimately, they translate into the presumption of an asymmetrical capacity for secrecy. The external control of the capacity for containment, and the aesthetic display of power, are the fundamental, albeit problematic, marks of the Mende big person.

AN AESTHETICS OF CONSUMPTION

Strategies of incorporation are crucial to the introduction of potent substances inside the body. Consumption is the most basic of such processes and, in its multiple forms, is a key activity of big people. It also can be one of the main avenues for a big person's downfall and bodily "shrinking"—for example, as the medium for poisoning him or her—and thus it is regarded with a great deal of ambivalence. Although sharing food is the prime gesture of generous hospitality, it also tests the level of trust between the parties. Upon returning to Kpuawala from events sponsored by leading chiefdom figures, one would normally be asked whether one "had been given," an expression whose surface abstractness belied its specificity: had one been well fed? But when I visited a town that had sided with Kpuawala's political rivals during the 1986 national elections, the question was not asked and none of the people accompanying me accepted any food or drink—for fear of poisoning, I was later told. Thus, although eating was a sign of wealth, physical health, and patronage—marking the generosity of food givers toward recipients—it could also be the avenue for bodily waste and death. This underscores the fact that processes of incorporation do not always fill the body with potent substances, which then radiate in their effects beyond bodily boundaries. On the contrary, instead of leading to a healthful expansion, incorporating harmful substances may lead to the body's destruction and consumption—a collapse into its hollowed-out self in illness. In this sense, the powerful body of the big person does not merely inspire fear and respect. Rather, it may trigger a sociopolitical struggle for the accumulation of power, which may lead to the destruction of a powerful opponent.

In the Mende anatomy of power, the abdominal cavity is where these invisible struggles take place, the locus of powerful agencies and processes. It is the area implied in any generic reference to the insides of persons, objects, and spaces. Indeed, the Mende word for inside translates as "inside the belly" (*ko-hu*). William Murphy points out that for ethnic groups in this part of West Africa, having a "deep belly" where one conceals one's knowledge is a valued attribute of powerful people (Murphy 1981: 670). If having a "deep belly" and concealing hidden capacities within one's body are key aspects of Mende power, control over others is also often expressed by metaphors of incorporation. People are said to "eat" others when they beat them in some contest or game (*i ngi mɛa*). The consumption metaphor also extends to other processes—for instance where money is concerned. When a bride's parents receive bridewealth for her, they turn to her and ask whether they should eat the money (*muaa mɛ?*) that is, whether they should spend it and thus consider the marriage final. When talking of individuals who spent all their wealth, people in Kpuawala would say that they ate it all up, or they might simply make the motion for gobbling everything up, a sweeping hand gesture across their mouths. The ultimate form of consumption is "eating" people through witchcraft or through human sacrifice (see Gittins 1987: 160–166; Harris and Sawyerr 1968: 74 ff.). In Kpuawala, people linked the latter to a desire for "bad medicine" (*hale nyamui*) that could endow one with power, charisma, and wealth—particularly for political purposes. To obtain this medicine, one would often be required by the medicine man (*halemɔ*) to "give a person" (*i numui ve*), to kill somebody, whose vital organs and substances were used to prepare the concoction.

Bad medicine normally required specific bodily parts (internal organs, as well as skin from the forehead and the palms of hands and feet) and substances such as fat and blood. Thus what is taken from the victim's body is a combination of inner organs and fluids, and those parts of the body surface usually associated with the interface between an individual and his or her social environment. The forehead is thought to be the seat of a person's fame and reputation (Boone 1986: 181; Harris and Sawyerr 1968: 126), and the palms of hands are the point of contact among people in greetings or, in prayer, among people, God, and the ancestors. Feet trod the earth under which ancestors are buried, and it is under the feet of a patron that dependents place themselves (*ngi gɔwɔbu*). But these body parts were rarely said to be consumed directly by the client who was seeking a particularly coveted political post or great wealth in the diamond business. More often, the medicine man was said to use the bodily parts to make preparations with which he soaked items of clothing worn by his client. Thus steeped in potent properties, these special clothes were worn under regular clothing.

Here too, the source of power was concealed under or inside one's external appearance in order to be effective. The focus on clothes that invest a wearer with special powers is rooted in Mande hunting and warfare lore. Mande hunters and warriors of the past wore special shirts with amulets and other attachments to make them invulnerable to enemy weapons or animal attacks, as well as to endow them with the accumulated powers of their victims, whose bodily parts or substances became part of their clothes (McNaughton 1982). In Wunde, such shirts are still kept and handed down as heirlooms and worn on ritual or ceremonial occasions. The heterogeneous appendages attached to clothes expand the bodily volume of the powerful through the layering on their bodies, of fragments from other animal and human bodies. In the case of hunters and warriors of old, these appendages could be either displayed on the outside or concealed in internal pockets and hidden pouches. But in the more recent and extreme applications of protective medicine—for example in the current civil war, or to gain power in the national, modern political sphere, or to acquire the new, fabulous forms of wealth introduced by technologies of mineral extraction—the incorporation of these trappings always seemed to take the bad and concealed form. In a way, this concealed form of medicine mimics the power and wealth it seeks to produce, which are often located in concealed sites: underground, off-shore, or the arcane workings of corrupt state bureaucracies.

Bad medicine is, by and large, disapproved of in Mendeland as a strategy for acquiring power (Gittins 1987: 129 ff.), and accusations of ritual murder or "cannibalism" have always been a useful component in political strategies aimed at discrediting adversaries or unpopular leaders, both historically and in contemporary Sierra Leone (Beattie 1915; MacCormack 1983: 60). Eating a person is the manifestation—to a greater degree—of the kind of hubris that can get one in trouble for not respecting social inferiors or for exploiting one's dependents. It reflects an excessive greed for power, which inevitably results in trespassing the boundaries of legitimacy. It also signals that the dangerous crossing of the threshold between visible and invisible realms of power (and secret transaction) may lead to a catastrophic ending.

In March 1990, the case of Alhaji Tokowa, which involved a Mende man who had reportedly sought bad medicine in pursuit of wealth, had gained national attention through the media and popular culture—taped songs, plays, and so on. The case was brought to trial in the capital city, Freetown, where this wealthy Muslim (his title, Alhaji, suggested that he had made a pilgrimage to Mecca) was accused of murder along with four other people, including the victim's mother. Unlike most cases of suspected ritual murder, in this case the victim's body and other evidence were found, so that it was possible to prosecute in a court of law. The defendants were eventually executed for the crime. Alhaji Tokowa was alleged to have killed his sister's daughter, a pregnant young woman, after luring her to his farm under the pretext of needing her help. This act was supposed to ensure his election as Chiefdom Speaker in an area at the heart of diamond territory, where holding a position of authority meant having access to considerable wealth and political influence.

In Kpuawala gossip, in the national news, and in the tapes of prominent Mende performers like Amie Kallon and Salia Koroma that helped bring the event to national attention,[26] much was made of the fact that this man was an Alhaji, that he had undertaken a pilgrimage to Mecca, and that he was therefore supposed to be a devout Muslim. Other topics that invariably surfaced in discussions of the case were the man's insatiable greed and his willingness to sacrifice his own pregnant niece to it. The Alhaji's greed seemed aptly conveyed by the nickname by which he was known, *Tokowa*, which translates as "big hand" or "long arm" (*l/toko wai*). His close relationship to the victim was also the subject of speculation, for people in Kpuawala said that a stranger would have been an easier target, one more difficult to identify.

In spite of the sometimes passionate indictments I heard expressed about the Alhaji Tokowa case, nobody seemed to question the basic principle of giving or taking a person in order to achieve wealth or power. The opposite conditions of being in someone's hands and being able to dispose of somebody are the criteria underlying most relations of patronage and dependence. Alhaji's victim was in many ways the quintessential dependent: she was a sister's child. She belonged, then, to the category of kin he could rightfully address and treat, as we have seen, as his "slaves."[27] The victim was also a woman, and women were among the most common casualties of ritual murders in Sierra Leone and elsewhere (see Nwaka 1978: 197). Thus one dependent is sacrificed to acquire many dependents and to attain "big personhood," a process of multiplication that has long been central to the logic of sacrifice itself, as well as these particular forms of murder (Beattie 1915; Nwaka 1978: 198).

The comments surrounding Alhaji Tokowa's story in Kpuawala suggested that his main faults were *excessive* ambition and greed, which induced him to sacrifice the social ties that produce positive power and wealth. Even before his extreme bid for political office, his wealth was suspect because it was founded on his role as a middleman in the diamond business rather than on the visible, apparent work connected, for example, with agricultural production and labor. This distinction between (1) good forms of wealth and labor, achieved through physical effort and with and for the benefit of an extensive network of social relations and (2) bad forms of wealth that produce only personal gain and originate outside the community (such as from Lebanese diamond dealers or multinational mining concerns) is not unique to Sierra Leone.

The juxtaposition elsewhere of rural, underexploited economies with extractive systems, where raw materials bring in disproportionate incomes from the international market to a very few, often generates the same suspicion of sudden, great wealth with no apparent labor. In her study of Yoruba popular theater in the aftermath of the Nigerian oil boom between the mid-1960s and the 1970s, Karin Barber suggested that representations of very great, sudden wealth were always negative, regardless of the source of such enrichment (Barber 1982). There is a sense, in Kpuawala as in the Nigerian setting described by Barber, that the rapid attainment of success or great power involves special deals with evil forces. Remember that in commenting on the wealth of Bockari a couple of men suggested that his good crops were paid for with the death of several of his newborn babies, sacrificed to *ndile*, the python spirit. In cases such as these, the secrets contained within a big person are about Faustian pacts with evil agencies; in order to safeguard one's own wealth and success, one sacrifices those of one's offspring, whose multiplication is itself another sign of potency.

Consuming persons in acts of ritual murder is an illegitimate shortcut to excessive power and wealth, through the agency of bad medicine. Kpuawala people gossiping about specific instances were ambivalent toward these practices. They subscribed to the view that having total control over others was essential to increasing one's prestige, and yet the complete autonomy demonstrated by a big person's readiness to sacrifice even the most intimate of relatives was deeply disturbing to them. Incorporation posed a moral dilemma when excessive accumulation resulted in the destruction of human lives (especially those of one own's kin). The moral solution to this dilemma was to incorporate persons into one's domestic unit, as dependents. Having dependents while at the same time being oneself relatively autonomous in relation to those above oneself in the social hierarchy was the key to becoming a big person (Geschiere 1997).

CONCLUSION

The making of Mende *kpakonga* (pl.) is predicated on controlling bodily and discursive processes that transmit potent knowledge, substances, or agencies to the body. In particular, the capacity for containing powerful secrets within "deep bellies" is crucial to the big person's accumulation of power. Although a big person's power goes far beyond bodily boundaries, which are constitutive of identity, this external dimension is secondary to the secret concealed in the body. Secrecy has primacy over its aesthetic display, and the latter may sometimes contradict the positive value of bigness, as suggested by the ugliness of the Bamana *boliw*. In other words, the cultural forms through which power becomes manifest in a big person are not always intelligible within an aesthetics of desirability.

Processes of incorporation are crucial to the containment of powerful knowledge and capacities, but these are not unambiguously positive, as the dangers of witchcraft and other forms of spirit possession illustrate. Although consuming in all its forms, and sealing the thresholds of a "full" body container, are essential to Mende conceptions of power, these processes can also lead to the loss of bodily control, and to death of the self, when poison or destructive spirits are the object of consumption.

By the same token, big persons command fear and respect. There is always a fear that they may become excessively greedy, engaging in destructive forms of consumption rather than in socially productive gestures of generosity.

Indeed, the behavior of big persons' dependents also underscores ironically the *inter*dependence between people in these hierarchical relationships. The strategies available to those above others (*mamɔ*) are limited and constrained to some extent by those who are "for," or under, them. These constraints derive in part from the interests of those who are formally subordinated to others in particular contexts. As we saw in the earlier analysis of marriage and other relations of dependence, including slavery, being for someone entails specific returns, such as being fed and clothed in exchange for labor or receiving goods and money to contribute to funerals of close relatives. When patrons fail to meet these obligations, those entrusted to them can and do legitimately challenge their authority. The generosity displayed through the aesthetic surplus surrounding big persons' bodies must be continually reproduced, as the abundant clothing and food they exhibit are given away to their dependents in acts of generosity. Once this generosity ends, and the big person is suspected of greedily hoarding—of containing wealth for his or her own consumption—he or she can rapidly become suspected of witchcraft. Thus the foundation of the big person's status is also the basis for subordinates undermining that very status.

Status and authority, then, are context-variable, relative attributes that are easily lost or challenged if people exceed their legitimate roles and do not meet expectations connected with those roles. These attributes are not simply a feature of the pragmatics of power relations. They are also recognized in Mende ideology, which conceives of power not as fixed and inalienable but as linked to specific spatiotemporal contexts and situations and to particular bodily states.[28] This attitude informs a range of behaviors, from the striking Mende generosity and respect toward visiting guests and strangers—regardless of their appearance and status—to the lack of deference displayed on some occasions toward high-ranking people by their social inferiors. The two phenomena are different sides of the same coin: strangers must be treated generously because one might be in their position someday, whereas a powerful person here, today, may become nobody—an anonymous person (*nu gbama*—tomorrow, under different circumstances.

Clay, Palm Oil, and Temporality

Hojo a bɛɛ numa, kɛya ngulɔ?
If white clay is flattering to appearance, how about oil?

> *Refrain from a Sande initiation song,*
> *Kpuawala, Sierra Leone, April 1990*

"If clay is flattering to one's appearance, how much more will oil be?" Gbesse said laughing, to his friend Braima, at the sight of their wives splattered with white clay. Mariama and Mama Kɔɔ stood next to each other on a wooden table facing the external wall of Gbesse's Kpuawala house, which had recently been repaired and covered with a new layer of mud. Over the fresh, smooth, brown mud, the women were smearing pasty white liquid from a bucket placed between them on the table, with the short palm rib brooms they normally used to sweep houses and yards. As soon as Gbesse had pronounced the words, the two women picked up a song in counterpoint, in which the line above made up the refrain. As they sang, they adapted their working rhythm to the music. Gbesse continued:

> They smear clay on Sande initiates (*mbogbonisia*) at the time of cooking *Gani*.[1] When they smear it on, people will say: "... how about oil?" They are thinking about the time of pulling out Sande.[2] That is what makes the Sande coming out a pleasure.

Gbesse's cue, and the Sande song it evoked, pointed to the relationship between two key stages in women's initiation. New Sande initiates appear covered in white clay on their first public appearance after the initial seclusion period. This sight makes people's thoughts leap ahead to the final coming-out ceremony, when the whitened skin that distinguishes *mbogbonisia* (girls undergoing Sande initiation) for the duration of their initiation gives way to beautiful, shiny bodies glistening with perfumed palm oil.[3]

For several reasons, this anticipation of the end of Sande initiation would be attractive to two men such as these. Braima had sponsored the initiation of his own young wife, Mariama, not too many years earlier and could still remember his Sande troubles—his efforts to produce the surplus required for initiation expenses and the marriage to follow. However, Gbesse's explanation implied more than the relief from troubles: he spoke with genuine relish about the way he had looked forward to beginning married life and the possibility of having children and his own farm that came with it. The final Sande ceremonies were also anticipated as a time of great celebrations. Braima and Gbesse reminded me of the 1985 Sande initiation, when the young men in Kpuawala had organized an all-night dancing party and hired a D.J. from Kenema town, who came with a rented generator. The event had attracted large crowds of outsiders to the community and had been deemed a great success, despite protests from observant Muslims among town elders who disliked the fact that alcohol and marijuana were consumed on these occasions. The bittersweet stories emerged, their memory revived by the site of clay-spattered women and by a song's refrain.

Men are in the audience at Sande initiations, as well as at this particular work scene, which had triggered their memory. If they have thoughts about the relationship between white clay and oil, how do women react to these substances? During the 1985 initiation that Gbesse and Braima referred to, one Sande elder told me that clay on the *mbogboni*'s skin signaled her difference from other women around her, at a time when she was no longer secluded in the secret society bush. After the *Gani*, *mbogbonisia* remained in partial seclusion until the end of their initiation—they returned to the Sande enclosure for the night—but were allowed to join their households for daytime work. Men had to avoid girls in this liminal state if they encountered them in town or on farms. This avoidance was necessitated by the fact that initiates at this stage were considered especially seductive. They were still virgins and yet already excised and prepared for sexual activity. Kaolin clay marked this liminal stage, but it also beautified the skin by eliminating its flaws. One Sande woman told me during preparations for the final coming-out ceremony, when initiates were taken to the river to wash and then had oil smeared on their bodies, that if it had not been for the weeks they spent covering themselves in clay to get rid of rashes, blemishes, and so on, the initiates would not have had such beautiful, smooth skin on this day.

Thus the white clay smeared daily on the Sande initiates' bodies had the cosmetic purpose of acting as a protective shell, beautifying the reflective skin that would emerge in the end. Clay was a mask that concealed the initiate's body until the end of initiation. Although it was emphasized as *the* identifying feature of Sande initiates in everyday contexts, white clay—as we shall see—concealed a more powerful aesthetic transformation, one that occurred later in initiation and was marked outwardly by smearing with oil the bodies of *mbogbonisia*. In ordinary contexts outside initiations, people who saw somebody plastered in white clay joked about that individual's being a *mbogboni*, regardless of his or her sex and age. In other words, the reaction of Gbesse and Braima at the sight of their clay-splattered wives was common: there was a strong identification between clay-covered bodies and Sande initiates. Men too went through a phase during initiation when clay was smeared on their limbs, but they were never seen publicly with their entire bodies covered with it.[4] However, the fact that clay could be used on male *and* female bodies at initiation and in other context points to a discrepancy between its uses in practice, and its ideal association with Sande initiation. In this connection, note that the *mabɔle* in her hybrid initiation went through "the clay stage," but skipped "the oil stage" of Sande initiation. This suggests that the final beautification of women's bodies with the substance referred to as hot oil (*ngulɔ gbandi*) was a more critical step than earlier ones in Sande initiation.

Despite a "clay-centered" idiom and the public focus on this substance in connection with Sande initiation, the fact that clay can be thought of as a mask for the potency of oil is underscored by lapses in its use. In 1993, on the occasion of a Sande initiation held despite the interruptions of the ongoing war, I witnessed an argument between a Sande elder and a *mbogboni* who was unwilling to smear clay on her body on a daily basis. The girl had begun the initiation process *the previous year* and had undergone *Gani*, but she had not gone through the final ceremonies. Like other families trying to maintain a semblance of normalcy during the war, the girl's family had not been able to amass the resources to pay for initiation, because rebels had stolen the rice harvest during an incursion in the area. Furthermore, the girl's family had no prospective husband to help them out, so the rest of the Sande cohort had completed the initiation, leaving her behind.

The girl had returned to live with her family and hoped to secure in the future the wherewithal to complete her initiation. Kema, the Sande elder who was half-heartedly rebuking her, commented that "today's girls" were not as obedient as they used to be, but she did not seem particularly upset with this transgression. She too must have seen the impracticality of

demanding that the *mbogboni* wear clay every day for a year, and perhaps longer, until her coming-out ceremony. Kema commented that the
girl did not want to wear clay and that this was not proper form for
someone who was still in the middle of her initiation, but she did not
threaten her with any punishment. At the same time, nobody seemed to
doubt that at some point the girl would be pulled out of Sande, clay or no
clay. Thus the saying that clay is beautiful, but oil is even more so,
seemed to provide at multiple levels a clue to clay's encompassment by
this other, sticky, shiny, and hot substance.

Hot oil had an excess of heat because women cooked palm oil several
times to transform the red, dense liquid first processed from palm fruits
into the clear and light substance they mixed with perfumed herbs to
beautify their skins. The attractive surface coolness of clay concealed
bodily heat and sexuality. In an analogous manner, the cool white clay
that women applied to the exteriors of Kpuawala houses deflected attention from what transpired within their walls.

CONSUMING CLAY AND OIL

Kaolin clay and water are linked metonymically and analogically. On the
one hand, clay is a wet substance that women collect in water. Clay and
water are both wet, cooling substances. On the other hand, in order to be
usable as a cosmetic, clay must be dry—that is, entirely free of water.
First clay is freed of all impurities until only a very fine-grained, grey
paste is left. This is shaped in balls, which are set out in the sun to dry, at
which point they turn white. Clay balls are then stored in a dry place, and
women break off fragments as needed. The kaolin powder is often mixed
with other substances that impart a pleasant scent or medicinal properties
to the clay. Then the mixture must return to its original mud form,
through the addition of water, to be smeared on the body. Without
returning to a partially liquid state, clay does not stick to the skin in such
a way as to perform its cooling, beautifying, and healing functions. When
clay dries and hardens on the body surface, then, it repeats the transformation from wet to dry, and from soft to hard and cooling substance,
that first brought it into existence. The substance's material properties
mimic the process through which it is produced.

Similar cooling properties pertain to clay as an edible substance in certain contexts. A Sande elder once mentioned that during initiation, initiates prepared plates of white clay mixed with sugar and sent them to
favorite younger sisters or friends "so that they may know that Sande is

'sweet' (*ma nɛɛngɔ*, which means 'pleasant' as well) and will want to join too." The gift of white, sweetened food, of kaolin clay and sugar, builds anticipation for sweet things to come. Clay, then, was the substance of anticipation not only for men like Gbesse and Braima, but for women as well. The sight of clay triggered in men memories of anticipating of the end of Sande initiation, but on the body of real initiates it was also a warning to keep away. By contrast, girls went beyond the visual and consumed clay in anticipation of their own future Sande initiation.

However, the sweetness of clay was deceptive as well. Indeed, this same image of clay became for some women, later in life, a cruel reminder of the pain experienced as they finally underwent Sande initiation. A Mende woman professional who lives in Europe once told me that the last thing she remembered about the moments preceding her clitoridectomy during Sande initiation was a song she and her companions were made to sing at the top of their voices as they stood in line near a waterhole in the bush, unable to see where the girls ahead of them were being led. The song told of crossing the water to find the driest and whitest clay possible, and of how only well-trained (*makɛngɔ*) girls would be rewarded with such a precious find. This sweet (and loud) song about clay drowned out the cries of pain from girls undergoing clitoridectomy. "Had we only been able to hear," said my friend, "we would have been too scared. We would have run away before our turn came." Bittersweet memories, indeed.

Clay also had cooling properties as a food in the context of pregnancy, particularly to relieve heartburn. One day I came upon a visibly pregnant Salimatu on her husband's rice farm. She was clutching a ball of white clay in her hand, and the white residue around her mouth suggested that she had been eating it as well. At the time, I found it natural that she should appear embarrassed at being caught in the act of eating clay. She smiled shyly while involuntarily concealing the clay behind her, even though she realized I had seen her eating it. She explained that only clay cooled her stomach when it was upset. I thought that her embarrassment derived from the fact that she had been caught eating a nonfood—a substance meant to cover the external surfaces of houses and bodies. However, in light of clay's associations with virginity and excision in the context of Sande initiation, Salimatu's embarrassment might have had to do with the fact that clay was consumed as food only in the secrecy of Sande, or when concealed in sugar. In any event, the episode suggests that clay provides a smooth coating not just for the exteriors of bodies and houses, but for inner surfaces as well.

Oil too is consumed in different forms; indeed, it has stronger associations than clay with food and bodily health. Clay evokes the dry season, when women can lower themselves in relatively empty waterholes to collect it; this is also the season when it is most in demand to provide relief from the heat and for ritual uses. By contrast, palm fruit harvesting is associated with seasonal ends and beginnings. Palm oil is processed early and late in the dry season, when rains have swollen the fruits but are not so frequent that the tree trunks are too slippery—making palm trees too dangerous for men to climb to harvest fruits. Red palm oil is a preferred, healthful base for the sauces with which people eat rice. The dark, bitter oil extracted from the fruit's kernel is also eaten, but it is associated with the rainy season and its hunger. Given a choice, people usually preferred palm oil to kernel oil, and they often expressed a very strong distaste for the latter. Extracting kernel oil is also more time-consuming, because kernels must be individually cracked with a stone if machinery is not available, and the nut in them must be dried and pounded into a grainy substance in a mortar. Kernel oil is then processed similarly to palm oil: women add hot water to the pounded pulp and, after moving it around to free its oils, skim it off the water's surface. They next cook the oil they obtain to free it from impurities, and finally they let it cool off before putting it in bottles and empty kerosene tins or drums for storage.

Palm kernels are usually given to women for their labor in processing palm oil. These kernels are more durable than palm fruits—which rot quickly once they ripen. Even palm oil can go rancid within a year. By contrast, kernels can be stored for a considerable amount of time without deteriorating. This durability makes kernels a good backup source of oil when palm oil is scarce—hence its associations with hunger and the rainy season. Paradoxically, at the turn of the century, the durability of kernels, compared to the ephemeral palm oil, made them a much more valued export item on the international market. Thus unlike the kola and cloth trades, which involved commodities that were valued locally as well as abroad, certain stages of the trade in palm products were characterized by the parallel production of palm oil for local consumption and kernels for export.

SLAVES, OIL, AND THE SHIFT TO LEGITIMATE TRADE

[There was] a revival of world demand for vegetable oils
and oilseeds in the early twentieth century. In 1902, . . .
a new process was invented by which soft vegetable oils

could be hardened and purified for use in top-quality
soap and margarine manufacture. This process of
hydrogenation . . . revolutionized (sic) the position of
palm oil and especially palm kernels within the world
market. Palm kernel oil proved particularly amenable to
the hydrogenation process and, along with coconut oil,
became a staple ingredient in margarine.

Martin (1988: 48)

The palm tree is to the Mende what the bison is to
certain Indian tribes of North America.

Addison (1918: 7)

There is a larger historical irony in the fact that palm oil marks the key
transformation in Sande initiation, despite the apparent importance of
clay. During the nineteenth century, the demand on world markets for
West African palm products was crucial to the transition from the slave
trade to legitimate commerce (see Hart 1982: 57–58; Hopkins 1973:
125). In *From Slaves to Palm Kernels*, historian Adam Jones covered this
transition on the Sierra Leone coast for two centuries beginning in 1730.
Jones documented the rise in European demand for palm tree products
beginning in 1860 (Jones 1983: 104), which also marked a shift in
regional power relations. The Atlantic slave trade had increased the political and economic importance of the coast, but the shift to legitimate
trade signaled the regional ascendancy of the inland territories where
most palm produce was obtained. These palm-producing areas were in
Mende territory, so the sociopolitical and economic transformations
brought about by the rise in the trade in palm products coincided with
the beginning of Mende hegemony in the region (Jones 1983: 134).

   Like kola nuts and cloth, then, palm trees and their produce are a key
material (and economic) element of Mende history and sociality. And like
kola and cloth, oil could be an ambiguous expression of political conflict,
or its mediation. It marked a historical shift in the configuration of a
regional political economy, and of a Mende place in it. The circulation of
palm products marked a shift of power centers away from the coastal
contact zones, where European and African traders dealt in slaves, to the
interior hinterlands from which palm oil originated. Palm oil also greased
the wheels of the Industrial Revolution in Britain, which made it an especially appealing expression of colonial relations and resistance to them.
No small wonder, then, that on the eve of decolonization, the palm tree

was chosen as the symbol for the Sierra Leone People's Party, which was founded and led by Mende politicians and which, after a hiatus of several decades, came back to power in the 1996 elections.

European demand for palm oil was much greater than that for West African kola and cloth, which were sought after as much for trade elsewhere in the colonial empire as for home consumption. Instead, the Industrial Revolution fueled demand for palm oil not only to lubricate its machinery but to wash up the working-class subjects who made it possible and whose lives were increasingly shaped by its rhythms, values, and filth. At first, Europeans imported palm oil from the fruit's red flesh, which was used to make candles and margarine. After a slump in the market brought about by the economic crisis at the end of the nineteenth century, palm kernels were in greater demand than oil, because in the meantime Lever had invented the technique of hydrogenation. This made better margarine, as well as "self-washing" soap, with which working-class consumers who inhabited hard-water areas could wash off industrial grime (Martin 1988: 45). It was not only Europeans who provided a market for soap: the production and marketing of soap and ideals of cleanliness constituted a key arena for cultivating African consumers as well (see Burke 1996). In a further irony, imported, tinned British margarine was popularly viewed as the epitome of sophisticated European food in Sierra Leone. It was also among the most widely circulating imported commodities, and the empty tins of a particular brand were the standard measure for selling small quantities of rice. However, there was little awareness in rural Mendeland that margarine—this imported, quintessentially British colonial food—originated in palm kernels exported from the West African coast and thus was returning full circle to its source.

The historical shift in market demand from palm oil to palm kernels also had implications for gender relations. It meant a shift in the relative trading value of a commodity that was locally valued and consumed, and was primarily controlled by men, to one that was devalued and owned by women.[5] This gave women an avenue for acquiring wealth through the sale of kernels (see Hofstra 1937). It was relatively easy to control the circulation of palm fruits, because they were perishable, and therefore a timely interference with the harvest could have a disproportionate impact. As I mentioned earlier, in Wunde chiefdom the nineteenth-century warrior Ndawa interrupted the colonial trade in palm oil by prohibiting the fruit's harvest in the territory he controlled, a move that in 1888 triggered a punitive expedition from the British colonial government (Abraham 1978: 88–89; Fyfe 1962: 481–483). Furthermore, the men's Poro society historically exercised its stewardship over community land by putting its medicine on parts of the bush to prevent overharvesting of palm fruits and other collective resources. Indeed, in the 1980s and early 1990s, the Poro society in Wunde chiefdom still played this role.

However, it was difficult to control in the same way the trade of kernels and processing of their oil. Kernels could be stored anywhere, and their value did not depend on timely harvest and processing. Women often owned kernels in small quantities, which they cracked and processed when they were on demand. A further processing stage produced *gulɔ gbandi*, hot or heated oil, the clarified oil that women used to beautify their skins. Thus palm tree products were smeared on the body's surface; used for lighting or as a lubricant; employed for bedding, for thatching, or as the material for the twine from which hammocks and nets are made; and consumed as alcoholic beverage or food. Clearly, this tree is at the center of Mende material life.

As is true for most sources of so many different products, the palm tree's many uses also gave it a key place in everyday symbolic life. This symbolism ranged from the fluidity of palm oil to the politics of stoppages in its flow in the colonial trade. It encompassed the durability of hard kernels, which, despite their stone-like hardness, could be cracked to disclose a secondary, concealed source of sustenance and livelihood—one that could be stored longer and was handled in smaller quantities by small-scale women traders. Oil generated the heat that protected bodies in the rainy season and the light that illuminated nights during periods when imported kerosene was scarce. Oil revealed the beauty concealed by clay masks and made the world stick to the body's surface after it had been enclosed in clay's protective shell. It made the skin shiny—attractive of light and attention—and reflective. It was the ultimate subject of mediation, the grease that gave life in the form of oil consumed as food (which gave health), and of ointment for the skin. Given the association of death with the body's "drying out" and, conversely, of oil with life-giving fluids like blood, palm oil kept death's dryness away as women intensified its use toward the end of their lives. And despite the greater value attached to the red oil derived from the palm's fruit, the less prized kernel oil—the oil that women got to keep as compensation for their processing labor—has historically proved to be the more economically lasting and politically elusive.

Sao and Jina (1990)

CHAPTER 6

Children and Their Doubles

For reasons similar to those underlying the dialectical construal of big persons, Mende representations of childhood are fraught with ambivalence. Given that power is inscribed within an order of concealment, people who are most manifestly devoid of it, like children, might in fact conceal it in unexpected ways. Anthropologists and social historians have pointed out that the social construction of childhood as a time of social and psychological innocence is a relatively recent phenomenon and not a very widespread one at that (Ariès 1962).[1] However, the notion of childhood as a condition set apart from adult practices and concerns still prevails in the popular imaginary of the privileged strata in Euro-American societies. Among other things, this perspective informed the focus, in the Western media coverage of the Sierra Leone conflict, on children both as victims and as perpetrators of atrocities. By contrast, one finds that the tendency to construe childhood as ambiguous is revealing of attitudes shared across a wider spectrum of material, social, and historical contexts. As Giovanni Levi pointed out in a comparative analysis of the history of youth,

> We encounter both the realm of symbolic meanings, promises, threats, potential, and fragility implicit in youth, and the subsequent ambiguous attention, composed of simultaneous expectations and suspicions, that societies devote to it. It is in this hybrid state of mind—a mixture of attraction and alarm—that societies always "construe" youth as an unstable social reality, and not merely as a fixed juridical or demographic fact.
>
> *(Levi 1997: 2)*

However, this comparative analysis of representations of youth is still at an embryonic stage in Africa. In particular, Alma Gottlieb (1998) called attention to the need for a better understanding of early stages of childhood, such as infancy and toddlerhood. In Sierra Leone, it is necessary to pay attention to this stage, because it is considered an especially ambiguous period characterized by uncertainties regarding a child's survival, moral development, and communication with adults.

I argue here that central to the social construction of infancy (the "attraction and alarm" that infants generate in adults) is the perceived relationship of infants with the world of spirits, which generates loyalties in conflict with the world of the living. As a result of this relationship, infants are presumed to develop unusual powers of vision and the powers to move across different sensory domains. Like the *kpako*, infants and children are thought to operate according to a modality of concealed power that triggers an aesthetics of wonder and repulsion and thus to generate contradictory practices. In turn, the social construction of infancy takes place through social and material processes of naming (persons, events in their lives, and so on) and of addressing (children as stand-ins for elders, namesakes, or a dead twin). These discursive practices transform children into potential instantiations of those after whom they are named, a fact that carries consequences for both namesakes. Thus children named after powerful namesakes, as we shall see, are often addressed as though they were big people, and at the same time, the adult namesakes may find themselves treated in familiar, belittling ways by the child's kin. Though this temporary suspension of social norms regulating legitimate behavior serves to confirm the strength of those norms, this practice also points to the potential reversibility of hierarchical relations.

Furthermore, a dynamic of the insignificant is at work in the cultural representation of childhood. As I argued earlier with respect to the paradoxical importance of small and apparently insignificant objects and animals, it is precisely when children are regarded as insignificant—as liminal beings between the world of animality and madness—that they are perceived as potentially most dangerous. Hence children share with the *kpako* a position between autonomy and interdependence and bigness and smallness. This idea was captured by Jina, whom I mentioned earlier, in her explanation for why she took "Child *sowεi*" as her name when she was initiated into the highest rank of the women's Sande society:

> *Ndopo joo*, I stand where big people (*kpako*) do not dare: you see, a child can provoke embarrassment and bring disgrace. I can be a great danger, a big ras-

cal. You see a small child, and you think that you are bigger, but he or she must be the very one you fear. If you see a small person, and you grow big inside—you grow arrogant—you will not notice her or his power. If you show disrespect, you will lose respect. That's why I say, I'm the Child *sowɛi*.

A few months before making this statement, Jina had jumped into the middle of a performance by the *ndoli jowɛi*, the Sande masquerade, wearing only a white brassiere, shorts, and head tie, and her clowning about had turned an otherwise solemn event into an occasion at once humorous and tense. She warned those who made fun of her, ignoring her role as a *sowɛi*, that she would subject them to public ridicule if they did not make amends and show her the respect she was due. A child does not immediately command the respect and attention of her seniors. And yet underestimating the potential threat posed by children leads to the big person's downfall. Children without visible authority can "stand where adults do not dare," and from this vantage point, they gain access to knowledge that can bring grief to their social superiors. Because they do not yet embody distinct social identities, children can cross boundaries between ordinary and ritual practices, and between public and secret discursive domains, which adults are more reluctant to transgress. They have not yet incorporated social values of shame and respect—that is, a concern for their reputation—and thus they move freely in zones of danger.

Infancy is seen as the most dangerous phase of life, in part because of the powers activated during the birth struggle. In that context, infants can endanger their own and their mothers' lives by harboring witch spirits who complicate pregnancy, labor, and delivery. This danger is linked to the perceived ambivalence of infants about leaving the "beforelife."[2] Infants and twins are believed to derive special powers from their relationships with doubles in the world of spirits, and these different kinds of pairs undermine stable and unitary notions of the self. Infants are thought to be able to see spirits and recognize witches, who dissemble their true nature under the appearance of ordinary humans or animals. However, witches are said to put an end to this order of visibility once a child learns to speak and hence threatens to reveal their true identities.

Infants are suspected of lacking a commitment to live among humans, because of their links with powerful agencies in the world of spirits, where they are thought to exist before birth. In contexts where poor health conditions lead to high rates of infant mortality, it is not uncommon to attribute to the children themselves an "aversion" to staying alive, as an explanation for what is perceived as inevitable by the aggrieved adults who are left behind (see Scheper-Hughes 1992: 270–272). Thus infants who die are buried in rubbish heaps instead of graveyards and are not mourned formally. They are denied even the opportunity of leaving in their burial a sign of their passage in the landscape, to be interpreted by posterity. Though painful to the immediate family, early death is seen as an ever present possibility for the very young. Once I saw the distraught mother of a three-year-old dead child being rebuked by a male relative when she started wailing loudly in the way that characterizes the formal mourning for deceased adults. He told her to stop that disgraceful display; after all, it was only a child. In spite of this rebuke, the woman kept on, as I had seen others do in similar situations. Indeed, to explain this mother's grief, one mother told me that the child was "already a little big" (sɛmbɛngɔ klo), that he had been weaned, and that he already walked. She added that the older the child, the more one grew attached to it, and its death therefore hurt. Thus the absence of a socially sanctioned mourning is quite independent of the sense of grief experienced at the death of a child by immediate relatives.[3]

Children are *nu vuli* (sing.), "real persons," but at times they also are likened to animals, or "living things" (*fu haiŋ*). Like animals, infants are unable to control their behavior, or their bodily functions. They relieve themselves whenever and wherever they please and are unable to master hunger. Unlike adults, for whom a relationship of trust is the precondition for both the acceptance and the shared consumption of food, children are seen as reversing this order by making feeding the premise for creating intimate bonds. "Like an animal," a mother once told me about her infant daughter, "she grows attached to anyone who feeds her." However, given the way in which adults *do* use food to create and express bonds of affection (surreptitiously cooked meals sent by a woman to her lover; delicacies saved by the hunter for his wife), it is perhaps more accurate to say that children lack the skills for *concealing* this relationship. Even older children, despite the fact that they have learned to control other bodily functions, seldom conceal their hunger. After large communal gatherings where food is served, it is not uncommon to see children swarming around a basin of leftovers, fighting among themselves and gorging themselves with big fistfuls of rice. Only the intervention of adults ensures that smaller or less aggressive children do not go hungry.

In Mende, uninitiated children are referred to as *kpowanga* (pl.), a term that also means "mad" and "mentally deficient." In other words, until children are taught how to use knowledge so that they might achieve real understanding, they are capable only of imperfectly perceiving the world around them and are unable to operate in it according to codes of prescribed social behavior. A kind of understanding is realized in the course of initiation into the women's Sande or the men's Poro society, and in other more specialized esoteric sodalities. Two processes overlap in initiation: one assumes the moral and ideal attributes of Mende men and women at the same time as one learns how to interpret the surrounding world. A third element contributing to initiation's status as a critical event is that it is a defining moment for the formation of gendered selves. In Mende, men and women are by definition Poro men and Sande women. Conversely, *kpowanga* of either sex are scarcely differentiated in forms of address, status, and sometimes even dress. In contrast with the teleological structure of initiation, a classic rite of passage for transforming the uninitiated into men and women, Mende ideas about infancy point to the fact that the self's life journey is not construed according to a narrative of linear progress. Rather, as children grow, they gain certain powers but lose others. The *mabɔle's* initiation, which begins in Sande but without completing the process there ends out of Poro, suggests that even here unpredictability and fragmentation may govern the logic of events. These processes are related in part to the fact that knowledge is transmitted in a contingent manner. As Vandi's story about the *gɛgbɛwuli* (see Chapter 1) suggests, the meaning of language events and social relations is never wholly accessible. Rather, knowledge is acquired in isolated fragments in the context of relations of mentorship with powerful persons. Knowledge of the self is coextensive with the discovery of the narratives that emerge from traces left by history in language and the social landscape. In what follows, I begin with an analysis of naming practices, which are one of the ways in which these relations of mentorship are established, to look at how ideas about the material self are construed in often contradictory ways.

BISMILLAH: NAMING AND MASKING THE DOUBLE

"What's the use of their having names," the Gnat said,
"if they won't answer to them?"

   "No use to *them*," said Alice; "but it's useful to the people that name them, I suppose. If not, why do things have names at all?"

       . . . .

   "This must be the wood . . . where things have no names. . . . Well, at any rate it's a great comfort," she

said as she stepped under the trees, "after being so hot,
to get into the—into the—into *what*?. . . I mean to get
under the—under the—under *this*, you know!" putting
her hand on the trunk of the tree. "What *does* it call
itself, I wonder?. . . And now, who am I?"

Lewis Carroll, Through the Looking Glass

Luc de Heusch pointed out that among the Luba of Congo, the name of
the ancestor is associated with the realm of the sacred—that is, with the
logic of interdiction. Local forms of address avoid proper names and
instead use the intermediary of nicknames. Thus the function of the name
is "to transform the person into a character," whereas the nickname is a
form of masking, which involves the whole person in the present. The
nickname masks the social actor—who belongs to the ancestral lineage
specified by the unspoken name—thus protecting him or her from possible attacks by witches (de Heusch 1973: 236). Hence the links between
nomination and the logic of secrecy.

A similar gesture is enacted in other forms of name concealment, such
as forgetting. In the inverted world of *Through the Looking Glass*, Alice
forgets the words to describe the world around her when she wanders
into the woods where things have no name. She also suffers a more profound loss. Unable to remember her *own* name, Alice ends up question-
ing the nature of her true self: "Who am I?" In the woods she encounters
a Fawn who tells her that in order to learn its name, she must move away
from this place. Without being able to name her surroundings, Alice
almost loses her sense of balance and must clasp her arms around the
Fawn's neck to find her way out. In the woods with no name, where
everything is both anonymous and synonymous, and hence the same,
Fawn and child can walk together without fear. Once the woods are left
behind, names and words are recovered, but so too are difference and
fear: as soon as the animal is able to identify itself as a Fawn, and Alice as
a "human child," it bounces fearfully away from the girl's embrace.
Though names are essential to Alice's recovery of language, self, and spa-
tiality—to the extent of inducing her to go elsewhere in pursuit of the
name that eludes her—she pays a great price for this knowledge. Once
she is out of the woods, the recovery of names—and identities—brings
about difference, with its corollary of fear and separation.

Mende ideas about the language of naming share features of both
Alice's story and the Luba conception of naming discussed by de Heusch.
In particular, the sites where naming is dangerous (such as the forest, or

woods) are also where other powerful secret practices take place, such as hunting, warfare, and initiation, which here too are linked to the need to protect the self from witch attacks. This same concern for protection guides Mende naming practices that pair selves with different forms of doubles (for example, namesakes), thus producing a form of synonymity that also entails a measure of anonymity. Some names individuate a person; others leave opaque not only elements for identifying an individual's history but even his or her sex. The act of naming creates identities anew in a social context and embeds them in the mythical narratives of a given community (see Ricoeur 1970: 19–34). These narratives tell of family relations, historical circumstances of one's life, and even personal quirks. However, it would be a mistake always to seek direct information about personal or communal history in nicknames, for their contingency may be of a more fundamental nature. Some nicknames originate not in a deliberate act of naming but in a slip of the tongue. In these cases, the relationship between a name's apparent meaning and its history is not directly accessible. Instead, it has to do with a linguistic event—a category mistake similar to that involved in creating metaphors—whose significance can be appreciated only by those who were present at the occasion or heard it narrated.

In a fundamental way, names point to intimate aspects of the self—to that which is most one's own. The Mende word for "name" also denotes possession. Thus in *nya nda wɛɛ*, "my own house," the placement of *nda* between the personal pronoun *nya* and *wɛɛ* (house) leaves ambiguous whether it reinforces the possessive "my" or the object of possession, the house. Because the naming ceremony (in Mende, *la hei*, "the sitting of a name") marks an infant's first official foray out of the big house after birth, it entails an opening to others. Most Wunde people have one of a limited number of birth names from the Muslim repertoire: names like Mohammed or Momoh, Moiforay, Moriwa (Mende for "big Muslim"), Braima (Ibrahim), Kadiatu or Kadi, Mussu, Maama (Mariama), Fatima, and so on. During the ceremony, infants hear their names for the first time, whispered in their ears by their namesakes and followed by the recitation of the *al-Fatiha* (the Opening, or Beginning)—the first chapter of the Qur'an. Note that the beginning of the *al-Fatiha* (and, more generally, the words with which Kpuawala Muslims often begin any activity, from a day's work, to a meal, to legal and political gatherings) also involves invocation of the name *par excellence*: *b' ism illah*, "in the name of God." Naming God—doing something *in God's name*—makes God witness and protector, thus ensuring an auspicious *beginning* to all solemn Kpuawala ceremonial gatherings. Given how contentious such events can become, it is as though invoking the name of God to open them expresses recognition that there is no gainsaying their outcome. The naming of God, or speaking in the name of God, has the ritual effect of announcing an auspicious beginning to potentially conflictual interactions. In the same way, the child's naming ceremony is punctuated by auspicious wishes for a long and good life, which conceal uncertainties about how that life will unfold.

But the dangers of the beginning can be far greater than those of the ending, as the naming ceremony makes clear. This was the time when the protective power of the Name was associated with the choice of a namesake. During naming ceremonies, namesakes brought out the infant from the house's veranda three times if a girl, four if a boy, each time stopping to whisper in turn in each ear the sequence of the name and the *al-Fatiha*.[4] The namesake then held up the child to the gathered community, repeating its name out loud for the first time, some seven days after birth. In the secret, whispered communication of the Name that preceded its utterance out loud, the namesake performed publicly an act of concealment. At the same time, the act of naming had the symbolic effect of opening an infant's ears to the world of language. The name had to be spoken not only to ensure that babies took possession of their name but also to endow them with sensory capacities—hearing in particular.

Initially a covert whisper, later an audible statement, both moments of naming are public and coincide with a baby's first exit "in front" of the house, as the ceremony's name implies. In Mende, the naming ceremony is referred to as *gbua le ngitii ya*, or "bringing out into the clearing," on the house's public side, to face the community in its central gathering places. In the ceremony, the sharing of a name is also accompanied by the transmission of vital substances from the elder to the younger namesake. This is underscored by the fact that the namesake spits lightly on a baby's forehead before whispering his or her name and reciting the prayer of Opening. Saliva, or "mouth water" (*nda nj/ya*) can also be said to be the water of one's self, of one's name (*nda*). This semantic overlap among saliva, mouth, and name suggests another reason why a name is only whispered during the ritual gesture. It is because these gestures have to do as much with the namesake as with the baby whose life has just begun. In other words, the older namesake in the pair protects his or her *own* identity by whispering their shared name to the baby.

If naming conferred something profoundly ownable, it also marked a person's social link to others. And here is a Mende paradox similar to

Alice's, whose distinct identity was forgotten in the sameness of the woods where things have no name: the identities of Mende babies are endlessly referred and deferred to others, their namesakes. As elsewhere in West Africa, in Mende the fact that many individuals shared a limited number of names carried with it the potential for confusing identities instead of distinguishing them (see Palau Marti 1973: 321–322). Thus the practice of naming everybody after someone else produces a synonymity that is a kind of dangerous anonymity, as I mentioned above. Naming *after* denotes a spatiotemporal relationship that crosses generations and hierarchical distinctions. *Pomɛi*, the Mende noun for "back," also means "corpse" and, in adverbial form, "after, behind" (see Innes 1969: 125). *Pomɛi* is left behind by the end of a life but is also a placenta (*ndo pomɛi*), a child corpse, or that which comes after the child's birth. As we shall see in the case of twins, there is a presumption that death enables the beginning of most lives.

Infants begin their lives with a referral to a dual form of otherness: the otherness of "the name of God" and the otherness of their namesakes, who fall in one of two categories. If a baby is named after an important, not necessarily related member of the community, the *tɔma* (namesake) relationship established through this act entails to some extent a sharing, or reversal, of roles. Here synonymity may well be an effort to minimize hierarchical and age differences. By contrast, when a baby is named after a grandparent, this identification renders the name unspeakable, at least for the intervening parent, who always addresses the child as "father's" or "mother's *tɔma*." On the one hand, this practice pushes even farther the identification of a child with his or her *tɔma*, by naming exclusively that relationship. On the other hand, it deprives the child of its own name and identity, by reflecting only the relationship of subordination to the grandparent *behind* him or her. Thus names that link individuals *within* a family produce not so much a circular or reversible relationship of sameness as one where difference separates hierarchically ordered generations like points along a line in time and space. Significantly, people referred to ancestors beyond the generation of grandparents as *maada fɔli*, or *mama fɔli*, the queue behind grandfather or grandmother, as though these ancestors were lined up *behind* them.[5] This also meant that deceased kin beyond the third ascending generation became nameless— an anonymity facilitated, ironically, by the repetition of names in namesake relations. Thus when people in Kpuawala tried, at my prompting, to recite their genealogies, they eventually lost track of the narrative, because they confused the identities of several kin across different generations who had the same names.[6] Like Alice in the woods where there were no names, these people lost their orientation because of the enchantment produced by repeating over and over the *same* names. Heroic ancestors did stand out of the anonymous line to be remembered individually, but in such cases the names remembered were not those given at birth in relation to a namesake. Instead, they tended to be nicknames or appellations, such as those of warriors or great healers—names that were by definition distinctive and descriptive of particular historical events or personal traits and hence were not duplicated.

SILLY NAMES

Mende nicknames sometimes originate in chance slips of the tongue. One has to pay attention to the specific logic of concealment governing these naming practices, as Freud suggests in *The Psychopathology of Everyday Life*. Freud argues that forgotten names or "accidental utterances" follow a specific logic and provide clues to "the thought contents, which, though striving for concealment, nevertheless unintentionally betray themselves. In doing this, the mistakes often perform the most valuable service" (Freud 1938: 78). Understanding nicknames—what in Mende are called *baabaa lɛisia* (pl.), "silly names"—and the circumstances in which they are acquired sheds light on the production of social meaning.

Silly names convey a great deal about historical contingency and individuality, but they also work as much to conceal their bearers as to identify them. They can be the most unique names, those owned by a single person in the community, but also generic and opaque. Nicknames often point to a physical peculiarity of an individual, as in the case of Moiforay, a boy whose deformed back made some call him "hump" (*ŋɔŋɔ*). Although this physical deformity sometimes made Moiforay the butt of jokes, ordinarily he was treated like any other child his age. Another one of his nicknames, *Kojɛ* (the name of a feared rock-dwelling spirit), suggested that his physical difference was also seen as a sign that he had special powers. In any case, Moiforay, who was being raised by his grandfather, was a favorite grandchild: he received constant attention, got the best food morsels, and accompanied his grandfather everywhere.[7]

Other nicknames were related to the circumstances surrounding a child's birth and thus placed the event within the broader context of a familial or communal history. For example, the nickname of one little girl Bɔte Cɔpɔ ("Butter Cup") evoked the Blueband brand margarine cans that, once emptied by urban consumers of their imported contents, became ubiquitous as the smallest measuring units for rice and other dry goods. She was born during a particular hungry season when food was so scarce that finding even a single butter cup of rice required enormous effort. In relating the nickname's story, the girl's father spoke of the hardship of wandering on flooded paths in search of rice to buy, for the hungry season was also the season of rains and cold. The man stressed that he barely found enough rice for sale to enable him to ensure his family's survival that year, let alone provide the traditional "nursing mother's rice" (*kuima mbɛi*), the unusually rich meal that a man was expected to offer his wife after she had delivered a baby.[8] In naming his daughter for this object, the margarine tin, the man memorialized that particular time in his own life, which was a time of hardship for others in the community as well. As it turned out, the name also placed her birth in a larger temporal context, for this unit of measure stopped being used in rural Sierra Leone in the 1990s, when different brands of imported margarine (which came in containers of different sizes) broke the monopoly that the British Blueband variety had enjoyed. Thus "Butter Cup's" name pointed to a particular moment in Sierra Leone's postcolonial history. Her nickname linked her birth to the memory of an especially hard rainy season in Kpuawala, but also constituted a link to—a material trace of—the history of everyday life in Sierra Leone.

The nicknames of two Kpuawala young men illustrate how these names tend to remain unique, and hence to become associated with particular individuals, even when they refer to similar historical or life events. Both men were said to have been born during Sande initiations and hence in the secret enclosure from which all men and nonmembers were excluded. The anomaly of being born male in an exclusively female domain translated in Mussa's case into the name "Bad Night" (*kpindi nyamui*), and Quee was given the nickname Kpangu, from *kpanguima*, the name of the society's initiation enclosure. Whereas Kpangu's nickname referred generically to the site of Sande initiations, Bad Night's pointed specifically to his birth on their first night. (This night of confusion and crowds ends with the performance of clitoridectomies on new initiates.) Thus names have an individualizing *and* a temporalizing dimension, as they recapitulate significant events in the lives of their bearers or of their families, communities, and nation. They are also related to key aspects of their bearers' dispositions and social roles. For example, people often connected the circumstances of Mussa Bad Night's birth with his prodigious abilities as a performer of the *Falui* dancing masquerade. However, even though they locate in time the individual, names that denote a person's place in the birth order, and nicknames such as Butter Cup and Bad Night, can belong to people of either sex. Bad Night would make sense only as a boy's nickname in the context of a birth that occurred during Sande initiation, but there are other kinds of bad nights in which a baby girl would be just as likely to receive this appellation.

New names are acquired by virtually everyone at initiation, a time homologous to birth, in which the symbolism of transformation is pervasive. Like other names, initiation names are more generic than nicknames, indicating only an individual's order of initiation in his or her cohort. For example, the first person of her cohort to be initiated in Sande is named Kema, a name that throughout a woman's life marks her as a leader among others of her sex (see Little 1951: 127). By contrast, nicknames linked to initiation share the general characteristic of being more individualizing and historically specific. They are also more restricted in use, often being employed only among members of a particular initiation cohort. For example, Satta acquired the nickname Magic, *Njosso*, because of her terrified reaction to a performer's tricks during entertainments at the time of her initiation. Within two years of her initiation, Njosso had already earned a reputation for strength and endurance to pain. During her first pregnancy, despite being a teenage bride with no experience, Njosso never complained about labor pains and waited until the last moment even to alert a midwife that she was about to give birth. Nonetheless, her nickname and the story of fear that was associated with it stayed with her, surfacing occasionally in remarks by her mother and her initiation mates.

Other nicknames were taken by members of Sande and Poro as they rose in the ranks of these societies through successive initiations. But here the nicknames were actively chosen to mark a personal feature for which one wanted to be remembered, as were great warriors, healers, and rulers of the past. Upon being initiated into the leadership of Sande and Poro, members are asked what name they want to take. In stating their choice, they accompany it with a riddle or proverb to explain—though rather ambiguously—their selection. A popular Sande name in Mendeland was Cool Heart (*li lɛli*), which underscored its bearer's equanimity and peacefulness. Other names stressed a leader's watchfulness (*Ngaa Bɛɛ*, "I will scrutinize, I am aware of all that is going on"), firmness (*Lomɛi*, from *toma*, "post, I stand firm"), deceitful nature (glossed with the term for "child," *Ndopo*). These names were used freely to address their bearers, even outside the domains of Sande and Poro. They were borne proudly, pointed to valued qualities, and were circulated widely, along with their histories.

Thus in the Wunde region, the name Ndawa (Big Name/Mouth) belonged to one and only one heroic warrior of the past, the founder of an important local lineage. The practice by warriors of adopting battle names is widespread and has a long history. In the Sierra Leone civil war, battlefield leaders of all factions adopted nicknames that referred to specific events in their military exploits or carried intimations of their particular fighting styles. Sam Bockarie, since 1998 a prominent R.U.F. field commander, explained that he chose the nickname Maskita, "Mosquito," because he was small but insidious well beyond his size. Like the insect after which he was named, he kept on buzzing unseen around the enemy and stinging. Other battlefield toughs chose names like Rambo, after the Hollywood film warrior character known for solitary acts of heroism and for his loyalty to a government that, for its part, found him expendable.

The layering of nicknames upon initiation names, matronymics, patronymics, and place names added specificity to common names, like Ibrahim or Mohammed. Thus names were used cumulatively to specify identity or selectively, and cryptically, to elude recognition. Whereas nicknames provided valuable openings into personal and social history, other names tended to stress a person's relationship with a twin, as we shall see, or a namesake—thus sacrificing the individual and the contingent to relations with doubles.

TƆMA—SIGNS AND SIMULACRA

Namesakes address each other as *tɔma* and often playfully reverse roles, the junior namesake taking liberties with the senior one, and the latter respectfully addressing a younger, ordinarily subordinate person, as though she or he were senior. This role reversal has a social dimension as well, for it is acknowledged and performed by the whole gamut of the namesakes' relations. For example, when Mbeindu, the Kpuawala chief's daughter, had a baby girl and named her Mariama after me, she began addressing me as *nya loi*, my child, instead of with the respectful *ngɔ* she had used before, in recognition of my seniority in age and status. As the namesake of Mbeindu's daughter, I was identified to some extent with her. Mbeindu would playfully address her infant daughter as *pumɔ*, "white/Western foreigner," and ask her about her writing and learning of things Mende. Kpuawala people often called their newborns after benefactors to whom they dedicated their offspring in gratitude, or after people of status in the hope of a similarly successful life for their namesakes.

Thus in these cases, the *tɔma* relationship was constructed to bridge significant age and status gaps, relativizing both through the playful pairing of opposites. This relationship between namesakes adds a different dimension to the mixture of fear and disdain for children expressed by Jina in her choice of "Child *sowei* " as her *sowei* name. One of the reasons one should be wary of children is that one never knows who they are associated with through such auspicious naming practices.

The word *tɔma* evokes an absent double not just among humans but also more generally in the Mende world. Most domestic plants and animals, and varieties found in inhabited settlements, were thought to have a *tɔmaseli* in the bush. Although it incorporates *tɔma*, and hence the notion of creating a paired link through a name, this word also means "sign, evidence" (see Innes 1969: 145). For example, a town weed I never saw eaten in Kpuawala was said to have its *tɔmaseli* in a vegetable grown on farms or in gardens for consumption. One of Kpuawala's Sande society elders claimed that this town variety was among her most powerful secret medicines—one that, used in a particular way, could stop bleeding almost instantly. The woman seemed to be especially pleased by the fact that a common, lowly weed had such potency. She pointed out that it grew abundantly and in plain sight throughout the village and that it was pulled out and thrown away by people who knew nothing of its medicinal use.

Animals, too, were thought to have their *tɔmaseli* in the wild. The bush cow was a greatly feared animal, which around Kpuawala was believed to be dangerous to humans and destructive of crops. I never saw a bush cow, but I was often shown what were supposed to be traces of its passage: trampled rice fields and destroyed hunting traps. Its *tɔmaseli* was the domesticated cow, which was not found in rural villages in this area of endemic sleeping sickness but was a common sight at markets and towns where Fula cattle herders from the North brought them to be slaughtered and sold. In the *tɔmaseli* relationship, town and bush varieties do not necessarily share a name. Town and bush spinach are both *hɔndi*, but domesticated cows (*nikɛi*) and bush varieties (*tewui*) have different names. In both cases, people see the two versions as related, each one a sign of the other. It is difficult to predict which of these paired entities is the more powerful. In the spinach case, the potent medicine is the common weed that grows in town, whereas the version consumed as food is cultivated on rice farms or in gardens on the settlement's edge. By contrast, the bush cow is more dangerous and powerful than its village counterpart.[9]

One of the two *tɔmaseli* conceals hidden powers, while the other becomes a simulacrum for the absent other. Whether an entity's hidden powers are best concealed by staying in plain view, like the town spinach,[10] or by being where it is seldom seen, the notion that most objects and living beings have doubles with altogether different attributes creates a world where it is difficult to distinguish the simulacrum from the real, the benign from the dangerous, and the powerful from the weak. The effect of these simulacra, and of the different ways in which visibility, familiarity, and concealed powers intersect, is to undermine any stable notion of which of two (or more) possible scenes of interpretive action must be brought to bear in particular circumstances. The plainly visible is not all it appears to be and may conceal invisible potency that is known only to a few. Furthermore, the familiar in town can be a sign of its powerful double in the bush, whose life unfolds mostly out of the range of ordinary human beings and can be divined only by clues left in the landscape, such as the damage discovered in the wake of a bush cow's passage. This makes the paired relationship between human or other namesakes a special case of the more general tendency in Mende epistemology to conceive of everyday working objects like fishing nets, mortars, and rice fans as doubles for powerful tools of the extraordinary world of the invisible. The underlying logic of both the namesake relationship and the concealed powers of ordinary objects is that everything may have a double reference or use that is not immediately knowable, or visible. Identities take their shifting character from this relationship with their double. As they cross into different domains, things, animals, and people reveal traits that are concealed in their simulacrum, which is but a sign, a stand-in for something else. This logic of surface simulacra referring to concealed, powerful doubles also echoes the shape-shifting of witches between animal and human forms, as they move from bush to farm and human settlement (see Cosentino 1982; Kilson 1966: 51–52).[11]

The *tɔma* relationship also undermines the notion that hierarchies are fixed. The playful reversal of *tɔma* roles, where a wealthy, senior person can be addressed as a child by his or her namesake's relatives, is a reminder that power can be located in unpredictable sites and can be easily lost. In such cases, the tension between attraction and repulsion comes into play. This tension is played out toward individual members of the *tɔma* relationship, as well as in their dialectical relationship as a pair. Thus on the one hand, each *tɔma* can be alternately the object of deference and of unwanted excessive familiarity, both out of proportion to the person's actual social status. On the other hand, one *tɔma* always invokes the absent member of the pair and thus the appropriate mode of relating to that other.

This form of pairing is a site of transformation and of potential plays of secrecy. In the Mende collective imaginary, the site of transformation *par excellence* is the forest, which is the place where power and wealth can be gained or lost. In West African forest and savannah belt societies more generally, the bush is represented as the site of "the wild and uncultivated space. . . . [It] is introduced as a third party between the 'being' of the village and its question, whenever this question imposes itself as an enigma" (Cartry 1982: 211). The enigma referred to is that of the strange encountered in the village, in ordinary social life (Ibid.: 210), or on the farm. Indeed, these linkages are made outside this region too, as suggested, for example, by the shared etymological origin in Indo-European languages of words for "forest," "strange," and "alterity."[12] The forest is where Vandi's hunting riddles are situated, evoking the logic of the trace and of its interpretation (see Chapter 1). In the forest there are no obvious names but only signs that may be intelligible, at least for a time, for those who can identify their doubles.

I now turn to twinship, a relationship between doubles that in some ways evokes notions of power opposite to those existing between *tɔma*s. Whereas this relationship—whether between forest and town varieties of plants, animals, or humans—has to do with the order of difference and with the possibility of reversing an individual's status and power, twinship is by definition a relationship of sameness. Here even hierarchical differences based on age are absent. And yet it is in the context of Mende ideas about the birth of twins that the virtual nature of relations with doubles, and the nature of names as traces of the absent, become apparent.

TWINS AND VIRTUAL DOUBLES

In 1990 Sebatu gave birth in Kpuawala to identical twin boys. As is customary throughout Mendeland, they were named, in order of birth, Sao and Jina (see Gittins 1987: 177; Jackson 1977 for Kuranko parallels). Sebatu complained that she did not have enough milk to feed both babies properly, and by my next visit, three years later, both had died. These were the only twins born in Kpuawala during the years spanned by my research. And yet twin names were even more common than the limited number of Muslim names I kept encountering. Twin names were not differentiated by sex: both men and women could be called Sao and Jina.

Although twin names, like many nicknames, may mask a child's gender, bodily practices and manipulations do mark differences. As we noted earlier in connection with the naming ceremony and initiation, these practices include the gendered tempo that regulates the iteration of ritual gestures three times for girls and four for boys. This extends to bodily manipulations and healing practices from the moment of birth. From the cutting of umbilical chords in three- and four-stage gestures, to the performance of three and four skin incisions to insert protective medicine against convulsions, this gendered pattern belies the discursive ambiguity surrounding uninitiated children. In one Kpuawala family, the only three surviving adult siblings by the same father and mother had twin names. The first two brothers were called "big" and "little" Sao (*Sao wai* and *Sao wulo*), which suggests that each was the firstborn of a set of twins, and the youngest sister was Gbesse, the name given to the last born in a set of triplets or to the first child born *after* twins (see Gittins 1987: 177).[13] None of these individuals had surviving twins. When asked why they were given these names, most people said that at one time they had had a sibling, but it had died.

As I found out more about the circumstances of twin births and deaths, it became apparent that in most cases the two events coincided. In other words, many so-called twin births produced only a single live baby. In these accounts, only one child issued alive at birth, whereas the other was assumed to have "wasted" in the womb and died. How, then, did people distinguish between single and twin births? Mostly through the interpretation of signs. They determined the presence of twins through premonitions in dreams—either the pregnant woman's or someone else's. Furthermore, midwives examined the placenta for clues to the presence of a deceased twin. Thus the term used to refer to the placenta gains its full significance in the context of Mende representations of twinship. The placenta is not merely what is "left behind" by a live baby; it is often perceived as containing a dead fetus. Twinship may be a concealed relationship, one determined only *a posteriori*. It is constructed on the basis of interpreted remains and traces. Twinship may also be confirmed later in life by the fact that the surviving sibling or Gbesse is endowed with powers of divination. The lone survivor of twins can couple ordinary human agency with that of spirits, thanks to his or her links with a double who has remained in that other world. This perspective on twinship as a relationship encompassing more *and* less than multiple siblings born at the same time adds another dimension to Mende ideas about the relationship between presence and absence, the visible and the invisible.[14]

As I mentioned above, Mende twin names are the same for men and women and are the only names not to specify their bearer's sex. Twinship endows both males and females with the same divination powers. Thus if human twinship generally challenges the notion of age-based seniority because it presents us with the anomaly of simultaneous, multiple births, the absence of gender connotations in their names elides another axis of hierarchical differentiation. However, the inclusion of Gbesse, who can be born several years later, and of single infants in the category of twinship also undermines the notion that simultaneous birth is a key element in this relationship. No distinction appeared to be made in Kpuawala between Gbesse as the third member of triplets and Gbesse as a single child born several years after a set of twins. This suggests that twinship involved a broader category of sibling pairings, one transcending temporal and hierarchical differences. Indeed, it raises altogether more encompassing questions about the phenomenology of gestation and birth, given that what one saw at birth was not necessarily what was there (a single baby may have a dead twin, who operates in the spirit world) and that the event of twin birth itself could be fragmented into multiple occurrences. The temporal gap between the birth of a presumed twin and that of Gbesse is minimized in part through the suspension of ordinary prohibitions against sexual intercourse until an infant is weaned (Gittins 1987: 173). Everything was done to encourage a mother of twins to get pregnant again, thus speeding up the arrival of Gbesse and the completion of the twin birth.

Given the beliefs about special vision of infants in general, Mende twinship represents the potential of maintaining these powers past the age when most ordinary children lose them in order to learn to speak. Divination is the ability to see, and communicate with, spirits. These powers come from the virtual relationship of twins with the world of spirits. Given that this is the world inhabited by dead, unborn twins, single twins are endowed with greater powers (through their relationship with their invisible doubles) than twins who have a visible, live double. The logic is carried even further by the mediating role of Gbesse, the third, who brings twinship to a close. One might say, with Georg Simmel, that Gbesse, the witness to the existence of doubles, produces a specific social form that "transcends both members of the dyad" (Simmel 1950: 136). Through her mediation, Gbesse can strengthen the relationship between a twin and her double, but she may also disturb it by interrupting the "pure and immediate reciprocity" of relations between such similar—indeed, often identical—beings. Ultimately, what is striking about Mende twinship is that it is often marked only by naming practices. Like *tɔma*, the term of address for namesakes, only the names Sao, Jina, and Gbesse offer clues to the existence of a special relationship between individuals and their visible or invisible doubles.

Beliefs and practices surrounding twinship in Africa have been described as ranging from celebration and special attention to revulsion, if not outright neglect. In parts of Uganda, twins were celebrated because they stood for the only possible sibling relationship where age-based hierarchy was nonexistent in a context where this hierarchy was a source of social tension (Abrahams 1972). Among the Dogon of Mali, perfection and the origin of the world were linked to an original and androgynous twin pair. But with the first humans came sexual differentiation and single births, which brought about incest and other proscribed behaviors (Griaule 1965: 18–22). By contrast, in parts of West and Central Africa, twins were regarded as anomalous because, as a case of multiple births, they were seen as closer to the world of animals and bush spirits than to that of socialized human beings (Douglas 1956; Fortes 1973: 295; Turner 1967). In some cases, the strength of twins is exemplified by their capacity to mediate between the human world and forest spirits (see Cartry 1982: 217). Among the Luba of Congo, the relationship in Dogon thought among twinship, single birth, and incest was reversed: the mythical original twins, a male and female, practiced incest until a single, later-born male sibling killed and replaced his half-brother in his half-sister's affections (de Heusch 1973: 239). Thus, similarly to Mende beliefs about the greater powers of Gbesse in relation to the twins born before him or her, a single child born after the twin pair exercised even greater power than the latter and put an end to their incestuous relationship. In a different vein, the Tonga of Mozambique emphasized the importance of the child born after twins in correcting the anomalies that the twins represented. A mother of twins, who as "children of the sky" were thought to have threatened the proper relationship between sky and earth, could not resume sexual relations with her husband until she had another child by a lover (Junod 1936, II: 387–392). Thus whereas the Mende suspend taboos against sexual relations between a nursing mother of twins and her husband in order to speed up the arrival of Gbesse, the Tonga go a step further, decreasing the chances of another twin birth by prescribing a different sexual partner. In both cases, it is the child born *after twins*—the third—who offers the hope of containing the dangerous anomalies of twinship. The Tonga attempt to ensure that child's arrival by going beyond the mere suspension of the ordinary regulation of sexual practices to sanction their transgression in an illicit union.

The birth of an infant may mask a struggle resulting in the death of a twin, with whom the survivor maintains a lifelong, ambivalent relationship. The very powers that result from this relationship, like those of divination, are not unambiguously positive. Several among the Kpuawala "twins" I knew had serious, recurring headaches, which they associated with the fact that they were twins and with their work as diviners. The pain in their heads was a sign of these powers, but it was also a reminder of the burdensome relationship with an invisible double, whose presence some rejected—for example, by refusing to practice divination. Gbesse comes in to mediate visible altercations between Sao and Jina in ordinary life, or to mediate invisible conflicts manifested in a twin's illness, in cases where only one is among the living. The arrival, later, of a third "twin" is necessary to balance the struggle between identical opposites. In this role, Gbesse fits at a different level in the Mende aesthetic of power that locates in figures that transgress simple polarities the possibility of existing without resolving dialectical tensions. As we have seen, Gbesse complicates the notion of temporal simultaneity and duplication of the self that is embedded in twinship. Like the *mabɔle*, he or she represents an interstitial zone between sharply defined identities. In both cases, however, there is a feminine element that operates this mediation: the *mabɔle* is a woman, and three—the number represented by Gbesse—is a female number. One might say, in the words of Luce Irigaray, that the feminine consists in a capacity for mimesis, which facilitates the transition from one element of difference to the other, without reducing either one to the other (Irigaray 1985: 74–78). The mimetic style situates itself in between; it remains always elsewhere (Ibid.: 76). Thus the *mabɔle* and Gbesse's roles point to this in-betweenness as the possibility of experiencing new forms of sociality that transcend the closure of binary oppositions, without resolving them.

CONCLUSION

As we have seen, twinship in Mende is marked more often by names than by the visible presence of a double. Names can be strategically deployed to elaborate, or conceal, alternative narratives of the self (and of community). Their own dynamic of concealment makes them a site of ideological elaboration. Because they are so explicitly linked to the self—that which is most one's own—and to key transformative events within the life narrative, names operate like mnemonic markers, like landmarks on the terrain that one inhabits. One must work against the grain, particularly against the tendency names have to fix and make intelligible a purportedly transparent self. In Mende, the self is woven into multiple levels of meaning and thus cannnot be revealed in its totality in any single instance.

As Jina pointed out, the social insignificance of children—their marginality to the world of adults—makes them potentially dangerous. In part this is because of what they are allowed to witness, given the assumption that they do not really understand what they see and hear. I sometimes encountered village elders holding meetings in clearings along forest paths, in order not to be heard by people in the settlement. When this happened, the gathering fell silent until I had moved on, well out of earshot. By contrast, the elders in the meeting seemed not to take notice of the children who often lay at their feet on such occasions. These were the grandchildren/namesakes, foster children, or Qur'anic students who accompanied them everywhere to attend to their needs and run errands on their behalf. These children were often old enough to distinguish between different forms of knowledge: a boy once told me in hushed tones that while he was with his grandfather he had heard that the Poro society was to hold a meeting that night. The fact that he had taken care to ensure that nobody could hear when he told me about the meeting suggested that he was aware that this was secret knowledge. Only a form of social invisibility could account for the fact that uninitiated children had access to this information.

Aspects of personal, communal, and even national history are embedded in names, though not necessarily in an accessible form. Names also point to one's position with respect to different doubles, twins, or nicknames. Thus names may provide knowledge of historical contingency in contracted form, or may say very little about the individual as such, because they communicate a kind of anonymity, a "stand-in" status for doubles located elsewhere. The latter trait undermines any notion that identities may be stable or fixed: roles can be reversed at any time, and one never knows whether one is faced with reality or its simulacrum. Hence the reversibility of orders of identity into orders of difference.

These ideas about the self are reflected in Mende attitudes toward childhood. Twins must resist the call of their doubles to return to the world from whence they came, and their parents go to considerable pains to keep them among the living. Namesake relations enable children to take liberties with powerful adults in which even other adults may not engage. Conversely, an adult is always susceptible to being treated as a child, if only by the latter's senior elders. Like Alice in Wonderland, people can experience miniaturization and enlargement, or infantilization and magnification of status, in rapid succession. Like her, too, they can exercise a limited control on these processes by treating their bodies with potent substances or by ingesting such substances. In any case, none of these conditions is stable, and the development of sense (and of the senses) comes at the price of other abilities. Thus the trajectory between childhood and adulthood cannot be seen as an unambiguous progress. Rather, it involves a constant confrontation between liminal and powerful beings at the boundaries between licit and illicit practices.

The social construction of gendered selves is also informed by ambiguities. At one level, gendered selves are signaled by the initiation of "idiots" into Sande and Poro, out of which come women and men. However, in practice the process is a gradual one wherein gender is defined, and contested in principle, by distinct bodily practices, rhythms, and symbolic postures well before this stage. Furthermore, gendered practices are embedded in the history of the community and in its practices of production and reproduction. Finally, the potential (and, at the same time, the threat) that children present to a society of adults, who refer to them as either idiots or potent mediators, generates both fear and respect, hardship and tenderness. One never knows whether a child will live long enough or well enough to achieve Mende ideals of the powerful self.

Conclusion

In the preceding chapters, I have presented the elements of a Mende cultural logic, without suggesting that together these account for a normative, seamless whole. Instead, I have emphasized how conflicts central to this cultural logic are in a mutually constitutive relationship with contingent historical events. Invoking culture is always a political act, one that appeals to what binds society together even though there may be internal contradictions. By focusing on figures of mediation such as particular kinship relations (which echo the historical legacy of slavery), or the *mabɔle*, Gbesse, and others, I have called attention to the dynamic way in which the same processes can bind together or irremediably separate members of a society.

In Sierra Leone, historical processes of cultural and linguistic mediation are characterized by a local variant of creolization, which has created highly unstable contours for the particular social field that might appear to be bound together. There is no such thing as a Sierra Leonean community, no matter how isolated, in which ethnic homogeneity is not disturbed by the presence of strangers who do not subscribe to the hegemonic cultural order. In a sense, it is precisely a recognition of the historical struggle generated by this mobility and admixture that is signaled by the ambivalent cult of the "stranger" in this region of West Africa. The sociopolitical conditions that allow people to engage in practices that reify cultural differences are also deployed in the strategic management of multiple identities. These multiple identities produce familiarity and belonging in the face of continuous encounters with the alien, and individuals use them to extricate themselves from the terrain of potentially dangerous forces, which are in turn concealed behind the apparently familiar. As Ernesto Laclau has written, "there is no major historical change in which the identity of all intervening forces is not transformed. There is no possibility of victory in terms of an already acquired cultural authenticity. The increasing awareness of this fact explains the centrality of the concept of hybridization in contemporary debates" (Laclau 1996: 50).

This process of Krio-lization in Sierra Leone (a hybrid formation of the national *lingua franca* and a historical reference to a specifically Sierra Leonean cultural creolization) has been made possible, paradoxically, by the shrinking *local* specificity of a Mende cultural identity and idioms, in exchange for their surge onto the *national* stage. In the streets of Freetown, popular culture and its media—music, print material, jokes, and catchy Krio neologisms coined to express current events and figures—borrow heavily from what is perceived as distinctive of different Sierra Leonean ethnic groups, and Mende in particular. Musicians and performers such as Amie Kallon and Salia Koroma, who sang in Mende alone, were appropriated by an audience that cuts across ethnic identities. The cultural, then, translates the local specificities of events in Mendeland onto the national scene. Thus, in 1990, one of the hit audio tapes on sale in most of Sierra Leone's towns and cities was Amie Kallon's Mende song about "Alhaji Tokowa." As we noted earlier, it concerned a ritual murder committed within a family of the rural hinterland, in the pursuit of diamond wealth. The Freetown shopkeeper who sold me this tape, and who played it continuously, had heard its contents translated and debated by Mende friends. He told me he liked the song because, like most young Sierra Leonean men, he "felt" the themes reflected in it: greed, the elusive and diabolical nature of diamond wealth, the hypocrisy of certain religious posturings, and betrayal within the family and between the generations. This intrusion of a local Mende event onto the scene of postcolonial national culture translates at the level of the imagination the expansiveness and hybrid character—military and political, as much as cultural—attributed historically to the Mende in folk and scholarly constructs. In turn, this expansiveness accounts for, and is predicated on, the hybridity and appeal of Mende popular culture.[1]

The surge of Mende popular idioms, icons, and events onto the national Sierra Leonean scene illustrates how liminal cultures can be sites for productively reinscribing the resources of the past in the service of the present, rather than merely being part of a received normative tradition. With respect to this process, Homi Bhabha writes that

> The "right" to signify from the periphery of authorized power and privilege does not depend on the persistence of tradition; it is resourced by the power of tradition to be reinscribed through the conditions of contingency and contradictoriness that attend upon the lives of those who are "in the minority." The recognition that tradition bestows is a partial form of identification. In restaging the past it introduces other, incommensurable cultural realities into the invention of tradition.
>
> *(Bhabha 1994: 2)*

The very appropriability of Mende idioms of self-making underscores their continued productivity for navigating an unstable and changing sociopolitical scene, which ranges from local rural settings to the new networks of strangers, refugees, diamond diggers, war children, and wandering fighters, well beyond the confines of Mende language and territory. This idiom of fragmentation and mobility over time infects the language and practices of everyday life, with its unpredictable turns.

The focus on fragmentation (and conflict) does not lead to an irrational view of Sierra Leonean cultures, as suggested during the 1990s in some of the war journalism and scholarly literature on this region.[2] Rather, it can lead us to an understanding of ambiguous practices and figures of mediation that have not been sufficiently addressed before. Whereas the figure of the double has been an emblematic icon of mediation in Sierra Leonean popular culture and in the scholarly literature, I have pointed to the prevailing significance of another figure, the figure of the third—Gbesse and the *maƂole*. These figures expose the impermanence of clear-cut dichotomies, such as those between child and adult, between indigenous and stranger, between male and female, between town and farm, and even between identity and its double. Instead of resolving dialectically one into the other, these figures keep those paired relations in productive tension, thus opening up ordinary experience to multiple layers of meaning. The figuration of mediated space allows social actors to perceive conflicts as ways to establish new forms of sociality. In other words, these forms may be a prelude to new configurations of community on which the very possibility of conflict resolution is predicated, but where outcomes are not necessarily benign. Thus the stranger and the refugee are seen as both dangerous enemy and welcome guest; birth as a sign of both life and death (in the case of a single twin); and marriage potentially as both alliance and betrayal (as observed in the formation of political alliances and in the context of witchcraft accusations). The outcomes of these mediations are not *a priori* overdetermined, and this creates a situation of instability that, under circumstances like the civil war, can create paralyzing levels of social anxiety about the actual identity and intentions of persons and about the hidden meaning of events.

The *mabɔle*, whose identity defies any sharp distinction between male and female domains, is emblematic of the tension her cultural and political mediations entail. Indeed, her very name may be the remnant of a past event in this region's history that marked a turning point in the political status of women. The *mabɔle*'s significance emerges primarily in the context of Poro rituals. But in Kpuawala and elsewhere, as I have documented, it is in her ordinary life that the conflicts raised by her gender ambiguity emerge. The *mabɔle* Jenne's fumbling response to the challenges of Sande midwives who were delivering a baby in the big house where she lived suggest that real conflicts were presenting themselves to her, as she weighed her identity as a "socially male" figure in the context of Poro society rituals against her roles as mother, wife, and woman living among women. Her status changed according to the perspective articulated by her Sande interlocutors. Thus at first nobody had paid attention to her presence in an ordinary (female) domestic context, the big house. She almost got away with remaining there during the course of this childbirth, and she had done so before, at the very least when she delivered her own offspring. However, in this particular instance the head midwife called attention to Jenne's "male" identity and required that she be excluded from the secret, Sande-controlled event of childbirth. Hence the *mabɔle*'s variable power, which depended on the context, in the face of unpredictable shifts in identities and events. What limits this unpredictability is the set of specific skills that individuals can bring to bear to shape the outcome of events in their favor. Jenne, for example, might have remained in control of her movements if, instead of meekly assenting when she was first addressed, she had answered the challenge with resistance.

The necessity of this space of contestation symbolically represented by the *mabɔle*'s ambiguous relation to the social field can be felt at times of political upheaval or of outright war. Then, the ability to remain in control in a regime of ambiguity is crucial, for the potential transformations of friends into enemies, and of guests into intruders, are matters of life and death. It is precisely in these situations of conflict that it is most productive to maintain, rather than resolve, ambiguity. Thus remaining in control does not necessarily imply that one overcomes conflicting views about the meanings of events and identities—a tension that is often more explicitly at the center of ritual contexts. Such contexts, in which the *mabɔle*, masks, and other forms of cultural performances become visible in public, and therefore represent the dangers entailed in what they stand for, are the (unconscious) training ground for mastering conflicts. In this way, ritual events are always sites for contesting and refashioning the sociopolitical order.[3] In the context of the civil war, Paul Richards addressed how the domains of cultural rituals articulate with historical contingencies by framing the rebels' forced conscription of youth in relation to rites of passage.

> With initiation already deeply etched in the lives of many young people in the Upper Guinean forests, capture may serve to recapitulate aspects of the experience. Villagers apply an initiation "model" to the disaster that has befallen them; they perceive that their children have been taken from them by force (as in initiation) and turned into alien creatures by the power of rebel magic. Offered rudimentary schooling in the bush, and instruction in skills of guerrilla warfare, many captives quickly adjust to their lot.
>
> *(Richards 1996b: 30)*

A similar example of the deliberate appropriation of ritual practices with a view to refashioning the social order, rather than reproducing it, is provided by the reinvention of the figure of the *kamajɔ*, the traditional hunter, for deployment in the Sierra Leonean civil war. As we have seen, the magic rituals deployed by the hunting societies were partially handed over to younger militia members recruited for the war. These, however, were sometimes a mimicry of purportedly traditional practices, of which they took only the surface appearance. The redeployment of hunters points to the multiple uses of ambiguous ritual practices, which can lend themselves to reproduce a particular sociopolitical construct or to change it, albeit under the guise of continuity. Another key trope of the regime of ambiguity associated with the civil war was the figure of the *sobel* that entered Sierra Leonean popular idioms between 1992 and 1997. In 1993, Kpuawala people justified this neologism by saying that during the preceding year, they had been attacked and scared away from the village by three separate groups of armed and uniformed fighters, all of whom subjected them to the same abuses and theft, even though they claimed disparate identities. *Sobels* were also referred to as "soldiers by day, rebels by night," an expression that blurred the very boundaries between the war's opposing sides—the government military forces and the rebels purportedly fighting them (see also Richards 1996b: 7, 13–14). This figure of the popular imagination turned out to be prescient: in 1997 the civilian government brought to power the previous year through a multiparty ballot was toppled in a coup organized by rebels allied with rogue elements of the Sierra Leone Army (the AFRC, led by Johnny Paul Koroma, who had been freed from prison for the occasion). Thus the *sobel* ceased to exist as such when it shifted from a figure of popular idiom and imagination to an actual historical embodiment. Here, then, the regime of ambiguity was not conducive to the management of conflict—that is, to the mediation of opposites. Rather, it prefigured a sinister development that led to an even harsher phase of the war, one eventually characterized by the systematic unleashing of terror on the civilian population through campaigns of mutilation, rape, and murder (Human Rights Watch 1999).

The careful management of ambiguity seen at work in the case of the *mabɔle* and the *sobel*—that is to say, the management of multiple layers of hidden meanings, and their interpretations—can bring about reversals of fortune. However, these layers of meaning are also hidden in the landscape. Hence the management of ambiguity often has to do with the control of natural resources and of their cosmological, political, and economic significance. Social conflicts about meaning are intrinsically bound up with the properties of substances and with the technologies for their extraction. Thus, as we have seen, the temporary alluvial diamond-mining settlement can be a site for technological experimentation that leads to reversals of fortune. However, these reversals often reduced people to poverty when the promises of instant wealth did not materialize. Young men who were at the forefront of this search for easy wealth were then forced back to the rural villages they had come from, and they were then at a disadvantage for the social and political negotiations required to gain access to new agricultural resources.

The rural Sierra Leone population living on the margins of mineral-rich enclaves exploited by local big people or multinational business was aware that this prosperity depended on the value of natural resources concealed in the ground—a value of which they had been unaware when they inhabited the land that was now being mined. Economic prosperity, for them, was associated with the skillful manipulation of esoteric phenomena and of the mineral substances, which were linked cosmologically to the concealed domains of ancestors and spirits located beneath the visible landscape. This aspect strengthened their belief that secret knowledge of substances, places, events, and persons was crucial for reversing personal and collective destinies. The occult economy of extraction not only is controlled by individuals but also is appropriated by state agents at different levels, and it even invests the very forces of production and reproduction (Comaroff and Comaroff 1999: 284). This is a more general feature of African modernity, which is often characterized by the heterogeneous links among postcolonial state politics, witchcraft, and the social rise of actors on the global scene who enrich themselves with local resources, while remaining locally invisible (e.g., Geschiere 1997: 140–164).

A LOGIC OF HISTORICAL CHANGE

The dialectics of modernization in Sierra Leone has not followed a unilinear trajectory toward progress, however this term may be understood. This despite the fact that observers of the Mende and surrounding societies interpreted the social, political, and economic instability they witnessed as an aspect of a trajectory of historical change that would lead to progress and civilization. Administrators and anthropologists of the colonial era brought with them a vision of the civilizing mission and its intended effects. They assumed that the combination of an end to slavery and internal warfare, and the advent of formal education, trade, and modern lifestyles, would cumulatively lead to permanent peace and progress in the region (Alldridge 1910; Little 1951; Migeod 1926; Wallis 1903). The historical experience of Mende and surrounding societies points to no such teleology. Instead, as Jean and John Comaroff have suggested for South Africa, there are both dialectical and dialogical aspects to historical experience, in which dialectics is understood "not to refer to tight teleological processes, unfolding according to one or another rigid historical 'law,' but to the mutually transforming play of social forces whose outcome is neither linear nor simply overdetermined" (Comaroff and Comaroff 1997: 410).

The history of social struggles is embedded in language, material objects, and historical narratives. In Sierra Leone, the collective memory and landscape are replete with evidence of military, political, and social advancement followed by reversals, and of crises turning into moments of opportunity. These changes are understood by the people interpreting them partly in light of magical interventions and partly as the result of concrete political mediations. As I have shown throughout this book, the fact that achievements are thought to be inherently precarious, and appearances deceptive, is not just a matter of fatalism and a belief in magical agency. These interpretations are equally grounded in a rational and realistic understanding of the arts of political mediation and discourse. The logic of unpredictability—with its own distinctive forms of concealment and shape-shifting—is a rational expectation, given the awareness of the multiple levels at which power works. As the deployment of the *sobel* during the civil war demonstrates, this logic is not merely one of dissimulation: it foreshadows real potential transformations of sociopolitical categories and boundaries.

The strategic emphasis or concealment of the legacy of slavery, especially in the idiom of marriage, offers a good example of the paradoxical reversals of historical experience. The confrontational language of enslavement—and of in-laws as "splitters"—embedded in marriage crosses a history where this relationship was the hub of contradictory tensions and where it created, but also eroded, relations of inequality. Kpuawala elders were unwilling to provide details of local history that could clearly reveal which contemporary lineages in the village were of slave or dependent origin, to some extent because such clarity would do violence to the social logic of incorporation that over time tended to silence any clear-cut distinction between kin or slave dependents. By contrast, after the 1926–1927 British ordinances ending domestic slavery in Sierra Leone, the women who sought divorces on the grounds that they had been slave wives embraced this identity, if only to end undesirable marriages. Depending on the circumstances, the legacy of slavery could either offer additional opportunities to find freedom from the constraints of binding allegiances or reproduce the potential for mutual exploitation through the denial of that same history.

Thus a regional history of instability and danger articulates critically with cultural forms—social idioms, practices, and performances—that are rooted in an interpretive ethos of ambiguity. This is not to say that there is a functional correspondence between the sociopolitical instability of the region and the cultural logic of ambiguity at work there. Nor am I making a culturalist argument about the overdetermining effect of the register of ambiguity and its institutionalization in secret societies upon this unstable history. Rather, my intention is to move away from origin accounts and to show instead how new, sometimes unpredictable dynamics are set in motion at critical junctures in the making and unmaking of the social order. The civil war waged intermittently in Sierra Leone since 1991 echoes, sometimes explicitly, a violent history (for example, in the appeal to hunter-warriors and their magic or in direct statements of retribution against the corruption of postcolonial political regimes). But the task of the anthropologist attentive to history cannot be merely to explore the origin of this violent present in a (mythic) past, which would take for granted structural continuity and do away with contingency. As the historical cases discussed here suggest, the fact that violent conflicts often erupt does not overdetermine their outcome. History also shows that the conflicts themselves have produced new social forms, images, and idioms, some of which have a very limited life span, like the *sobel* idiom alluded to previously. Others, like the women's big house that was key to the organization of the rural economy in the days of slavery, underwent more gradual transformations. Today the "big house" may still be a separate building, but in many cases it is only a house in name— a name given to a room at the back of the house that is occupied by women, or linked to narratives about rural life in urban settings where this form of domestic sociality is sometimes entirely absent. This should alert us to the importance of understanding history not only as a site of causal explanations but also as a source of particular forms—symbolic, linguistic, practical—that social actors deploy to rework the social fabric in response to contingent events. These new social and cultural forms are the effect of a dialogical mediation between the present historical situation and a past repertoire of ideas with which social actors critically engage. For example, the civil war has shifted our attention to youth in a continent that is demographically the youngest in the world and has made us rethink our benign notions of childhood in the face of the atrocities committed by child combatants. At the same time, the war has demonstrated how adept the young can be at organizing themselves amid the collapse of age-based moral hierarchies, which have always been taken for granted in these societies.

In this book, I have provided the elements for framing a narrative about Sierra Leone in the present by looking at the relationship between traces of historical memory and the potentially occult economy within which the circulation of everyday objects takes place. The historical and political economies of this region are embedded in the material world of everyday practices and substances. Thus the symbolism, seasonal cycles, and technologies of harvesting and consuming kola nuts recapitulate a history of socioeconomic inequalities at the level of material objects. The role of kola over the span of five centuries as a stimulant food for local and regional consumption articulates with that of trade currency, to produce an economy of fetishism. What is inscribed within this general economy is the circulation of social forces and dynamics that have created networks of exchange ranging from Afro-Portuguese Christians on the Atlantic Coast to Arab-speaking Muslims on the trans-Saharan trade routes. As William Pietz pointed out, the "irreducible materiality" of such fetishistic objects makes them concrete expressions of cultural and linguistic gaps, but also sites of cultural translation, around questions of value. Fetishistic objects, then, are best understood as repositories of complex historical memories and sociocultural links specific to the West African coast.[4] Thus named hairstyles and clothing patterns, for example, fix in time the significance of particular historical events and also act as mnemonic clues to these events. Hence certain domains of material culture and consumption become the privileged bearers of collective memory and act as a temporal index to a disjunctive history of local engagements with events at national, regional, or global levels.

In 1986, when I collected from elders the narratives of Kpuawala's origins, I hardly expected that their stories about villagers founding the settlement by taking up permanent residence on a farm to escape aggression would be reenacted only a few years later, as people fled the threat of the civil war. Nor did I expect to see the generosity of villagers stretched to the limit to accommodate the influx of war refugees that doubled the size of settlements. And yet I had been told time and time again that Mende hospitality was linked to the region's past instability and to the population mobility it generated. The past I had heard narrated did not directly justify or explain the war, nor did it account for the acts of social cohesion that defied it, but it did provide the elements through which people made sense of the present or contested how others did so. And it was the embeddedness of that past in everyday places, words, and objects that made it usable for such purposes.

In the future, the war known in Sierra Leone as the "war of theft" (*huma gɔɛ*)—the civil war that began in 1991—will assume its place among the events that constitute the timeline for remembered experience. Like the "O.A.U. time" or the "A.P.C. time"[5] of waste and graft that preceded it, it might find itself memorialized in a hairstyle or cloth pattern, in new words like *sobel*, or in the much more sinister vocabulary of the lottery of mutilation that took place in wartime. The everyday objects, words, and places of war will find their way into narratives and social relations, in a manner analogous to those of slavery and violence left behind by a buried past in the peacetime of my pre-war fieldwork. History shows that in the past Sierra Leoneans successfully deployed a range of strategies—including secrecy—to live in the proximity of death. Secrecy does not offer the teleological certainty of realizable political projects. However, Sierra Leoneans have lived this social instability before, and they have sometimes turned it into a creative, though violent, opportunity to refashion themselves vis-à-vis their own institutions.

Notes

INTRODUCTION

1. There is a considerable scholarship on masking and power in this region, especially in connection with secret societies (e.g., Bellman 1980; d'Azevedo 1973; Eberl-Elber 1937; Harley 1950; N'Diaye 1964; Phillips 1978). On the politicization of urban secret societies and their masked performances in Sierra Leone in connection with party politics, see Nunley (1987). More general theoretical questions have also been raised about the significance of masking for a cultural aesthetics of secrecy (e.g., Bellman 1981, 1984; Boone 1986; Hommel 1981; Phillips 1980, 1995). Finally, scholarship on this region's civil war has linked its violence to the central role played in it by forms of dissimulation, including masking and cross-dressing (see Ellis 1999; Moran 1995).

2. Meanings are deferred and made ambiguous in magic squares in ways that can make them inaccessible even when they are in full view and visible to people who are literate in Arabic. To make and decode one of these squares, one needs to know where to enter and exit its grid, in order to link letters and numbers in a meaningful sequence. Even when more explicit writings provide clues to the relationship between a text and the object on which it is inscribed, information is still missing about the performative practices required to deploy words and things to bring about desired effects. Repetition is key to the effectiveness of ritual gestures and words, as are the time and place of their performance. Thus certain magic amulets must be made on specific days of the month, only at night, by the light of seven candles, and after a given set of prayers; and the same sequence of words must be written and erased a given number of times for them to become potent. This information about the deployment of sacred words is usually absent from the text itself, though crucial to its production and to the symbolic logic of its effectiveness.

3. For this archeology of meaning, see Ricoeur (1970).

4. On the sociopolitical characteristics of diamond mining as a "dig-and-quit" activity that produces a small and highly portable (and hence concealable)

source of wealth, see Richards and Fithen (n.d. 1–2), and Smillie, Gberie, and Hazleton (2000).

5. For more highly developed, public forms of history telling, one needs to go to the areas farther north, as has been noted by Innes (1974), Jackson (1977), and Miller (1990: 68–113).

6. I am less interested in the rhetorical effects of irony or surprise, which one might read into the constant references to a culture of ambiguity and indirectness, than in Mende constructs of these concepts and the distinctions between them, which underscore an unpredictability of outcomes, beyond the intentions of social actors. Indirectness operates, for example, in proscriptions against direct questions on certain topics, a feature thoroughly analyzed by Bellman (1984) for the related Kpelle region of Liberia. By contrast, to remain at the discursive level, ambiguity has to do more with the ways in which information is provided in encoded form, rather than withheld.

7. Politically, Muraro points out, this emphasis on metaphorical processes helped liberation movements (including those of feminist liberation) in challenging dominant power configurations by undermining the totalizing bent of representation (Muraro 1980: 64). However, she also argues that the crisis of this once liberatory strategy is underscored by its replacement by imitation—by a theoretical emphasis on the mimetic in art, politics, and culture.

8. The two operations are part of an inseparable, "bipolar" system, however (Jakobson and Halle 1956: 96), and each taken on its own is only partial in its ability to structure concepts (e.g., Lakoff and Johnson 1980: 52).

9. The first emphasis of this literature pertained to the body of work on the role of the women's Sande and the men's Poro initiation societies as key elements in the social organization of this, the Upper Guinea Coast region of West Africa. For example, see contributors to Adams (1980), Butt-Thompson (1929), d'Azevedo (1962), Hoffer (1974) Horton (1971), Little (1965, 1966), MacCormack (1975), and Rodney (1970: 67–68). The emphasis on gendered politics had to do instead with a long history of European interest in the fact that in this region, both women and men had access to socially and politically prominent offices. This feature of social organization was reported in European accounts of the region from the sixteenth century onward (e.g., Alldridge 1901: 166, 181; Fyfe 1962: 3, 67; Guerreiro, cited in Rodney 1970: 66). Women's access to political office was also the focus of renewed attention in feminist scholarship in this region beginning in the 1970s (Day 1988, 1994; Hoffer 1972, 1974; cf. Moore 1988: 133). Indeed, by the 1980s, the "compensatory" emphasis of this scholarship in producing accounts of female domains without paying much attention to how these fit into an overarching gender system had given way to studies that problematized the very opposition between male and female, but still within the parameters of esoteric cults, public office, and their symbolism (e.g., Bledsoe 1984; MacCormack 1980).

10. To some extent, the effort to demistify secrecy in Bellman's work, but also in that of Zempléni (1976, 1996) and Murphy (1990)—the effort to situate it in everyday life, rather than in esoteric domains—is made possible by a deeper understanding developed through long-term fieldwork. Piot pointed to the fact

that the more competent he grew in the language, the more he became aware of the banal contexts in which secrecy was deployed (see Piot 1993: 354).

11. For a critical assessment of anthropological studies of bounded communities, see Clifford (1992), Gupta (1997), and Tsing (1993). Such criticism has often pointed to the relationship between particular field site choices—ranging from "island cultures" to remote rural villages—and the synchronic representation of "other" cultures as consistently patterned and outside of time (e.g., Fabian 1983). As my own argument in later chapters suggests, the very construction of remoteness needs to be problematized.

12. The proliferation of anthropological writings on the landscape (e.g., Bender 1993; Feld and Basso 1996; Hirsch and O'Hanlon 1995) has been attributed to the fact that the landscape allows us metaphorically to speak of many indeterminate things; it is "a concept in between" (Morphy 1993: 205). Though some of this work is phenomenological in nature and explores linkages among landscape, individual or social memory, and collective histories (e.g., Kahn 1996; Küchler 1993; Stewart 1996), this dimension has also been linked to the political contestation of the landscape and its meanings (e.g., Santos-Granero 1998) and the misrecognition of its industrial features when this has been constructed as an idyllic rural space (Frake 1996).

13. For a theoretical analysis of the detail in modernity, see especially Bachelard (1964), Schor (1987), and Stewart (1996).

14. See Hoskins (1998) for an evocative study of "biographical objects" in Indonesia, objects linked by Sumbanese individuals to their selves and their social biographies. By focusing on how the lives of particular people and objects are intertwined over time through memories of key events, texts, and formulaic expressions in the communities in which they are embedded, Hoskins gives new ethnographic depth and specificity to studies of "the social life of things" that have proliferated since the 1980s in anthropology (e.g., Appadurai 1986; Miller 1998; Munn 1986; Weiss 1996).

CHAPTER 1

1. Wallis's cry against nature's indifference must also be seen in the context of this particular crime, in which a young American female missionary was raped and killed by African men. As others have shown, this kind of event played on key colonial anxieties about sexual and racial boundaries, in which white women and their bodies figured prominently (see McClintock 1995; Stoler 1991, 1992: 332–333). In the multiple permutations of these anxieties, the brutal policing of racial boundaries was often justified as being required by the threat that dark-skinned men posed to the bodily integrity of white women. Nature itself was construed in highly sexual terms in the colonial landscape, which was often represented as a mysterious (dark) female body open to European male penetration (see Comaroff and Comaroff 1991: 98–108; McClintock 1995: 1–9).

2. The buttress roots of the cotton tree could easily conceal a standing man. In rural Sierra Leone, particularly during periods of intense warfare in the late nineteenth century, concentric palisades were built around war towns, and these

were allowed to take root, thus leaving a telltale circular pattern in tree growth that to this day helps identify former settlements in forest areas. See Alldridge (1910: 181) and Malcolm (1939: 47) for descriptions that provide clues to the vegetation and natural features left behind by abandoned fortified settlements.

3. What these modern "hunters" do *not* lack is technological know-how and training, ranging from the computer (the CDF's Web page was up and running before the official Government of Sierra Leone Web page) to weapons and indoctrination.

4. Paramount Chiefs themselves have had roles that blur the distinction between traditional and modern domains and warfare. Hinga Norman was an example of the way modern Sierra Leonean Paramount Chiefs straddle local and state politics and, in this case, warfare. A Sandhurst-trained military man, he became Paramount Chief of the Jaiama-Bongor Chiefdom during the civil war, and in 1994 he organized local militias with sophisticated modern weaponry and training to defend the civilian population of his chiefdom from RUF rebel attacks (Muana 1997: 83). His strategy was successful enough to eventually win him a ministerial post in the national government.

5. The relationship between concealing and revealing is addressed for this region by Bellman (1981: 1–2) and more generally by Simmel (1950: 332). Reeck (1976) uses the expression "deep Mende" to refer to an ethos of ethnic authenticity in the face of colonial modernization projects and historical efforts by Christian and Muslim proselytizers to bring about change in religious beliefs and practices. In my experience, though, the expression "deep Mende" (*Mende ndɔwungɔ*) was used almost exclusively to refer to the realm of discourse, rather than to distinctive cultural practices—which were referred to as *Mende hinda*, "Mende things."

6. See LaFontaine (1977) and Cohen (1971) for a discussion of the political implications of ritual secrecy, especially within the context of initiation and secret institutions.

7. The term used by Joadi was *puubla*.

8. Queen Elizabeth II.

9. Every year after the rice harvest, Joadi left his farm in the chiefdom neighboring Wunde to travel around the area performing the songs, dances, and stories for which he was well known. He was an illiterate farmer, like most of his audience.

10. "A narrow gauge (2 ft., 6 in.), a single track, extremely tortuous alignment and steep gradients, . . . together with the general meandering nature of its course, imposed on the railway's speed an effective limitation of around 20 mph for safe and comfortable travel" (Kaindaneh 1993: 24). Clarke (1969: 104) points out that the Sierra Leone Government Railway's "ludicrously narrow gauge" was due to cost containment as well as to difficulties of the terrain. He also refers to a "dubious suggestion" that this gauge was chosen "to remove the possibility of a link with the neighboring French colonial territory" of Guinée (Clarke, ibid.). The explicit colonial goal in building the railway had been to link the Sierra Leonean hinterland more closely to the capital, to bring produce from the provinces, and to export signs of progress there from the city (Alldridge 1910; Blyden 1872). Yet the fact that the Sierra Leone railway was

then constructed as a miniature version of the technology of the day also reflected ambivalence toward this project. Whether to save money or to prevent linkages with the French rail system across the fragile and ill-defined borders of its area of influence, the British colonial government from the beginning undermined the prospect of the railway as an efficient and affordable means of transportation.

11. The noted West Indian intellectual and educator E.W. Blyden was the first to recommended that such a railroad be built after his expedition to Falaba in 1872 on behalf of the Sierra Leone colonial government, to open up the north to colonial trade (Public Records Office, London: 267/316).

12. The British referred to the 1898 insurrection as the "Hut Tax War," whereas in Mendeland it is simply referred as "The Whiteman's War," *puu gɔɛ*. This suggests a difference of opinion as to the war's precipitating causes. Mende participants and witnesses who were interviewed at the time by the British commissioner sent to inquire into the causes of the insurrection made it clear that a combination of factors precipitated the war, including (1) the declaration of a formal protectorate over the Sierra Leone hinterland in 1896, (2) the establishment of permanent outposts of a Frontier Police Force in the region, and (3) the imposition of taxes beginning in January 1898 (Chalmers 1899, I: 44–52). In particular, chiefs had made it clear for some time that they objected to the abuses of office perpetrated by the Frontier Police personnel sent out to remote outposts with little supervision by their superiors and that they resented the loss of sovereignty implied by the demand that they begin paying taxes to the British Protectorate government (Ibid.: 11–14).

13. The feeder road that linked the Wunde chiefdom to the country's secondary road system dates to this period.

14. However, in the 1990s the arrival of state-of-the-art satellite technology made telephone poles and wires obsolete. A cursory look at the Freetown press reveals the appearance of advertisements for cellular phones by several competing companies in a single issue, as well as articles on the expansion and upgrading of communication technologies.

15. Kambawama, the place of the many, or big, graves, was situated at the site of the nineteenth-century warrior Ndawa's fortified towns, described in colonial records as "a cluster of thirteen towns" (Abraham 1978: 89). The name was said to be linked to the size and dense population of the settlement in the past and to the fact that "many people came to die here." For an analysis of how supporters of the Wunde candidate on the 1986 ballot used this history of past warfare in efforts to gain political legitimacy for their man, see Ferme (1999).

16. On the use of "youth wings" for the purposes of thuggery in modern electoral politics in Sierra Leone, see Abdullah (1997: 49).

17. Janet Roitman's work on the "garrison-entrepots" of the Cameroon-Chad basin explores such enclaves (which in this case are also military garrisons) as sites of specific political and economic subject-formation, whose location on state borders challenges classic notions of state sovereignty (see Roitman 1998).

18. On the notion of the linkages between African modernities and the resurgence of magic and economies of the occult that threaten the deployment of an authentic political vision, see Comaroff and Comaroff (1999) and Geschiere

(1997). For an analysis of occult economies in early modern Europe, see Certeau (1970) and Levi (1988).

19. For a better-known case of a spirit with similar attributes and powers, see the rich literature on the cult of Mammy Wata in West Africa and elsewhere (e.g., Drewal 1988).

20. On history as forgetting versus remembering, see Renan (1990 [1882]); on the necessity of forgetting a past of struggle and division in the history of nation building, which is centered on the possibility of conjuring up a cohesive community, see Nora (1984) and Benjamin (1969: 253–264).

21. For a detailed study of Mende farming knowledge, particularly with an eye to agricultural practices that apparently do not maximize productivity but in fact strategically minimize risks from weather and pest damage, see especially Richards (1986).

22. As the term, big farm implies, this was an extended household's main farm; it was considered the household's primary labor commitment, as well as being the main source of its food.

23. These hamlets were often inhabited by domestic slaves or dependent strangers, who did the bulk of the farming work (cf. Little 1951; Siddle 1968). Kpuawala elders pointedly avoided saying whether there might be any descendants of slaves among them.

24. For an analysis of the semiotics—and particularly the indexical nature—of the relationship between farming and social activities and places, see Nancy Munn (1986) and Christine Hugh-Jones (1979).

25. In this particular case, other, larger political and environmental events that were also used for time reckoning over longer periods of time (earthquakes, the transition to independence, the beginning of APC single-party rule, etc.), helped place the woman's birth date at around 1956, or 30 years earlier. This suggested that the fallow period for this particular plot, which was quite close to the settlement and hence would not have been used too often for farming, was about 10 years. Work on fallow patterns in this region has suggested that it ranges between 7 and 15 years (Johnny, Karimu, and Richards 1981).

26. Rice farming presents special labor problems because of the relatively short growth cycle of rice compared, for example, to yams, which are the staple in other parts of West Africa. This produces labor bottlenecks at critical times in the rice-farming season, so successful farmers tend to be people with the necessary social skills and capital to mobilize large groups of clients who can help clear, burn, and plant at the right time (see Johnny, Karimu, and Richards 1981: 606).

27. Throughout the 1970s, development schemes designed to intensify swamp cultivation in Mendeland failed to persuade farmers to abandon upland rice. The strong sociocultural preference for upland rice farming is summed up by the designation of paddies as "swamps" (kpete) rather than "farms" (kpaa).

28. Men did all the earlier work. They cleared the forest and cut down trees, burned them when dry, broadcast rice, and hoed the ground. At this point, women and children took over, the former keeping birds and other pests away, the latter planting their own crops among the rice, weeding, and so on until the time of harvesting, which was a collective effort. This temporal division also meant that the bulk of men's work was done before the rains and in concentrated

spurts of intensive labor, whereas the women's and children's work was more drawn out and time-consuming and took place during the rainy season.

INTERLUDE 1

1. Though it is not my intention here to enter into the details of hair symbolism, anthropologists have long noted that hair is cross-culturally the object of symbolic and ritual elaboration. In its dual capacity as a living, growing, and pliable extension of the body *and* as inert, dead matter that can be severed from it, hair lends itself to mark crucial bodily and social transitions during the life cycle. Leach (1958) situated his powerful anthropological critique of—and efforts toward a rapprochement with—psychoanalysis in a cross-cultural exploration of "hairdressing" symbolism related to rites of passage. Since Leach, anthropologists have analyzed the gendered symbolism of hair styling, covering, and uncovering, and in the process they have also paid more attention to the political dimensions of these practices, both in Africa and elsewhere (e.g., Delaney 1994; Houlberg 1979). My focus is on how hair plaiting is related more generally to weaving practices of which it is a particular instance. I am also interested in how shifts in women's hairstyles are associated with particular events, thus becoming mnemonic devices in a popular history reckoned through material change.

2. In the 1890s, during his first trek to the Sierra Leone hinterland, District Commissioner T. J. Alldridge noted that women in one northern location wore a new, named hair style, which he photographed (Alldridge 1901: 290).

3. Urban African street signs for hairdresser shops provide whimsical pictorial records of these fashions. Male and female styles are portrayed in detail, and given names ranging from "American boy" to "Rasta lady" and "rocket head." For an analysis of women's hairstyles and their names with reference both to cultural history and to more recent sociopolitical events in Nigeria, see Houlberg (1979).

4. See Wass (1979) for a history of the main patterns in wax prints and their varying fortunes on the West African market. In the 1970s several European producers interviewed by Wass kept thousands of patterns in production, introducing up to 200 new ones every year and taking out of production those for which there had been no demand for the preceding two years (Wass 1979: 479). This rapid change in demand for particular patterns makes them an ideal dating device for particular events—not to mention the fact that there were also special patterns commissioned for particular events (e.g., Wass 1979: 493, plate 18). Picton (1995: 29, 118) reproduces commemorative fancy prints commissioned by the United Africa Company as early as 1928 for events ranging from the installation of a new Asantehene in Ghana (1929) to the silver jubilee of Great Britain's King George V and Queen Mary (1935). He sees this practice as one aspect of "the mediating influence of local [African] traders" in European cloth production.

5. See Cordwell, in Nielsen (1979: 495), for a discussion of how political sentiments were conveyed subtly, by wearing such specially commissioned patterns upside down or with a leader's portrait placed so that one would sit on it. More explicit political and social messages were inscribed, for example, on the *kangas* worn by Kenyan women. In the late 1950s and early 1960s (the height of the emergency declared to fight Mau Mau), the colonial government recognized the

subversive potential of the clothing medium for expressing political messages and attempted to ban some *kanga* patterns with particularly explicit political phrases (Hilger 1995: 45). Conversely, President Daniel K. Arap Moi and the U.N. used this feature to their advantage, commissioning the incorporation of special *kanga* phrases to promote unity and peace or the U.N. Decade for Women Conference in Kenya (Hilger, ibid.).

6. Alldridge included this in a 1901 book on Sierra Leone (Alldridge 1901: 99–100), with alterations. In the book, which was intended for a broader audience than the specialized 1894 article journal, Alldridge omitted the entire passage that included the material italicized here. The omitted passage contained a critical assessment of English traders who cheated in cloth transactions from the point of view of both "quantity [and] quality" among a people who produced excellent cloth of their own and who were "shrewd" as well. By contrast, in the book version, perhaps catering to the bourgeois sensibilities of his English readership, Alldridge adds the following decorative advice: "A very primitive method of treating indigo produces the most beautiful light and shade that is a real pleasure to the artistic sense, and goes charmingly with blue china" (Alldridge 1901: 100).

7. Note that although cloth eventually lost its use as currency (Wallis, 1903: 229), it retained its value as prestige gift and as souvenir much sought after by the foreign visitor. Hence the multiple, ambivalent meanings of "the country cloth culture," given that among the reasons for the economic and symbolic importance of cloth to the Mende was that it was so sought after by non-Mende.

8. For a detailed analysis of the role of European clothing, and in particular of "the Empire's old clothes," in creating a culture of consumption in colonial southern Africa, see Comaroff and Comaroff (1997: 218–273). Their analysis also pays attention to the status- and gender-specific variations in the adoption of European fabrics and clothing styles.

9. Whiteness and fair skin are here linked to good disposition and intentions, as elsewhere in Africa and in the wider Muslim world.

10. However, within contexts where cloth production has become a specialized craft, such as in Sierra Leone urban areas, dyeing is sometimes taken up by men (Wahlman and Chuta 1979).

11. In Mende, the language associated with cloth production does not evoke the gendered symbolism familiar elsewhere in Africa. Among the Dogon of Mali, the anthropomorphic naming of weaving equipment for parts of the human body has prompted the drawing of some parallels with speech (Calame-Griaule 1987: 82–83), and procreation (Griaule 1965: 73). In Morocco, where women weave (in contrast to West Africa, where men weave), similar links have been made between the idiom of childbearing and weaving (Messick 1987).

12. Ekejiuba (1995: 146–147) documents for Eastern Nigeria the modern use of handmade, older kinds of cloth as a form of wealth for protecting women against currency instability during the civil war and the boom–bust cycles of the oil economy since the 1960s, in part because of its continued value in "social payments" such as bridewealth.

13. In this, country cloth blankets shared some of the features Weiner (1989) described in the prizing of mortuary cloths as "inalienable possessions" and heirlooms in the Trobriands.

14. In Dogon cosmology, the processes of weaving and secrecy, or secreting words, are cosmologically linked in the language of weaving (Griaule 1965: 73–74).

CHAPTER 2

1. As Lévi-Strauss (1969: 12–25) and Bourdieu (1990b) would note, these boundaries also offer insights into the fundamental organizational framework of particular cultures.

2. As its name (a tribute to the British Broadcasting Corporation's World Service radio transmissions) implies, this was the meeting house where people went to hear the latest news and gossip. It was situated in the more populous of Kpuawala's two wards. This was not, however, where the town's official political and legal matters were addressed. For these, people convened at the meeting place in the chief's compound, in the neighboring ward (see page 147).

3. In taking this line of reasoning, I am following the argument advanced by Marilyn Strathern for gender relations in the New Guinea highlands and Melanesia more generally (see Strathern 1981, 1988: 59 ff.).

4. On the relationship between politics and economy of the sacred, see Bataille (1989, I).

5. Thus Victor Turner's symbolic and political analysis of ritual objects and spaces in Africa (Turner 1967: 20–25) gave way to analyses of how values are produced and transformed through the circulation of objects (e.g., Appadurai 1986: 3; Munn 1986).

6. In a similar vein, women who were asked what was essential to their appearance as women would most often cite well-plaited hair and cleanliness. In terms of dress, head ties were the distinct markers of a female identity and were often the only item identifying men in drag, or in transitional roles associated with female capacities, such as certain stages of initiation. Male storytellers like Joadi (mentioned in Chapter 1), virtually always performed dressed as women.

7. There is no comparable language associated with hammocks or fishing nets.

8. In Africa, this distinction between the solitary, gun-armed form of hunting and other techniques of catching game is common. It is documented, for example, for the Ndembu of Zambia, among whom separate hunting rituals exist for *Wuyanga*—hunting with guns—and *Wubinda*—all other forms of hunting (Turner 1967: 280–298). For the links between hunting and rituals, see Rosaldo (1980).

9. See Ferme (1994) for a more general discussion of this event in the context of an analysis of syncretism and secrecy in the face of local efforts toward Islamic reform.

10. The masquerades associated with the men's Poro society in this region have been analyzed by Bellman (1980), Harley (1950), and Siegmann and Perani (1980), among others.

CHAPTER 3

1. Historians have stressed the distinctive demographic character of slavery in Muslim Africa, which primarily affected women and children, as contrasted with

the predominantly adult, male makeup of the Atlantic slave trade (e.g., Curtin 1969; Willis 1985a: vii). This has been linked to the ideology of *jihad* and enslavement promulgated in Muslim legal texts, which encouraged the faithful to kill enemy warriors and capture their wealth, women, and children (Willis 1985b: 22). However, the preference for female slaves was also attributed to the fact that in the African societies affected, "status and wealth were measured by the length of the master's line, [and hence] the production of progeny—the motive force behind the institution of concubinage in Islam—became a reflection of the prestigious self. Women . . . formed the circulating medium of foreign exchange" (Willis 1985a: viii).

2. Typical of this ambiguity is the historical indeterminacy in early Islam of the Arab term *mawla* (pl. *mawali*), which could mean, among other things, freed slave, convert, ally, in-law, cousin, client, and protector (Pipes 1985).

3. Peter Ekeh has gone further, to argue that the traumatic history of slavery (and colonialism) accounts for the continued strength of kinship ties and the relative weakness of the state in postcolonial Africa (Ekeh 1990: 773–783). Ekeh attributes the modern African articulation of kinship and political institutions to the historical protections provided by the former against the threat of enslavement. By contrast, the Mende and other West African cases also suggest the role of kin groups in *bringing about enslavement!*

4. By contrast, among the Wolof of Senegal, where primogeniture was an important principle, the term Arab referred to offspring of a parent's older sibling (Labouret 1929: 245).

5. In Kpuawala, the preference for matrilateral cross-cousin marriage was linked, as we shall see, to concerns about marriage stability. There are parallels to this link elsewhere in Africa, as documented, for example, by Fallers (1957). However, my argument here is that encompassing factors such as population mobility, the changing conditions of dependent (formerly slave) farm labor, and the relative availability of land must also be taken into account to put marriage and its stability in a historical context. The fact that Gluckman (1950) and Fallers (1957) gave opposite accounts of the role of strong patrilineages in maintaining stable marriages (one argues for a positive correlation between the two phenomena, the other for an inverse one) suggests that it is not sufficient to understand marriage patterns in sociocultural terms, in relation to forms of kinship.

6. However, the immobility implied by this terminology, and by insignia of chiefly office such as thrones and staffs, is a relatively recent feature of Mende political might, one associated with the British colonial period and the prevalence of land chiefs. By contrast, a different rhetoric and symbolism characterized the war chiefs of the precolonial and early colonial period.

7. One must be wary of positing a direct correlation between kinship terminology and the assimilation to kin categories, let alone what this implies for behavioral prescriptions (Scheffler 1991). Schneider (1984) and others (e.g., Yanagisako and Collier 1987) have exhaustively criticized this line of inquiry on theoretical and empirical grounds. Thus it is important to relate marriage and kinship practices to broader historical and political forces that they may help

reproduce, as I do here with the context of slavery, and which in turn may shape their transformation.

8. In a different disagreement, the town chief, in spite of his seniority in status and age, deferred to one of his neighbors who was *kenyamɔ*, a person in a *kenya* relationship to him. The chief explained that a *kenya's* wrath and curse were worse even than a father's and hence were to be avoided at all cost. A *kenya's* curse could be lifted by him only after public acts of humiliation by his *njagbe*, his nephew or niece (cf. Harris and Sawyerr 1968; Little 1951: 110).

9. The expression for putting down an advance (on marriage payments, in this case), *tokola kula*, has overtones of physical bonding, because tokola's homophone means "arm or hand," so the expression also alludes to clasping someone's arm with something. In addition, a commitment to marry is described as "tying a rope on a young woman's arm" (*ngeya yili nyapo loko la*).

10. Here was the list of items that one Kpuawala young man bought at the Blama market during his future wife's Sande initiation, in anticipation of her coming-out ceremonies: 2 double lengths (*lappa*) of wax-died cotton cloth; 2 pairs of women's plastic shoes; 1 umbrella; 1 head tie (synthetic fabric); 1 double-length cotton head tie; 1 t-shirt; 1 towel; 4 sets of hair pins; 1 eye makeup pencil; 2 half-slips (*semi*); 3 pairs of underwear (*drossi*); 1 plastic carrier; 1 scented soap bar; hair styling gel; 2 brassieres (*kaki bobi*); 1 tailored knee-length woman's dress; 1 purse. The amount spent on these items, 615 Leones, represented a fortune for this young man. It was the equivalent of about 75 kilograms of dry cocoa beans or of several 50-kilogram bags of clean rice.

11. In the fourth *surah* of the Qur'an, on "Women," is the passage "you may marry other women who seem good to you, two, three, or four of them. But if you fear you cannot maintain equality among them, marry only one or any slave-girls you may own. This will make it easier for you to avoid injustice" (Qur'an 1956: 60).

12. A more encompassing ambivalence toward death itself is of course also at issue here. In his classic essay on the collective representation of death, Hertz linked this ambivalence to the necessity, at death, of transforming "the character of the corpse"—turning it into a new body within which what survived after death could be free of the world of the living (Hertz 1960: 43). A similar "act of liberation" applied to the other category of person involved in death: the surviving relative whose mourning ended with ritual washings, dressings, and celebrations that had parallels in the treatment of the dead body (Ibid: 64).

13. The bodily referents extended to the money offered to the bereaved by visiting mourners, which was referred to as *kasange*, "shroud." This was a way to link the donor's contribution to the purchase of the white shroud necessary for a Muslim burial. However, the syntactical construct implied that the money itself was a kind of shroud in which to wrap the corpse, and Harris and Sawyerr have documented for Mende burials the practice of placing money "in the grave-clothes" themselves (1968: 32).

14. Hertz remarked that the transitional periods characterizing burial and mourning, and people's ambivalence toward the dead, made death analogous to initiation (as well as to birth and marriage), rather than being linked to it only in

a metaphorical sense. In both death and initiation, a radical transformation of the person was effected: in one case a person moved "from the visible society to the invisible," whereas in the other he or she was removed from the community and reinstated in a new capacity (Hertz 1960: 80).

15. *nyaha gɔɛ* is a term also used for expressions such as "picking fruit."

16. The Native Administration system in Sierra Leone supported itself, among other things, through the collection of taxes and fees for licensing "traditional" practices such as marriages, naming ceremonies (birth certificates), and funerals (death certificates).

17. This cloth gift to a mother-in-law also echoed an earlier gift of cloth from her husband at the time of weaning a child. This cloth was intended to replace clothes worn out by repeated soiling and washing during the period when the nursing infant spent much of its time on the mother's back.

18. He had originally sought 1,500 Leones as retribution—the equivalent in April 1990 of about one bushel of rice—but was cajoled and begged (*manɛnɛ*) by his in-laws to accept a third of what he had requested, in light of their promise to be more attentive in the future.

19. Kenneth Little noted in the 1940s the prevalence of court cases brought by men against allegedly adulterous, wandering wives (Little 1951: 186). However, the outcome of such cases was not necessarily a permanent separation, particularly because sometimes, Little argued, husbands and wives conspired to unmask a lover in order to generate income from court fines against him. Little did not find a great concern over marriage instability during his work among the Mende, but he did note that the individual desires of marriage partners were becoming more important, and he attributed this change to modernizing trends in the country. By contrast, much of the anthropological literature on marriage instability in Africa attributed it to structural features of the kinship system. For example, consider Gluckman's argument that the contrast between Zulu marital stability and a high rate of divorce among the Lozi was due to the absence of strong unilineal kin groups among the latter (1950: 180), or Fallers's counterargument (based on the case of the Ugandan Soga) that it was precisely the tensions between kin and affines produced by a woman's continued membership in strong patrilineages of origin that accounted for high divorce rates and an "explicit public concern over marriage instability" by men (1957: 112–113). Yet other perspectives linked relative marital stability to how women gained access to resources necessary to their own and their children's survival (e.g., Potash 1978: 390).

20. The act of "watching food being prepared in the hope of being invited to join in eating it," *nɛhɛmei* (Innes 1969: 99), is despised and ridiculed among adults. One woman told me it was bad for a man to be a *nɛhɛmɔ* with his friends, for this would become a cause of friction between the man imposed on and his wife, who would have to stretch her daily food allowance for an extra mouth.

21. However, this threat was carried out with other Kpuawala strangers. In one case an older trader whose gambling and drinking had always been a source of friction with the Muslim political leadership of the community was finally chased out of town when he sided with the political faction that lost the 1986 elections. As elsewhere in this region, traders, both Mende and foreign, were the

paradigmatic strangers in Kpuawala (Brooks 1993; Shack and Skinner 1979). Although this particular man died within a year or so, most other people who had been evicted from the community were eventually able to return, unless they had committed crimes that had come to the attention of the Native Court system in the Chiefdom Headquarters.

INTERLUDE 2

1. *Cola nitida*, whose fruit is made up of two lobes, is native to the forest region of which Sierra Leone is a part. This variety is generally valued more highly in the trade than the other main West African species—*C. acuminata*—which grows further east, from Nigeria to Gabon (see Brooks 1980: 2), and which has four lobes rather than two. These two types are merely the most valued—and edible—of some 40 varieties of kola (Brooks, ibid.; for comparative perspectives on kola preferences, trade patterns, and ceremonial uses in West Africa, see also Drucker-Brown 1995; Lovejoy 1980; Uchendu 1964).

2. Kola produces colors ranging from dark yellow to rust and brown. The dark brown "country cloth" (locally spun and woven cotton) clothes of Mende warriors used to be kola-died. By the 1980s, nobody dyed cloth in Kpuawala; dyeing had become the specialized activity of small-scale industries in larger towns such as Bo. For their clothes, people in Kpuawala mostly bought lengths of patterned cloth or second-hand clothes from traveling salesmen, from local Fula, or in Blama, the nearest market town. Although beginning in 1952, imported chemical dyes and cottons replaced natural ones (Wahlman and Chuta 1979: 458), demand for traditional indigo and kola dyes among Western visitors has revived the use of these substances in both urban and rural Sierra Leone. One of the most popular patterns in these dyes was named "Peace Corps" *gara* in honor of the people who provided reliable marketing outlets for such cloth, and in the 1970s, revived its production as part of a program to promote Sierra Leone arts and crafts for export (see Wahlman and Chuta 1979: 461). *Gara*, the generic word used for dyed cloth, means "indigo" in the Mandingo language.

3. The fact that the member of this Malian family who was living in Blama also engaged in the diamond trade (Amselle 1977) points to how easily such ancient trading routes and connections can be converted to respond to demands for new commodities.

4. Ford's argument contradicts the notion, prevalent in the literature on kola in West Africa, that this was primarily a crop opportunistically harvested from self-propagating trees. In arguing that these trees were deliberately planted by farmers who in shifting the location of their fields also contributed to the spread of kola and other trees, Ford contributes important evidence to the growing literature that seeks to counter commonplaces about the links between deforestation and indigenous farming practices. Fairhead and Leach (1996a; 1996b), discussed earlier, have done some of the most interesting work to date on this issue.

5. See Amselle (1977), Cohen (1966), and Lovejoy (1980) for an analysis of the political implications of European interventions in the kola trade in French colonial West Africa and in British Nigeria.

6. Mende terms for money are *navo*, "that which shines," and *kɔpɔ*, from the English "copper."

CHAPTER 4

1. In discussing medieval iconography, Bachelard points out the lack of symmetry in the movement between small and large: "[I]t becomes normal for an elephant, which is an enormous animal, to come out of a snail shell. It would be exceptional, however, if we were to ask him to go back into it. . . . in the imagination, to go in and come out are never symmetrical images" (Bachelard 1964: 108).

2. In a critical study of "the house" in the life of Colombian peasants, and of the domestic economy literature, Gudeman (1990: 184) speculated that anthropologists might have spent more time analyzing this entity, instead of corporate descent groups or lineages, if they had taken seriously the model offered to Evans-Pritchard by his Nuer interlocutors: "A lineage is *thok mac*, the hearth, or *thok dwiel*, the entrance to the hut" (Evans-Pritchard 1940: 195). In a similar vein, Grinker took at face value the contention by Lese farmers in Zaire that they formed "houses" with their Efe forager partners in the forest, even though they did not reside with them, and argued that this was a cultural idiom for integrating women and ethnically different people into the same group (Grinker 1994: 113).

3. Children of either sex lived in the big house with mothers or grandmothers from birth. Boys left it when they were judged ready for "training" (*makɛmei*), a term that encompasses European and Islamic schooling, as well as apprenticeship in a craft or trade. Girls left their mothers' big houses to be initiated into Sande, which usually took place when a suitable husband was found.

4. Senior women in different Kpuawala big houses sometimes brought charges against other residents for leaving the front door open at night. In suggestive songs and conversations, women implied that a big house door found ajar at night or in the early morning hours was thought to be a sign that one of the resident women was having secret assignations with a human or spirit lover. They claimed that this endangered others in the big house by exposing them to the potential attention of wandering spirits while in the particularly vulnerable and weak state of sleep.

5. "Going behind the house" (*li pɛɛ woma*) was the expression used for urinating. Indeed, the areas behind houses were generally where a range of physiological and transformative processes took place: this was where food was processed and cooked and where human and other waste was disposed of.

6. If a man did not deal with the problem, this eventually became known because the bugs migrated into clothes and onto any piece of furniture on which people spent time. Thus visitors to an infested house would be bitten by bedbugs while sitting on chairs and hammocks too. Though nobody would openly acknowledge having a bedbug infestation (it was embarrassing), periodically word got around Kpuawala during evening gossip sessions. Someone would report having been bitten by bedbugs while visiting so-and-so in his house, or while lying in his hammock in the meeting place, and people thus forewarned would tactfully find ways not to sit where they might be bitten.

7. Historically, *puubla* were fair-skinned Europeans from "beyond the sea" (*njie woma*), especially traders and British Protectorate and colonial officers, but the term has come to encompass a whole range of outsiders, including African-American Peace Corps volunteers.

8. On this topic and its implications for women's powers, see Abu-Lughod (1985).

9. On women dismantling tents and beds among the Tuareg, see Labelle Prussin (1996: 78–93).

10. My surprise was of course a reflection of my own naïveté in construing rural Sierra Leonean life as devoid of such reminders of cosmopolitan, urban living. By contrast, there is a long history documenting the interpenetration between these dimensions in this region of the Atlantic world. In the eighteenth century, Matthews wrote of his surprise in visiting a chief on the Sierra Leonean coast and being put up in a house that was built in European style and furnished with expensive, fashionable imports from England including valuable silverware (1788).

11. *Kaamɔ* is the title given to Qur'anic teachers, but it has also come to include all teachers, including masters in a craft, such as carpenters or taylors. In Kpuawala I also heard the term used in connection with the relationship between a woman and her husband (the husband being the *kaamɔ*), and the joking context in which this was done had sexual overtones. Thus *kaamɔ* is someone who has taught one (from *kaa*, to learn) in subjects ranging from literacy to sex, and who has had more generally a role in "training" one for life, and as a result is in a position of hierarchical superiority with respect to his pupil. A *kaamɔ*'s curse was deemed worse than a father's in Kpuawala. Though women could train people in various skills, I have heard them addressed as *kaamɔ* only in the (rare) cases where they were Qur'anic teachers.

12. The project was the Bo-Pujehun Rural Development Project (or the Bo-Pujehun Project, as it was known), a joint venture run by the Sierra Leonean government and the German GTZ, which funded it. Throughout the 1980s, the Bo-Pujehun project oversaw most development activities in the Bo and Pujehun Districts. With the onset of civil war in 1991, it lost most of its assets and eventually closed down.

13. Gbesse is a Mende "twin name." It is given to both males and females who either are third in a set of triplets or are born after a pair of twins. Gbesse's given name was Mohammed, but it was never used to address him in Kpuawala.

14. By contrast, Ambulai's choice of a Muslim religious training for his son involved different expectations and opportunities. Qur'anic teachers did not charge fees but, rather, relied on their pupils' farming labor while they lived with them. The rewards to parents came in the form of religious blessing (*baraka*) and the fact that a *kaamɔ* was a lifelong mentor, as opposed to a paid schoolteacher. On Qur'anic schooling in West Africa and its integration into a more holistic "work discipline" and training ethos, see Saul (1984). Bledsoe (1986) also discusses the extension of this ethos to Western schooling.

15. The new town chief was a close political ally of the Paramount Chief and lived in the neighboring compound.

16. Lamin, Mami's husband, also had such a reputation for litigiousness that he was known in Kpuawala as "*Lamin kɔti*," or "law court." During the 1986 general elections, he sided with his relatives—the Paramount Chief and his brother—and this provided an opportunity for his enemies in Kpuawala to expel him from town, thus indirectly supporting his wife's efforts to make a final break with him.

17. Massa's sympathetic dealings with her co-wife were due in part to the fact that she too had "brought her hand" to this marriage arrangement (*loko wili*); that is, she had been involved in the decisions and negotiations that linked Hawa to the Kamara *mawɛɛ*. Massa often stated that she liked her co-wife and that she agreed with her husband's choice of Hawa. Many Kpuawala men consulted their senior wives about their plans to marry another woman, and some even said they preferred to send them as intermediaries to the families, to smooth the way for their own proposal. They explained that it was important for co-wives to get along and that the senior one needed to convey her approval so that a future junior wife's family would be reassured of her well-being. Finally, a husband needed his wife's labor to gather the resources for initiating and marrying another woman, and this was often withheld if she did not approve of his decision.

18. *Sowɛi* is the Mende name for the Sande society's most senior women, for its female ancestral spirits, and for the masquerade topped by a blackened, carved wooden headpiece that appears in public at some of the society's functions or for entertainment.

19. Note that the potential closeness among co-wives is marked by the Mende term for co-wife, *mbaa nyaha*, which includes the generic term of address used among women for close female friends (*mbaa*).

20. When disputes and misunderstandings arose among women in the big house, these were first addressed "under its eaves" (*pɛɛ wai bu*), rather than "at the feet" (*ngi gɔwɔ bu*) of the *mawɛɛ's* head. When Sebatu and Mama Kɔɔ did not get along together in their cooking hut, Mariama (who was the former's mother, the latter's mother-in-law, and the senior wife of the *mawɛɛ's* head) tried to resolve their differences. When she failed to do so, she called for a senior male elder to "bring his hand" to the mediation effort, all along expressing her embarrassment in having to do so, because women "should be able to take care of these things themselves." Thus the big house had not only its own code of solidarity and sociality but also its own hierarchy. This was not uncontested. As we have seen, the main reason why Mariama did not get along with Kema was that she resented the latter's leadership role in big house affairs.

21. The big houses in Kpuawala were locked at night on the inside with a metal or wooden latch, and though most could also be secured with a padlock on the outside, padlocks were reserved for individual (usually male) sleeping quarters and storage rooms, where valuable *mawɛɛ* property was stored. It would have been impossible to keep track of a key in the big house, with so many people constantly coming and going. If women wanted to keep valuable property with them in the big house, they procured themselves a *sɔboxi*, a wooden trunk, and locked that.

22. In the 1890s, Travelling District Commissioner Alldridge characterized "Upper Mendi" settlements as "closely packed towns" where buildings were crammed together, and paths between them difficult to follow, for defensive pur-

poses (1901: 288). Alldridge's photographs support the argument that houses were mostly round (Ibid., facing 136, 217), and that more open settlement plans and square or rectangular buildings became common only in the colonial period, often as a result of government construction projects—the building of police barracks, government rest houses, towns and housing along the railway, and so on (see also Harvey 1969: 64; Little 1951: 67–68; Migeod 1926: 123, 131, 142). Another feature introduced by European traders, missionaries, and administrators was the separation of living quarters from kitchens to reduce the danger of fires. This arrangement is now the prevalent one throughout rural and urban Sierra Leone.

23. Houses belonging to cults, such as Sande houses, also tended to be single-roomed, and if they were inhabited at all, it was only by senior members within the particular sodality.

24. *Nya ye kohu* ("the place inside which I live"), as opposed to *nya wɛɛ* (my house."

25. Though all Kpuawala *mawɛɛsia* were headed by a senior man, in some circumstances female kin and senior wives could take on this role. However, when they did so, it was usually specifically as stand-ins for brothers or husbands. Thus they did not challenge the "maleness" of this office, though there is evidence that this is not the case elsewhere in Sierra Leone (MacCormack 1977).

26. The disparity between the two wards, in terms both of area covered and of population, is visibly mapped in figure 3, where buildings drawn as solid black geometric forms belong to Gbangoya, while Buima comprises all the remaining, outlined, buildings.

27. See Richards (1996b) for a discussion of the long-term sociocultural implications of this history.

28. Vestiges of this history are recognizable in the language of kinship and marriage noted in Chapter 3, and of dependence and "ownership" of persons and their labor, that permeate relations among contemporary rural Mende, as we shall see.

29. In one Kpuawala *mawɛɛ* without a big house, women and children occupied an ordinary bedroom at the back of the residence where its senior men—two brothers—lived. This association of female residential quarters with the back of houses is widespread in Sierra Leone and in neighboring areas (see Jackson 1977; Littlejohn 1967). In their analyses, Jackson and Littlejohn relate these features to cosmologies where front is linked with public, male domains, and back is linked with domestic areas more closely associated with female productive and reproductive roles and with physiological processes of waste and rebirth.

CHAPTER 5

1. In this literature, the debates have focused on whether women's access to prominent public offices is linked to features of social organization such as exclusive initiation societies and matrilineal descent or to historical contingencies such as the weakening of political rule under colonialism. See, in particular, Abraham (1976, 1978) and Hoffer (1972, 1974). For an assessment of and contribution to this debate, see Day (1994: 481–484).

2. On the centrality of idioms of bodily expansiveness to African political discourse, see, for example, Bayart (1993: 60–86) and Price (1979). For a comparative perspective on this issue, see Godelier (1986: 162–188) and Sahlins (1963).

3. In some societies, this notion also translates into practices of bodily enlargement. Through deliberate fattening or enforced immobility, high-ranking people actually attain a larger size than most ordinary people, thus creating a visible sense of wonder (see Handy et al. 1965; Popenoe 1997). Popenoe's focus on female fattening in Niger also addresses the link among this practice, sexuality, and fertility. Indeed, the bulk of writing about the practice of fattening in relation to women centers not so much on questions of political power and office as on fertility and sexuality. For a sample of this literature in the same general region as my own research, see Paulme (1952) and MacCormack (1982).

4. Thus I agree with Murphy's analysis of the Mende sublime but move beyond his focus on the intentions of social actors in the deployment of *kabande*, to examine the negative potential—the unintended ways in which the very same systemic configurations of this idiom of power can lead to its collapse.

5. Whereas chiefly "eyes" and representatives act openly and legitimately on their leader's behalf, spies, or "shadow people" (*nɛnɛmɔ*), do so surreptitiously. In Kpuawala, election time and political tensions in the chiefdom were marked by an increased concern among residents about the likelihood that particular starngers or longstanding residents might be spying for local authorities.

6. There was and continues to be in Wunde an exposure to foreign rule by other West Africans, such as the Paramount Chief's Mandingo ruling lineage. But this is an instance of rule by a multilingual regional elite who has maintained strong ties in the Sierra Leone–Liberia–Guinea border region for at least a century and has intermarried in Mendeland over several generations.

7. The same respect and honor is accorded to newly initiated members of both Sande and Poro societies, who are called *maha ninɛi*, new chiefs. Like chiefs, initiates are carried back to town for the final ceremonies on other members' backs, under a canopy of locally woven cotton cloth (*kɔndi gulɛi*) or with umbrellas held above them.

8. Thus opponents of the Wunde Paramount Chief spoke about deposing him in terms of "taking the staff from his hands" (*a mu kɔlɔ gbua ngi yeya*).

9. Throughout the 1880s, Mende and Sherbro warlords fought a series of wars that were detrimental to trade in the Colony—which at that time comprised little more than the Freetown peninsula and a narrow contiguous strip along the Atlantic coast. Another source of concern for the British administration was the periodic disputes with Liberia and France over respective spheres of interests in the Sierra Leone hinterland (Fyfe 1962: 417–418). These factors induced the British to establish a protectorate in the territories adjoining the Colony, and thus formalize links that during the preceding century had been of an informal nature (cf. Abraham 1978: 80–111).

10. The choice of Qur'anic passages for this process is appropriate to a client's specific concerns. For example, one Muslim diviner and medicinal specialist in Kpuawala used the 106th *surah*, the Qureish, for clients seeking protection against evil spirits—a topic central to the passage, which is about God's protection being extended to the Prophet Mohammed's lineage. For people seeking a

positive outcome for something (a courtship, a harvest, etc.), he often used the *surah* of "help," the 110th; and so on. In each case, words that address a particular issue (protection, help and success) are written a prescribed number of times (as many as 1,111) on a wooden board and washed off. The water used to dilute the words and make them disappear is then imbibed by the client, in order to make things happen in the world. The fact that most work on charms and medicines had to be done at night to be effective added another dimension to this: it was the acts performed in the concealment and solitude of night that were most effective for making things happen during the day.

11. Londo was a favorite name for elders in the women's Sande society and for their masquerades (see Phillips 1995). On an event in which the ability to silence was central to the management of power, see Ferme (1994: 33).

12. Ndawa was a thorn in the side of British trading concerns, because in the 1880s the fighting in which he participated resulted in trade blockades that interrupted links between the interior and the coast near the Liberian border (cf. Abraham 1978: 85–89).

13. See, for example, Mukerji 1983 on the historical relationship between cloth production, trade, and consumption and the rise of merchant capital and the Industrial Revolution in Europe, and on the role of cloth in European imperialist expansion into South Asia, Africa, and elsewhere. Hollander (1975) analyzes the place of drapery and abundant cloth in the conspicuous display of wealth and power in European painting.

14. Mende takes this word from Sierra Leonean Krio. The term is originally Yoruba, from *aʃɔ*, "clothes," and *ɛbi*, "blood relations" (Fyle and Jones 1980: 15). Indeed, throughout Sierra Leone, different levels of "relatedness" are expressed on particular occasions—by kin groups, regional associations, clubs, church groups, chiefdom delegations, and so on—by wearing clothes made from the same bolt of fabric. But the genesis of this form of public display is also linked to the use of uniforms in colonial military and police forces, as well as in schools.

15. This is the opposite of the effects of the circulating "fame" and reputation of owners of important Kula valuables discussed by Munn in the Trobriands. There the names of owners of particularly valued shells remain associated with the objects and the events in which these change hands even after many years and circuitous ownership paths (see Munn 1986).

16. For a cultural and historical analysis of uniforms and clothes, particularly in relation to colonialism and consciousness, see Cohn (1996: Ch. 5) and Comaroff and Comaroff (1992).

17. Bockari's statement was consistent with studies of credit patterns in the region, which showed that farmers with relatively large households defaulted on loan repayments more often than poorer farmers. Most borrowing (up to 50% or so) was done for household subsistence during the hungry season or for ceremonial occasions (such as funerals and initiations), and these factors affected those with many dependents more than others (cf. Johnny 1985: 116). As we have seen in Chapter 3, failure to contribute to expenses for funerals and other rituals could cause serious conflicts among in-laws. The notion of "wealth-in-people" expressed by Bockari has been prominent in the literature on African political

economy (cf. Bledsoe 1980; Hart 1982: 23, 36–40; Hopkins 1973: 15; Meillassoux 1981).

18. Like many other languages, the Mende tongue uses the same word, *nyaha*, for "wife" and "woman," whereas "man" (*hindo*) is distinguished from "husband" (*hinɛi*).

19. *Jifa ina koimei i lo pɛɛla, ndoi ii humbu a wua.*

20. This use for medicinal purposes of water that had been in contact with Qur'anic verses further strengthens the symbolic juxtaposition of delivering words (or writing) and people. However, as I pointed out earlier in this chapter, *nɛsi* has applications in a broad range of physical and spiritual ailments beyond the realm of reproduction.

21. Such practices are also widespread in Sierra Leone as a whole. Thus Littlejohn reported that among the northern Temne, "the body is closed off like farms and houses; all space being penetrable by evil, that occupied by the body is no different from any other. . . . witches and demons can penetrate the body. A type of *Kanta* for closing the body which is popular among women is this: appropriate exorcising sentences from the Koran are written on a writing board and washed off into a bucket of water, used for lustration" (Littlejohn 1963: 8).

22. *Muaa hinga, mu gomɛ hale hindahu, mu bɛ hɔndɔ yila, hu ya lun!! Wua, wu wu nda hale nyanima, sɔlɛ ji wu piema.*

23. As mentioned earlier, the urgency of policing women's bodily boundaries had to do with the concern that a body emptied of healthy and life-sustaining substances might be open for occupation by witch spirits. Indeed, one of the most serious insults against an adult, circumcised woman was to refer to her as being "empty" (*ngi wopongɔ*). That this was an insult suggests that some kind of fullness was a requirement for being held in respect—and certainly for become a big person. By contrast, the idiom about male bodies, sexuality, and reproductive capacities did not emphasize dangerous openings and emptiness, nor was concern expressed about the uncontrolled loss of substances.

24. See Boddy (1989) for a study of analogous concerns with the symbolism of bodily—and social—enclosure in female pharaonic circumcision in the Sudan. There is a large, critical feminist literature on female genital mutilation, including Koso-Thomas (1987), on such practices in Sierra Leone. However, this literature seldom moves beyond the analysis of excision and other forms of genital mutilation in ideological terms. Understanding the cultural forms and historical context of these practices is essential to devising strategies for their eradication that might have a chance to succeed.

25. Paul Richards argued that there are parallels between initiation and the techniques of forced conscription of child fighters in the Sierra Leone civil war (1996b). One might add that the tattooing of these forced conscripts, in order to prevent their defection, also has a parallel in the bodily scarification that accompanies initiation.

26. The case had international exposure as well. In August 1990, the weekly *West Africa* reported that the defendant and five other accomplices had been sentenced to death for "the murder of a young woman for ritual purposes" (*West Africa* 1990: 2290).

27. See Chapter 3, especially notes 5 and 19, for a discussion of the coexisting tensions and intimacies that characterize this relationship in the historical context of slavery. More generally, the place of the mother's brother–sister's child relationship is a classic theme in the anthropology of Africa and in kinship studies, where the ambivalence and ambiguity of this relationship have been linked to the contradictory interests of kin and marriage groups in certain residential configurations, or to specific problems in social structure (see Kuper 1977: 174–188; Richards 1950).

28. This emphasis on literally *locating* power and outlining its boundaries is echoed in the pervasiveness of locatives in Mende language concerning the sociocultural order (cf. Murphy 1990: 27–28).

INTERLUDE 3

1. *Gani* is the name both of the meal and the occasion when Sande initiates first appear in public after their seclusion in the Sande enclosure, the *kpanguima*. For a detailed discussion of this and other aspects of Sande initiation, see Ferme (1994).

2. *Sande gbua* or "the pulling out of Sande," is the occasion that marks the end of an initiation, when the new initiates return to the community.

3. See Boone (1986: 18–23, 63–65, 119) for the contexts in which these substances are used by women and for the specific associations between Sande and clay, as well as "whiteness" in general (cloth, cotton, etc.).

4. However, this is not generally the case in this region. In particular, see Leopold (1983) for a comparative study of the shared metaphorical significance of white clay for Sande and Poro.

5. Martin (1988) analyzes for coastal Nigeria the relationship between this gendered shift in the trade of oil palm products and anticolonial resistance, including the "women's riot" of 1929 (see Martin 1988: 106–118).

CHAPTER 6

1. For example, Ariès points out that from at least the sixteenth century until the eighteenth, school children as young as five were armed. The historian's evidence comes from town edicts and school rules seeking to regulate the practice of children carrying weapons into schools (Ariès 1962: 315–316). Thus in Europe the social construction of an innocent childhood set apart from adulthood is coextensive with the development of a regimented schooling system and other disciplinary practices involving children. With regard to Mende ideas about disciplining and schooling the young in different settings, Bledsoe (1990) has pointed out that physical and psychological harshness is thought important to the proper training of children and is at the core of the widespread practice of sending them away in fosterage. However, the apparently callous treatment of children, especially foster children, by Mende adults may be more than a strategy to ensure a disciplined upbringing—and hence success in life. It may, as we shall see, bespeak a real uncertainty about how this life will turn out, and when it might end.

2. The term, *beforelife*, is used by A. Gottlieb with reference to the Beng of Côte d'Ivoire, in connection with their belief that babies are reincarnations of dead people and hence have a rich spiritual life preceding and following birth (Gottlieb 1998). Related beliefs exist elsewhere in West Africa. In Nigeria certain babies are thought to be prone to early death because they reincarnate other prematurely deceased infants (see Okri 1991; Palau Marti 1973: 324). Though reincarnation as such is not part of Mende cosmology, one finds here the belief that children, and infants in particular, have special links to the spirit world from which they have only recently arrived (e.g., Gittins 1987:89–90). In particular, Mende ideas about the links between the dead and their living namesakes seem to follow patterns more common in the Bantu world, where the dead are reincarnated only "in name" in their living *ngudi*, or namesakes (for example, among the Luba of Congo), with whom homonymy implies only a special protection and contiguity, or "doubleness," rather than actual reincarnation (de Heusch 1973: 235).

3. Hofstra (1940: 180–187) analyzed the relationship between grief and its social expression in different forms of Mende mourning but did not address the context of child deaths.

4. As elsewhere in West Africa, the numbers three (female) and four (male) have a gendered valence in the Upper Guinea Coast region (see Gibbs 1965; Sawyerr and Todd 1970). In other West African cases, the connotation is reversed, the three being the masculine number, whereas four has feminine associations (e.g., Calame-Griaule 1987: 33; Griaule 1965). In the mid–1980s, naming ceremonies in Kpuawala took place about a week after birth, but I was told that this was a Muslim practice and that "long ago" this ceremony would have taken place three days after birth for a girl, four days after birth for a boy. At the end of this ceremony, before partitioning the sacrificial food among the baby's maternal and paternal relatives, the namesake would press four 10-cent coins in the infant's right hand if he was a boy, three if a girl. By the 1990s, coins had been replaced by small-denomination paper currency in the appropriate number of banknotes.

5. The significance of grandparents as the borderline generation, the most senior to be recognized and respected through specified identification, is underscored by the fact that grandfather (*maada*) and grandmother (*mama*) are the terms of address for a chief, the highest political office at the local level.

6. Kenneth Little noted the significance of the fact that "terms analogous to 'family' and 'lineage' play a relatively small part in social identification" in Mende (Little 1951: 108), by comparison to more heterogeneous units including non-kin relatives within a limited generational span.

7. In the Mande epic of Sundiata, this mythic founder of the Mali empire was portrayed sometimes as a hunchback and in any case as a cripple. This sets an important precedent for the link between physical deformity and unusual, heroic powers in this region, which might account for Moiforay's treatment ranging from the deferential to the discriminatory (see Innes 1974).

8. Most people in Kpuawala considered three butter cups of rice to be the minimum required for the *kuima mbɛi*.

9. Note that resemblance in appearance between a plant or animal variety and its *tɔmaseli* also varies. Domestic cows and bush cows were thought to

resemble each other, whereas the two spinach varieties were different in appearance and dimensions. Instead, women mentioned the fact that they both spread through rhizomes as a shared feature of these spinach varieties.

10. The relationship between secrecy, or acts of concealment, and the visible has been explored in literary and psychoanalytic writings. Edgar Alan Poe's story "The Purloined Letter" was about a stolen letter that was concealed by being left in plain view, hanging in front of the fireplace in a public room. In "The Pattern in the Carpet," Henry James wrote about a visible yet unseen pattern. In their search for the uncanny in the familiar, psychoanalysts have long used these texts to explore by analogy how concealment works by familiarizing to the point of invisibility, rather than by removing an object altogether from consciousness and perception (e.g., Lacan 1991: 191–205).

11. In some cases, the shift from one to the other member of the paired relationship operates through language. In a study of the Yoruba-related Sabe of Dahomey (Benin), Palau Marti emphasized the importance of enunciating the proper, less widely known names (*eéki*) of plants, as opposed to their common names (*eéko*), in order to activate their healing powers. In a similar vein, successful hunters were those who knew the "other" names of animals and thus lured them to their deaths by calling them (Palau Marti 1973: 325). De Heusch has suggested that the relationship between these two name categories parallels that of being to appearance (de Heusch 1973: 236).

12. In a study of village-forest relations in Brahmanic ideology, Charles Malamoud showed that the Sanskrit word for "forest" derives from the word for "strange," which in turn shares the same root as the Latin *alius* and *alter* (Malamoud 1976). Hence the notion of forest as alterity—as the site of doubles for the familiar, domesticated village world.

13. However, live triplets were so rare that most people named Gbesse in Kpuawala were said to be born after twins. Indeed, Gittins (1987: 173) omits the possibility that Gbesse might be a member of triplets. In any case, what is consistent across Mendeland is the fact that Gbesse is considered a twin and hence an integral part of that paired relationship.

14. Gittins referred to "single" twins as *ngila-vele*, literally "one-two," to distinguish such a "pair" from the *felanga* (plural) used for live twins (Gittins 1987: 176). For his informants, single births resulted from the more powerful sibling "eating"—killing—the other. Thus single twins were seen as more powerful than those who belonged to a surviving pair, because the latter had to be roughly equals. In the Wunde region, people did not make the distinction between different categories of twins: all were called *felanga*.

CONCLUSION

1. Mende ethnogenesis has been the subject of historical debates. In European and other foreign archives, the name *Mende* did not refer to an ethnic group prior to the nineteenth century. These sources, as well as local oral histories, suggest that this relatively recent identification encompasses disparate groups brought together by successive waves of migrations from the North (see d'Azevedo 1962; Fyfe 1962: 119; Rodney 1970: 39–70).

2. Journalist and writer Robert Kaplan wrote an influential piece with echoes in the scholarly literature and international policy circles (1994; on its reception, see Richards 1996b: XIII-XX). Richards's book about the Sierra Leone civil war (1996b) was written largely to refute the "New Barbarism thesis," as the author calls it, of which works like Kaplan's were an example.

3. I have argued elsewhere that the inheritance of cultural forms that shape the practices and visions of a moral community makes itself felt even when a particular legacy is being subverted (Ferme 1999). On the interpretation of ritual as a site of reproduction versus subversion and historical transformation, see Comaroff and Comaroff (1993) and Turner (1967).

4. Although the Portuguese considered that Africans gave false (religious) values to made objects, they later proceeded to objectify humans as trade and cargo in ways that contradicted the very Christian principles that supposedly placed them above their human property. But they also more or less consciously participated in opening new routes for the discursive and material circulation of fetishes, increasing their potential as sites of cultural creativity and of the historical renewal of collective memories (see Pietz 1985; 1987; 1988).

5. The O.A.U. time was a reference to the expenditures linked with Sierra Leone's role as host country for the 1980 meeting of the Organization of African Unity (see Zack-Williams 1989). The A.P.C., or All People's Congress, was the ruling party in Sierra Leone for most of the 1970s and 1980s—a period marked by the dramatic deterioration of the country's economy and state services.

References

Abdullah, Ibrahim
   1997   "Bush Path to Destruction: The Origin and Character of the Revolutionary United Front (RUF/SL)." *Africa Development* 22(3/4): 45–76.

Abraham, Arthur
   1976   *Topics in Sierra Leone History: A Counter-Colonial Interpretation.* Freetown: Leone Publishers.

   1978   *Mende Government and Politics under Colonial Rule: A Historical Study of Political Change in Sierra Leone, 1890–1937.* Freetown: Sierra Leone University Press.

Abraham, Arthur and Habib Sesay
   1993   "Regional Politics and Social Services Provision since Independence." In *The State and the Provision of Social Services in Sierra Leone since Independence, 1961–1991,* edited by C. Magbaily Fyle. Dakar, Senegal: Codesria Book Series.

Abrahams, R. G.
   1972   "Spirits, Twins, and Ashes in Labwor, Northern Uganda." In *The Interpretation of Ritual: Essays in Honor of A. I. Richards,* edited by Jean S. La Fontaine. London: Tavistock.

Abu-Lughod, Lila
   1985   "A Community of Secrets: The Separate World of Bedouin Women." *Signs: Journal of Women in Culture and Society* 10:637–57.

   1990   "The Romance of Resistance: Tracing Transformations of Power through Bedouin Women." *American Ethnologist* 17 (1):41–55.

Adams, M. J.
   1980   Introduction. *Ethnologische Zeitschrift* (Zürich) 1:9–12.

Addison, W.
1918   "The Palm Nut Tree (*Elaeis guineensis*) and Its Uses." *Sierra Leone Studies* (o.s.) 1:7–19.

Adorno, Theodor
1997   *Aesthetic Theory.* Edited by G. Adorno and R. Tiedemann. Minneapolis: University of Minnesota Press.

Alldridge, T. J.
1894   "Wanderings in the Hinterland of Sierra Leone." *The Geographical Journal* 4(2):123–140.
1901   *The Sherbro and Its Hinterland.* London: Macmillan.
1910   *A Transformed Colony. Sierra Leone: Its Progress, Peoples, Native Customs and Undeveloped Wealth.* Philadelphia, PA: Lippincott.

Amselle, Jean-Loup
1977   *Les Négociants de la Savane: Histoire et organisation sociale des Kooroko (Mali).* Paris: Éditions Anthropos.

Appadurai, Arjun
1986   "Introduction: Commodities and the Politics of Value." In *The Social Life of Things: Commodities in Cultural Perspective,* edited by A. Appadurai. Cambridge: Cambridge University Press.
1988   "Introduction: Place and Voice in Anthropological Theory." *Cultural Anthropology* 3 (1):16–20.
1998   *Modernity at Large: Cultural Dimensions of Globalization.* Minneapolis: University of Minnesota Press.

Apter, A.
1999   "IBB=419: Nigerian Democracy and the Politics of Illusion." In *Civil Society and the Political Imagination in Africa: Critical Perspectives,* edited by John Comaroff and Jean Comaroff. Chicago: University of Chicago Press.

Ardener, Edwin
1972   "Belief and the Problem of Women." In *The Interpretation of Ritual: Essays in Honor of A.I. Richards.* Edited by Jean S. La Fontaine. London: Tavistock.

Ariès, Philippe
1962   *Centuries of Childhood: A Social History of Family Life.* New York: Knopf.

Asad, Talal
1973   *Anthropology and the Colonial Encounter.* London: Ithaca Press.
1993   *Genealogies of Religion: Discipline and Reasons of Power in Christianity and Islam.* Baltimore: Johns Hopkins University Press.

Austin, J. L.
1962   *How to Do Things with Words.* Cambridge, MA: Harvard University Press.

Bachelard, Gaston
1964 [1958] *The Poetics of Space.* Translated by Maria Jolas. Boston: Orion Press.

Bakhtin, Mikhail
  1981   *The Dialogic Imagination.* Edited by M. Holquist. Translated by
              C. Emerson and M. Holquist. Austin: University of Texas Press.
Barber, Karin
  1982   "Popular Reactions to the Petro-Naira." *Journal of Modern
              African Studies* 20 (3):431–450.
Barnes, J. A.
  1949   "Measures of Divorce Frequency in Simple Societies." *Journal of
              the Royal Anthropological Institute* 79:37–62.
Barthes, Roland
  1967   *Système de la mode.* Paris: Éditions du Seuil.
Bataille, Georges
  1989 [1967] *The Accursed Share.* Vol. 1. Translated by R. Hurley. New York:
              Zone Books.
Bateson, Gregory
  1972   *Steps to an Ecology of Mind.* New York: Ballantine Books.
Bayart, Jean-François
  1993   *The State in Africa: The Politics of the Belly.* Translated by M.
              Harper, C. and E. Harrison. London: Longman.
Beattie, K. J.
  1915   *Human Leopards: An Account of Human Leopards before the
              Special Commission Court. With a Note on Sierra Leone, Past
              and Present.* London: Hugh Rees.
Bellman, Beryl
  1975   *Village of Curers and Assassins: On the Production of Fala
              Kpelle Cosmological Categories.* The Hague: Mouton.
  1980   "Masks, Societies, and Secrecy among the Fala Kpelle." *Ethnolo-
              gische Zeitschrift* (Zürich) 1:61–79.
  1981   "The Paradox of Secrecy." *Human Studies* 4:1–24.
  1984   *The Language of Secrecy: Symbols and Metaphors in Poro Ritual.*
              New Brunswick, NJ: Rutgers University Press.
Bender, Barbara, ed.
  1993   *Landscape: Politics and Perspectives.* Providence, RI, and
              Oxford: Berg.
Benjamin, Walter
  1969   "The Work of Art in the Age of Mechanical Reproduction." In
              Illuminations. New York: Schocken.
Bhabha, Homi K.
  1994   *The Location of Culture.* London: Routledge.
Binger, L. G.
  1892   *Du Niger au Golfe de Guinée par le pays de Kong et le Mossi
              (1887–1889).* 2 vols. Paris: Hachette.
Bledsoe, Caroline
  1980   *Women and Marriage in Kpelle Society.* Stanford, CA: Stanford
              University Press.
  1984   "The Political Use of Sande Ideology and Symbolism." *American
              Ethnologist* 11 (3):455–472.

1990   "No Success without Struggle: Social Mobility and Hardship for
                Foster Children in Sierra Leone." *Man* 25 (1):70–88.
Bledsoe, Caroline and Kenneth Robey
1986   "Arabic Literacy and Secrecy among the Mende of Sierra Leone."
                Man 21:202–26.
Bledsoe, Caroline H. and William Murphy
1980   "The Kpelle Negotiation of Marriage and Matrilateral Ties." In
                The Versatility of Kinship, edited by L. S. Cordell and S. Becker-
                man. San Francisco: Academic Press.
Blyden, E. W.
1872   Report on the Falaba Expedition, dated 26 March 1872 and
                addressed to J. Pope-Hennessy, Administrator-in-Chief of the
                Government of the West African Settlements, enclosed in *Dis-
                patch*, 110 CO 267/316.
Bockari, J.
1955   "The Derivation of Mende Names for the Months of the Year."
                Sierra Leone Studies (n.s.). 4:208–210.
Boddy, Janice
1989   *Wombs and Alien Spirits: Women, Men, and the Zar Cult in
                Northern Sudan.* Madison: University of Wisconsin Press.
Bohannan, Paul
1954   *Tiv Farm and Settlement.* London: H.M. Stationery Office.
Boone, Sylvia
1986   *Radiance from the Waters: Ideals of Feminine Beauty in Mende
                Art.* New Haven, CT: Yale University Press.
Bourdieu, Pierre
1979   *La Distinction: Critique sociale du jugement.* Paris: Les Éditions
                de Minuit.
1980   *Le Sens pratique.* Paris: Les Éditions de Minuit.
1990a   "La Domination masculine." *Actes de la recherche en sciences
                sociales.* 84:2–31.
1990b   *The Logic of Practice.* Translated by Richard Nice. Stanford, CA:
                Stanford University Press.
Bravmann, René
1983   *African Islam.* Washington, DC: Smithsonian Institution Press.
Breitborde, L. B.
1991   "City, Countryside and Kru Ethnicity." *Africa* 61(2):186–201.
Brooks, George
1980   "Kola Trade and State-Building: Upper Guinea Coast and
                Senegambia, 15th–17th Centuries." Working paper 38, African
                Studies Center, Boston University.
1993   *Landlords and Strangers: Ecology, Society, and Trade in Western
                Africa, 1000–1630.* Boulder, CO: Westview Press.
Burke, Timothy
1996   "Sunlight Soap Has Changed My Life: Hygiene, Commodifica-
                tion, and the Body in Colonial Zimbabwe." In *Clothing and Dif-*

ference: Embodied Identities in Colonial and Post-Colonial Africa, edited by Hildi Hendrickson. Durham, NC: Duke University Press.

Butler, Judith
1990   *Bodies That Matter*. New York: Routledge.

Butt-Thompson, Frederick William
1929   *West African Secret Societies: Their Organisations, Officials and Teaching*. London: H. F. & G. Witherby.

Calame-Griaule, Geneviève
1987   *Ethnologie et langage: La parole chez les Dogon*. Paris: Institut d'Ethnologie.

Canetti, Elias
1984 [1960] *Crowds and Power*. Translated by Carol Stewart. New York: Farrar, Straus & Giroux.

Carroll, Lewis
1981 [1865] *Alice's Adventures in Wonderland & Through the Looking Glass*. New York: Bantam Books.

Carsten, Janet and Stephen Hugh-Jones
1995   "Introduction." In *About the House: Lévi-Strauss and Beyond*, edited by J. Carsten and S. Hugh-Jones. New York: Cambridge University Press.

Cartry, Michel
1982   "From Village to Bush: An Essay on the Gourmantché of Gobnangou (Upper Volta)." In *Between Belief and Transgression: Structuralist Essays in Religion, History, and Myth*, edited by M. Izard and P. Smith. Chicago: University of Chicago Press.

Cashion, Gerald
1982   "Hunters of the Mande: A Behavioral Code and Worldview Derived from the Study of Their Folklore." 2 vols. Ph.D. dissertation. Indiana University.

Castoriadis, Cornelius
1987 [1975] *The Imaginary Institution of Society*. Translated by K. Blamey. Cambridge, MA: MIT Press.

Census of Sierra Leone
1986   *The Preliminary Report on the 1985 National Population Census of Sierra Leone*. Freetown: Sierra Leone Government Printing Office.

Certeau, Michel de
1970   *La Possession de Loudon*. Paris: Julliard.
1973   *L'Absent de l'histoire*. Liguge, France: Maison Meme.
1984   *The Practice of Everyday Life*. Translated by S. Rendell. Berkeley: University of California Press.
1988   *The Writing of History*. Translated by Tom Conley. New York: Columbia University Press.

Certeau, Michel de, Luce Giard and Pierre Mayol
1994   *Habiter, cuisiner*. L'Invention du quotidien. Vol. 2. Paris: Gallimard.

Chalmers, Sir David
    1899   *Report by Her Majesty's Commissioner and Correspondence on
                 the Subject of the Insurrection in the Sierra Leone Protectorate,
                 1898.* London: Her Majesty's Stationery Office.
Cisse, Youssouf
    1964   "Notes sur les société des chasseurs Malinké." *Journal de la
                 Société des Africanistes* 34 (2):175–226.
Clapham, Cristopher
    1976   *Liberia and Sierra Leone: An Essay in Comparative Politics.* New
                 York: Cambridge University Press.
Clarke, J. I., ed.
    1969   *Sierra Leone in Maps.* London: Hodder and Stoughton.
Clifford, James
    1988   *The Predicament of Culture: Twentieth-Century Ethnography,
                 Literature, and Art.* Cambridge, MA, and London: Harvard Uni-
                 versity Press.
    1992   "Spatial Practices: Fieldwork, Travel, and the Disciplining of
                 Anthropology," in *Anthropological Locations: Boundaries and
                 Grounds of a Field Science,* edited by A. Gupta and J. Ferguson.
                 Berkeley: University of California Press.
Cohen, A.
    1966   "Politics of the Kola Trade." *Africa* 36 (1):18–36.
    1971   "The Politics of Ritual Secrecy." *Man* 6:427–448.
    1981   *The Politics of Elite Culture: Explorations in the Dramaturgy of
                 Power in a Modern African Society.* Berkeley: University of Cali-
                 fornia Press.
Cohen, William and E. S. Atieno Odhiambo
    1989   *Siaya. The Historical Anthropology of an African Landscape.*
                 Athens: Ohio University Press.
Cohn, Bernard
    1989   "Cloth, Clothes, and Colonialism: India in the Nineteenth Cen-
                 tury." In *Cloth and Human Experience,* edited by Annette B.
                 Weiner and Jane Schneider. Washington, DC: Smithsonian Insti-
                 tution Press.
    1996   *Colonialism and Its Forms of Knowledge: The British in India.*
                 Princeton, NJ: Princeton University Press.
Collier, Jane and Sylvia Yanagisako
    1989   "Theory in Anthropology since Feminist Practice." *Critique of
                 Anthropology* 9 (2):27–38.
Comaroff, Jean
    1985   *Body of Power, Spirit of Resistance: The Culture and History of
                 a South African People.* Chicago: University of Chicago Press.
Comaroff, Jean and John L. Comaroff
    1991   Of Revelation and Revolution, Vol. 1. *Christianity, Colonialism,
                 and Consciousness in South Africa.* Chicago: University of
                 Chicago Press.

1993   Introduction to *Modernity and Its Malcontents: Ritual and Power in Postcolonial Africa*, edited by J. Comaroff and J. Comaroff. Chicago: University of Chicago Press.

1997   Of Revelation and Revolution. Vol. 2. *The Dialectics of Modernity on a South African Frontier*. Chicago: University of Chicago Press.

1999   "Occult Economies and the Violence of Abstraction: Notes from the South African Postcolony." *American Ethnologist* 26 (2): 279–303.

Comaroff, John

1980   "Bridewealth and the Control of Ambiguity in a Tswana Chiefdom." In *The Meaning of Marriage Payments*, edited by J. L. Comaroff. New York: Academic Press.

1982   "Dialectical Systems, History, and Anthropology: Units of Study and Questions of Theory." *The Journal of Southern African Studies* 8 (2):143–172.

1987   "*Sui Genderis:* Feminism, Kinship Theory, and Structural 'Domains.'" In *Gender and Kinship: Essays toward a Unified Analysis*, edited by Jane F. Collier and Sylvia J. Yanagisako. Stanford, CA: Stanford University Press.

1989   "Images of Empire, Contests of Conscience: Models of Colonial Domination in South Africa." *American Anthropologist* 16 (4): 661–685.

Comaroff, John and Jean Comaroff

1987   "The Madman and the Migrant: Work and Labor in the Historical Consciousness of a South African People." *American Ethnologist* 14 (2):191–209.

1992   *Ethnography and the Historical Imagination*, Boulder, CO: Westview Press.

Comaroff, John and Simon Roberts

1981   *Rules and Processes: The Cultural Logic of Dispute in an African Context*. Chicago: University of Chicago Press.

Cooper, Barbara

1997   "Gender, movement, and history: Social and spatial transformations in 20th century Maradi, Niger." *Environment and Planning D: Society and Space* 15:195–221.

Coronil, Fernando

1997   *The Magical State: Nature, Money, and Modernity in Venezuela*. Chicago: University of Chicago Press.

Cosentino, Donald

1982   *Defiant Maids and Stubborn Farmers. Tradition and Invention in Mende Story Performance*. Cambridge, England: Cambridge University Press.

1989   "Midnight Charters: Musa Wo and Mende Myths of Chaos." In *Creativity of Power: Cosmology and Action in African Societies*, edited by W. Arens and Ivan Karp. Washington, DC: Smithsonian Institution Press.

Crosby, K. H.
1937   "Polygamy in Mende Country." *Africa* 10 (3):249–264.
Curtin, Philip D.
1964   *The Image of Africa: British Ideas and Action, 1780–1850.* 2
              vols. Madison: University of Wisconsin Press.
1969   *The Atlantic Slave Trade: A Census.* Madison: University of Wis-
              consin Press.
Davis, A. Glyn and Paul Richards
1991   *Rain Forest in Mende Life: Resources and Subsistence Strategies
              in Rural Communities around the Gola North Forest Reserve
              (Sierra Leone).* London: United Kingdom Overseas Development
              Administration.
Day, Lynda R.
1988   *"The Female Chiefs of the Mende, 1885–1977: Tracing the Evo-
              lution of an Indigenous Political Institution."* Ph.D. dissertation.
              University of Wisconsin.
1994   "The Evolution of Female Chiefship during the Late Nineteenth-
              Century Wars of the Mende." *The International Journal of
              African Historical Studies* 25 (3):481–503.
D'Azevedo, Warren
1962   "Some Historical Problems in the Delineation of a Central West
              Atlantic Region." *Annals of the New York Academy of Sciences*
              96 (2):512–538.
1973   "Mask Makers and Myth in Western Liberia." In *Primitive Art
              and Society*, edited by A. Forge. New York: Oxford University
              Press.
1977   "The Setting of Gola Society and Culture: Some Theoretical
              Implications of Variation in Time and Space." *The Kroeber
              Anthropological Society Papers* 21:43–125.
de Heusch, Luc
1973   "Le Sorcier, le Père Tempels et les jumeaux mal venus." In *La
              Notion de personne en Afrique Noire.* Paris: L'Harmattan.
1987   "Heat, Physiology, and Cosmogony: Rites of Passage among the
              Thonga." In *Explorations in African Systems of Thought*, edited
              by Ivan Karp and Charles S. Bird. Washington, DC: Smithsonian
              Institution Press.
De Lillo, Don
1997   *Underworld.* New York: Scribner.
Delaney, Carol
1994   "Untangling the Meanings of Hair in Turkish Society." *Anthro-
              pological Quarterly* 67 (4):159–172.
Douglas, Mary
1956   "Animals in Lele Religious Symbolism." *Africa* 27 (1): 46–58.
Drewal, Henry J.
1988   "Performing the Other: Mami Wata Worship in West Africa."
              The Drama Review 33 (2):160–185.

Drucker-Brown, Susan
   1995   "Court and the Kola Nut: Wooing and Witnessing in Northern Ghana." *Journal of the Royal Anthropological Institute* 1: 129–143.

Eberl-Elber, Ralph
   1937   "Die Maske der Männerbunde in Sierra Leone." *Ethnos* 2: 38–46.

Edwards, Joanna
   1992   "The Sociological Significance and Uses of Mende Country Cloth." In *History, Design, and Craft in West African Strip-Woven Cloth: Papers Presented at a Symposium Organized by the National Museum of African Art, Smithsonian Institution, February 1988*. Washington, DC: National Museum of African Art.

Ekeh, Peter
   1975   "Colonialism and the Two Publics in Africa: A Theoretical Statement." *Comparative Studies in Society and History* 17:91–112.
   1990   "Social Anthropology and Two Contrasting Uses of Tribalism in Africa." *Comparative Studies in Society and History* 32 (4): 660–700.

Ekejiuba, Felicia
   1995   "Currency Instability and Social Payments among the Igbo of Eastern Nigeria, 1890–1990." In *Money Matters: Instability, Values and Social Payments in the Modern History of West African Communities*, edited by Jane I. Guyer. Portsmouth, NH: Heinemann.

Elias, Norbert
   1978   The History of Manners. Translated by E. Jephcott. New York: Pantheon Books.

Ellis, Stephen
   1999   *The Mask of Anarchy: The Destruction of Liberia and the Religious Dimension of an African Civil War*. London: Hurst.

Etienne, Mona
   1977   "Women and Men, Cloth and Colonization: The Transformation of Production-Distribution Relations among the Baule." *Cahiers d'Études Africaines* 17 (1): 41–64.

Evans-Pritchard, Edward E.
   1940   *The Nuer*. Oxford: Clarendon Press.
   1951   *Kinship and Marriage Among the Nuer*. Oxford: Clarendon Press.

Fabian, Johannes
   1983   *Time and the Other: How Anthropology Makes its Object*. New York: Columbia University Press.

Fairhead, James and Melissa Leach
   1996a   *Misreading the African Landscape: Society and Ecology in a Forest-Savanna Mosaic*. Cambridge, England: Cambridge University Press.

1996b   "Rethinking the Forest-Savanna Mosaic: Colonial Science and Its
                Relics in West Africa." In *The Lie of the Land: Challenging
                Received Wisdom on the African Environment*, edited by Melissa
                Leach and Robin Mearns. Oxford, England: James Currey and
                the International African Institute.

Fallers, L. A.
1957   "Some Determinants of Marriage Stability in Busoga: A Refor-
                mulation of Gluckman's Hypothesis." *Africa* 27 (2):106–123.

Feld, Steven and Keith H. Basso
1996   *Senses of Place*. Santa Fe, NM: School of American Research
                Advanced Seminar Series.

Feldman, Allen
1991   *Formations of Violence: The Narrative of the Body and Political
                Terror in Northern Ireland*. Chicago: University of Chicago Press.

Ferme, Mariane
1994   "What 'Alhaji Airplane' Saw in Mecca and What Happened
                When He Came Home." In *Syncretism/Anti-Syncretism: The Pol-
                itics of Religious Synthesis,* edited by C. Stewart and R. Shaw.
                London: Routledge.
1998   "The Violence of Numbers: Consensus, Competition, and the
                Negotiation of Disputes in Sierra Leone." *Cahiers d'Etudes
                Africaines* 150–152 (2-4):555–580.
1999   "Staging *Pôlitisi*: The Dialogics of Publicity and Secrecy in Sierra
                Leone." In *Civil Society and the Political Imagination in Africa*,
                edited by John L. Comaroff and Jean Comaroff. Chicago: Uni-
                versity of Chicago Press.

Ford, M.
1992   "Kola Production and Settlement Mobility among the Dan of
                Nimba, Liberia." *African Economic History* 20 (51):51–63.

Fortes, Meyer
1973   "On the Concept of the Person among the Tallensi." In *La
                Notion de personne en Afrique Noire*. Paris: L'Harmattan.

Foucault, Michel
1980   *Power/Knowledge*. New York: Pantheon Books.

Frake, Charles O.
1996   "Pleasant Places, Past Times, and Shattered Identity in Rural East
                Anglia." In *Senses of Place*, edited by Steven Feld and Keith H.
                Basso. Santa Fe, NM: School of American Research Advanced
                Seminar Series.

Freud, Sigmund
1965 [1938]   *The Psychopathology of Everyday Life* Translated by J. Stachey.
                New York: Norton.

Fyfe, Christopher
1962   *A History of Sierra Leone*. London: Oxford University Press.

Fyle, C. and E. Jones, eds.
1980   *A Krio-English Dictionary*. Oxford, England: Oxford University
                Press.

Garine, Igor de
1995   "Sociocultural Aspects of the Male Fattening Sessions among the
            Massa of Northern Cameroon." In *Social Aspects of Obesity*,
            edited by Igor de Garine and Nancy J. Pollock. Amsterdam: Gordon and Breach.
Geschiere, Peter
1997   *The Modernity of Witchcraft: Politics and the Occult in Postcolonial Africa.* Translated by Janet Roitman and Peter Geschiere.
            Charlottesville: University of Virginia Press.
Gibbs, James
1965   "The Kpelle of Liberia." In *Peoples of Africa*, edited by J. Gibbs.
            New York: Holt, Rinehart and Winston.
Giddens, Anthony
1984   *The Constitution of Society: Outline of the Theory of Structuration.* Berkeley: University of California Press.
Gilfoy, Peggy Stoltz
1992   "The Eye, the Hand, and the Stripe: North African Designs in
            West African Strip-Woven Textiles." In *History, Design, and
            Craft in West African Strip-Woven Cloth.* Washington, DC:
            National Museum of African Art.
Ginzburg, Carlo
1989   *Clues, Myths, and the Historical Method.* Translated by John
            Tedeschi and Anne T. Tedeschi. Baltimore, MD: Johns Hopkins
            University Press.
Girard, René
1972   *La Violence et le sacré.* Paris: Éditions Bernard Grasset.
Gittins, Anthony J.
1987   *Mende Religion: Aspects of Belief and Thought in Sierra Leone.*
            Studia Instituti Anthropos No. 41. Nettetal (Germany): Steyler
            Verlag-Wort und Werk.
Glissant, Edouard
1996   *Caribbean Discourse: Selected Essays.* Charlottesville: University
            of Virginia Press.
Gluckman, Max
1950   "Kinship and Marriage among the Lozi of Northern Rhodesia
            and the Zulu of Natal." In *African Systems of Kinship and Marriage*, edited by A. R. Radcliffe-Brown and D. Forde. London:
            Routledge and Kegan Paul.
Goddard, T. N.
1925   *The Handbook of Sierra Leone.* London: Grant Richards.
Godelier, Maurice
1986   *The Making of Great Men: Male Domination and Power among
            the New Guinea Baruya.* Cambridge, England: Cambridge University Press.
Goodwin, Jan
1999   "Sierra Leone Is No Place to Be Young." *The New York Times
            Magazine,* 14 February 1999.

Goody, Jack
1958   "The Fission and Fusion of Domestic Groups among the
            Lodagaba." In *The Developmental Cycle in Domestic Groups*,
            edited by Jack Goody. Cambridge, England: Cambridge Univer-
            sity Press.
Gottlieb, Alma
1998   "Do Infants Have Religion? The Spiritual Lives of Beng Babies."
            American Anthropologist 100 (1):122–135.
Grace, John
1975   *Domestic Slavery in West Africa. With Particular Reference to
            the Sierra Leone Protectorate, 1896–1927.* New York: Harper &
            Row.
1977   "Slavery and Emancipation among the Mende in Sierra Leone,
            1896–1928." In *Slavery in Africa: Historical and Anthropologi-
            cal Perspectives*, edited by S. Miers and I. Kopytoff. Madison:
            University of Wisconsin Press.
Griaule, Marcel
1965   *Conversations with Ogotemmeli.* London: Oxford University
            Press.
Grinker, Roy Richard
1994   *Houses in the Rain Forest. Ethnicity and Inequality among the
            Farmers and Foragers in Central Africa.* Berkeley: University of
            California Press.
Gudeman, S.
1990   *Colombian Conversations: The Domestic Economy in Life and
            Text.* Cambridge, England: Cambridge University Press.
Gupta, Akhil
1997   *Culture, Power, Place. Explorations in Critical Anthropology.*
            Edited by Akhil Gupta and James Ferguson. Durham, NC: Duke
            University Press.
Guyer, Jane
1981   "Household and Community in African Studies." *African Studies
            Review* 24 (2/3):87–137.
1994   "The Spatial Dimensions of Civil Society in Africa: An Anthro-
            pologist Looks at Nigeria." In *Civil Society and the State in
            Africa*, edited by J. W. Harbeson, D. Rothchild, and N. Chazan.
            Boulder, CO: Lynne Rienner Publishers.
Hale, Thomas
1998   *Griots and Griottes: Masters of Words and Music.* Bloomington:
            Indiana University Press.
Handy, E. S. C., et al.
1965   *Ancient Hawaiian Society.* (revised edition) Rutland, VT: Charles
            Tuttle.
Hardin, Kris L.
1993   *The Aesthetics of Action: Continuity and Change in a West
            African Town.* Washington, DC, and London: Smithsonian Insti-
            tution Press.

1996   "Technological Style and the Making of Culture: Three Kono
                Contexts of Production." In *African Material Culture*, edited by
                M. J. Arnoldi, C. M. Geary, and K. Hardin. Bloomington: Indi-
                ana University Press.

Harley, George W.
1950   *Masks as Agents of Social Control in Liberia*. Cambridge, MA:
                Papers of the Peabody Museum, Harvard University.

Harris, W.T. and Harry Sawyerr
1968   *The Springs of Mende Belief and Conduct*. Freetown: Sierra
                Leone University Press.

Hart, Keith
1982   *The Political Economy of West African Agriculture*. Cambridge,
                England: Cambridge University Press.

Harvey, J. I.
1969   "Rural House Types." In *Sierra Leone in Maps*, edited by John I.
                Clarke. London: Hodder and Stoughton.

Hendrickson, Hildi
1994   "'Long' Dress and the Construction of Herero Identities
                in Southern Africa." *African Studies Johannesburg* 53 (2):
                25–54.

1996   *Clothing and Difference: Embodied Identities in Colonial and
                Post-Colonial Africa*. Durham, NC: Duke University Press.

Hertz, Robert
1960 [1907] "A Contribution to the Study of the Collective Representation of
                Death." In *Death and the Right Hand*, translated by R. Needham
                and C. Needham. Aberdeen, Scotland: Cohen and West.

Hilger, Julia
1995   "The *Kanga*: An Example of East African Textile Design" In *The
                Art of African Textiles: Technology, Tradition and Lurex*, edited
                by J. Picton. London: Lund Humphries Publishers.

Hirsch, Eric and Michael O'Hanlon
1995   *The Anthropology of Landscape: Perspectives on Space and
                Place*. Oxford, England: Clarendon Press.

Hoffer, Carol P. (MacCormack)
1972   "Mende and Sherbro Women in High Office." *Canadian Journal
                of African Studies* 6 (2):151–164.

1974   "Madam Yoko: Ruler of the Kpa Mende Confederacy." In
                Woman, Culture, and Society, edited by M. Z. Rosaldo and L.
                Lamphere. Stanford, CA: Stanford University Press.

Hofstra, Sjoerd
1937   "The Social Significance of Palm Oil in the Life of the Mendi."
                Internationales Archiv für Ethnographie 34 (5–6):105–118.

1940   "The Ancestral Spirits of Mendi." *Internationales Archiv für
                Ethnographie* 39 (1–4):177–196.

1942   "The Belief Among the Mendi in Non-Ancestral Spirits, and Its
                Relation to a Case of Parricide." *Internationales Archiv für
                Ethnographie* 40 (5–6):175–183.

Hollander, Anne
   1975   *Seeing through Clothes*. New York: Avon Books.
Hommel, William Louis
   1981   "Form and Meaning of Masks in Three Mende Societies." Ph.D.
                 dissertation. Indiana University.
Hopkins, A. G.
   1973   *An Economic History of West Africa*. New York: Columbia Uni-
                 versity Press.
Horton, Robin
   1970   "African Traditional Thought and Western Science." In *Ratio-
                 nality*, edited by B. Wilson. Oxford, England: Oxford University
                 Press.
   1971   "Stateless Societies in the History of Western Africa." In *The His-
                 tory of West Africa*, edited by M. Crowder and J. F. Ade Ajayi.
                 London: Longman.
Hoskins, Janet
   1998   *Biographical Objects: How Things Tell the Stories of People's
                 Lives*. New York: Routledge.
Houlberg, Marylin
   1979   "Social Hair: Tradition and Change in Yoruba Hairstyles in
                 Southwestern Nigeria." In *The Fabrics of Culture. The Anthro-
                 pology of Clothing and Adornment*, edited by Justine M. Cord-
                 well and Ronald A. Schwarz. The Hague: Mouton.
Hugh-Jones, Christine
   1979   *From the Milk River: Spatial and Temporal Processes in North-
                 west Amazonia*. Cambridge, England: Cambridge University Press.
Human Rights Watch
   1999   *Getting Away with Murder, Mutilation, Rape: New Testimony
                 from Sierra Leone*. Report released on 24 June 1999. Available at
                 http: www.hrw.org.
Innes, Gordon
   1969   *A Mende-English Dictionary*. Cambridge, England: Cambridge
                 University Press.
   1974   *Sunjata, Three Mandinka Versions*. London: School of Oriental
                 and African Studies.
Irigaray, Lace
   1985   *This Sex Which Is not One*, translated by C. Porter with C.
                 Burke. Ithaca, NY: Cornell University Press.
Isaacman, Allen
   1996   *Cotton Is the Mother of Poverty: Peasants, Work, and Rural
                 Struggle in Colonial Mozambique, 1938–1961*. Portsmouth, NH:
                 Heinemann.
Isaacman, Allen and Richard Roberts, eds.
   1995   *Cotton, Colonialism, and Social History in Sub-Saharan Africa*.
                 Portsmouth, NH: Heinemann.
Ishige, Naomichi
   1995   "Evaluation of Fatness in Traditional Japanese Society." In *Social*

Aspects of Obesity, edited by Igor de Garine and Nancy J. Pollock. Amsterdam: Gordon and Breach Publishers.

Jackson, Michael
1977   *The Kuranko: Dimensions of Social Reality in a West African Society*. London: Hurst.
1989   *Paths toward a Clearing: Radical Empiricism and Ethnographic Enquiry*. Bloomington: Indiana University Press.
1997   *Minima Ethnographica: Intersubjectivity and the Anthropological Project*. Chicago: University of Chicago Press.

Jakobson, Roman and Morris Halle
1956   *Fundamentals of Language*. The Hague: Mouton.

Jedrej, M. C.
1980   "Structural Aspects of a West African Secret Society." *Ethnologische Zeitschrift* (Zurich) 1:133–142.

Johnny, Michael
1985   *Informal Credit for Integrated Rural Development in Sierra Leone*, Studien zur Integrierten Ländlichen Entwicklung No. 6, edited by H.-U. Thimm. Hamburg, Germany: Verlag Weltarchiv.

Johnny, Michael; John Karimu, and Paul Richards
1981   "Upland and Swamp Rice Farming Systems in Sierra Leone: The Social Context of Technological Change." *Africa* 51 (2):596–620.

Jones, Adam
1983   *From Slaves to Palm Kernels: A History of the Galinhas Country (West Africa), 1730–1890*. Wiesbaden, Germany: Steiner Verlag.

Junod, Henri
1936   *Moeurs et coutumes des Bantous. La vie d'une tribu sud-africaine.* 2 vols. Paris: Payot.

Kahn, Miriam
1996   "Your Place and Mine: Sharing Emotional Landscapes in Wamira, Papua New Guinea." In *Senses of Place*, edited by Steven Feld and Keith H. Basso. Santa Fe, NM: School of American Research Advanced Seminar Series.

Kaindaneh, Peter M.
1993   "State Provision of Transport and Communication Services in Sierra Leone." In *The State and the Provision of Social Services in Sierra Leone Since Independence, 1961–1991*, edited by C. Magbaily Fyle. Dakar, Senegal: Codesria Book Series.

Kalous, Milan
1974   *Cannibals and Tongo Players in Sierra Leone*. Auckland, New Zealand: Wright and Carman.

Kandeh, Jimmy
1992   "Politicization of Ethnic Identities in Sierra Leone." *African Studies Review* 35 (1):81–100.

Kant, Immanuel
1978 [1798] *Anthropology from a Pragmatic Point of View*. Translated by Victor L. Dowdell. Revised and edited by Hans H. Rudnick. Carbondale, IL: Southern Illinois University Press.

Kaplan, Robert
1994   "The Coming Anarchy: How Scarcity, Crime, Overpopulation
            and Disease are Rapidly Destroying the Social Fabric of our
            Planet." *Atlantic Monthly*, February 1994:44–76.
Karlström, Mikael
1996   "Imagining Democracy: Political Culture and Democratisation in
            Buganda." *Africa* 66 (4):485–505.
Kilson, Martin
1966   *Political Change in a West African State: A Study of the Modern-
            ization Process in Sierra Leone.* Cambridge, MA: Harvard Uni-
            versity Press.
Kopytoff, Igor
1986   "The Cultural Biography of Things: Commoditization as
            Process." In *The Social Life of Things: Commodities in Cultural
            Perspective*, edited by A. Appadurai. Cambridge, England: Cam-
            bridge University Press.
Koso-Thomas, Olayinka
1987   *Circumcision of Women: A Strategy for Eradication*, London:
            Zed Books.
Küchler, Susanne
1993   "Landscape as Memory: The Mapping of Process and Its Repre-
            sentation in a Melanesian Society." In *Landscape: Politics and
            Perspectives*, edited by Barbara Bender. Providence, RI: Berg.
Kup, Adam
1961   *A History of Sierra Leone, 1400–1787.* Cambridge, England:
            Cambridge University Press.
Kuper, Adam, ed.
1977   *The Social Anthropology of A. R. Radcliffe-Brown.* London:
            Routledge.
Labouret, Henri
1929   "La Parenté à plaisanteries en Afrique Occidentale." *Africa* 2
            (3):244–253.
Lacan, Jacques
1991   *The Seminar of Jacques Lacan*, edited by J.-A. Miller. Book II:
            *The Ego in Freud's Theory and in the Technique of Psychoanaly-
            sis 1954–1955*, translated by S. Tomaselli. New York: W.W.
            Norton & Co.
Laclau, Ernesto
1996   *Emancipation(s).* New York: Verso.
La Fontaine, Jean
1962   "Gisu Marriage and Affinal Relations." In *Marriage in Tribal
            Societies*, edited by M. Fortes. Cambridge, England: Cambridge
            University Press.
1977   "The Power of Rights." *Man* 12:421–437.
Lakoff, George and Mark Johnson
1980   *Metaphors We Live By.* Chicago and London: University of
            Chicago Press.

Lamb, Venice and Alastair Lamb
1984   *Sierra Leone Weaving*. Hertingfordbury, England: Roxford Books.
Lattas, Andrew
1998   *Cultures of Secrecy: Reinventing Race in Bush Kaliai Cargo Cults*. Madison: University of Wisconsin Press.
Leach, Edmund
1958   Magical Hair. *Man* 88:147–164.
1961   *Rethinking Anthropology*. London: Athlone Press.
Leach, Melissa
1989   "The Politics of Palm Oil in a Mende Village." *Africana Research Bulletin* 16:3–23.
1994   *Rainforest Relations: Gender and Resource Use among the Mende of Gola, Sierra Leone*. Edinburgh, Scotland: Edinburgh University Press.
Leopold, Robert S.
1983   "The Shaping of Men and the Making of Metaphors: The Meaning of White Clay in Poro and Sande Initiation Society Rituals." *Anthropology* 7 (2):21–42.
Levi, Giovanni
1988   *Inheriting Power: The Story of an Exorcist*. Chicago: University of Chicago Press.
1997   Introduction to *A History of Young People in the West*, Vol. I. *Ancient and Medieval Rites of Passage*, translated by Camille Naish. Edited by Giovanni Levi and Jean-Claude Schmitt. Cambridge, MA: Harvard University Press.
Lévi-Strauss, Claude
1966   *The Savage Mind*, translated from the French. Chicago: University of Chicago Press.
1969   *The Elementary Structures of Kinship*, translated by J. H. Bell and J. R. von Sturmer. Boston: Beacon Press.
1982 [1979] *The Way of the Masks*. Translated by S. Modelski. Seattle, WA: University of Washington Press.
Levtzion, Nehemia
1973   *Ancient Ghana and Mali*. London: Methuen.
Lewis, Roy
1954   *Sierra Leone: A Modern Portrait*. London: Her Majesty's Stationary Office.
Little, Kenneth
1948   "The Mende Farming Household." *The Sociological Review* 40 (4):37–56.
1949   "The Role of the Secret Society in Cultural Specialization." *American Anthropologist* 51:199–212.
1951   *The Mende of Sierra Leone: A West African People in Transition*. London: Routledge.
1965   "The Political Function of the Poro, Part I." *Africa* 35 (4): 349–365.
1966   "The Political Function of the Poro, Part II." *Africa* 36 (1):62–71.

Littlejohn, J.
1963   "Temne Space." *Anthropological Quarterly* 36 (1) :1–17.
1967   "The Temne House." In *Myth and Cosmos: Readings in Mythology and Symbolism*, edited by J. Middleton. Austin: University of Texas Press.

Lovejoy, Paul E.
1973   "The Kambarin Beriberi: The Formation of a Specialized Group of Hausa Kola Traders in the Nineteenth Century." *Journal of African History*, 14 (4):633–651.
1980   "Kola in the History of West Africa." *Cahiers d'Études Africaines* 20:97–134.

MacCormack, Carol P.
1975   "Sande Women and Political Power in Sierra Leone." *West African Journal of Sociology and Political Science* 1 (1):42–50.
1977   "The Compound Head: Structure and Strategies." *Africana Research Bulletin* 6 (4):44–64.
1979   "Sande: The Public Face of a Secret Society." In *The New Religions of Africa*, edited by B. Jules-Rosette. Norwood, NJ: Ablex Publishing Co.
1980   "Proto-Social to Adult: A Sherbro Transformation," in *Nature, Culture and Gender*, edited by C.P. MacCormack and M. Strathern. Cambridge: Cambridge University Press.
1982   "Ritual Fattening and Female Fertility." In *Folk Medicine and Health Culture: Role of Folk Medicine in Modern Health Care*, edited by. T. Vaskilampi and C. P. MacCormack. Kuopio, Finland: University of Kuopio Department of Community Health.
1983   "Human Leopards and Crocodiles: Political Meanings of Categorical Ambiguities." In *Ethnography of Cannibalism*, edited by P. Brown and D. Tuzin. Washington, DC: Society for Psychological Anthropology.

Malamoud, Charles
1976   "Village et forêt dans l'idéologie de l'Inde brahmanique." *Archives Européennes de Sociologie* 17:3–20.

Malcolm, J. M.
1939   "Mende Warfare." *Sierra Leone Studies* (o.s.) 21:47–52.

Marcus, George
1998   *Ethnography through Thick and Thin*. Princeton, NJ: Princeton University Press.

Martin, Susan M.
1988   *Palm Oil and Protest: An Economic History of the Ngwa Region, South-Eastern Nigeria, 1800–1980*. Cambridge, England: Cambridge University Press.

Matthews, John
1788   *A Voyage to the River Sierra Leone, on the Coast of Africa, Containing an Account of the Trade and Productions of the Country, and of the Civil and Religious Customs and Manners of the Peo-*

ple; In a Series of Letters to a Friend in England. London: B. White and Son (1966 reprint, London: Frank Cass).

Mauss, Marcel
1973   "Techniques of the Body." Translated by Ben Brewster. Economy and Society 2 (1):70–87.

Mbembe, Achille
1990   "Pouvoir, violence et accumulation." Politique Africaine 39: 7–24.
1992   "Provisional Notes on the Postcolony." Africa 62 (1):3–37.

McClintock, Anne
1995   Imperial Leather: Race, Gender and Sexuality in the Colonial Contest. New York and London: Routledge.

McKenzie, Glenn
1998   "Sierra Leone's Cult of Killers: Militiamen Tap into Belief that They're Invincible." San Francisco Chronicle, 8 December 1998.

McNaughton, Patrick R.
1979   "Secret Sculptures of the Komo: Art and Power in Bamana (Bambara) Initiation Associations." In Working Papers in the Traditional Arts No. 4. Philadelphia, PA: Institute for the Study of Human Issues.
1982   "The Shirts That Mande Hunters Wear." African Arts 15 (3):54.

Meillassoux, Claude
1981   Maidens, Meal and Money: Capitalism and the Domestic Community. Cambridge, England: Cambridge University Press.

Messick, Brinkley
1987   "Subordinate Discourse: Women, Weaving, and Gender Relations in North Africa." American Ethnologist 14:210–225.

Migeod, Frederick William Hugh
1926   A View of Sierra Leone. New York: Negro University Press.

Miller, Christopher
1990   Theories of Africans. Chicago: University of Chicago Press.

Miller, Daniel
1987   Material Culture and Mass Consumption. Oxford, England: Blackwell.
1998   "Coca-Cola: A black sweet drink from Trinidad." In Material Cultures. Why Some Things Matter. Chicago: University of Chicago Press.

Mitchell, P. K.
1989   "Trade Routes of the Early Sierra Leone Protectorate." Sierra Leone Studies 6:204–17.

Moore, Henrietta
1986   Space, Text and Gender: An Anthropological Study of the Marakwet of Kenya. Cambridge, England: Cambridge University Press.
1988   Feminism and Anthropology. Minneapolis: University of Minnesota Press.

Moran, Mary
  1995   "Warriers or Soldiers? Masculinity and Ritual Transvestism
              in the Liberian Civil War." In *Feminism, Nationalism, and
              Militarism*, edited by C. D. Sutton. Washington, DC: Association
              for Feminist Anthropology.

Morphy, Howard
  1993   "Colonialism, History, and the Construction of Place: The Poli-
              tics of Landscape in Northern Australia." In *Landscape: Politics
              and Perspectives*, edited by Barbara Bender. Providence, RI: Berg.

Moynihan, D. Patrick
  1998   *Secrecy: The American Experience*. New Haven, CT: Yale Uni-
              versity Press.

Muana, Patrick
  1997   "The Kamajoi Militia: Violence, Internal Displacement and the Pol-
              itics of Counter-Insurgency." *Africa Development* 22 (3/4):77–100.

Mukerji, Chandra
  1983   *From Graven Images: Patterns of Modern Materialism*. New
              York: Columbia University Press.

Munn, Nancy
  1973   *Walbiri Iconography: Graphic Representation and Cultural Sym-
              bolism in a Central Australian Society*. Ithaca, NY: Cornell Uni-
              versity Press.
  1977   "The Spatiotemporal Transformation of Gawa Canoes." *Journal
              de la Société des Océanistes* 33 (54/55):39–53.
  1986   *The Fame of Gawa: A Symbolic Study of Value Transformation
              in a Massim (Papua New Guinea) Society*. Cambridge, England:
              Cambridge University Press.

Muraro, Luisa
  1980   "Maglia o Uncinetto? Metafora e metonimia nella produzione
              simbolica." *Aut Aut* 175/176 (April): 59–85.

Murphy, William
  1980   "Secret Knowledge as Property and Power in Kpelle Society:
              Elders versus Youth." *Africa* 50:193–207.
  1981   "The Rhetorical Management of Dangerous Knowledge in
              Kpelle Brokerage." *American Ethnologist* 8 (4):667–685.
  1990   "Creating the Appearance of Consensus in Mende Political Dis-
              course." *American Anthropologist* 92 (1):24–41.
  1998   "The Sublime Dance of Mende Politics: Aesthetics of Charismatic
              Power." *American Ethnologist* 25 (4):563–82.

Murphy, William and Caroline Bledsoe
  1987   "Kinship and Territory in the History of a Kpelle Chiefdom
              (Liberia)." In *The African Frontier*, edited by I. Kopytoff. Bloom-
              ington: Indiana University Press.

Myers, Fred R.
  1991   *Pintupi Country, Pintupi Self: Sentiment, Place, and Politics
              among Western Desert Aborigines*. Berkeley: University of Cali-
              fornia Press.

N'Diaye, Samba
    1964   "Masques d'ancêtres de la société Poro de Sierra Léone." *Notes
                    Africaines* 103: 73–81.
Newton, Esther
    1972   *Mother Camp: Female Impersonators in America*. Chicago: Uni-
                    versity of Chicago Press.
Nielsen, Ruth
    1979   "The History and Development of Wax-Printed Textiles from
                    West Africa and Zaire." In *The Fabrics of Culture. The Anthro-
                    pology of Clothing and Adornment*, edited by Justine M. Cord-
                    well and Ronald A. Schwarz. The Hague: Mouton.
Nooter, Mary
    1993   *Secrecy: African Art That Conceals and Reveals*. New York:
                    Museum of African Art.
Nora, Pierre
    1984   *Les Lieux de mémoire*, Vol 1. La République. Paris: Gallimard.
Nordstrom, Caroline
    1995   "War on the Front Lines." In *Fieldwork under Fire: Contempo-
                    rary Studies of Violence and Survival*, edited by C. Nordstrom
                    and A. Robben. Berkeley: University of California Press.
Nunley, John W.
    1987   *Moving with the Face of the Devil: Art and Politics in Urban
                    West Africa*. Urbana: University of Illinois Press.
Nwaka, Geoffrey
    1978   "Secret Societies and Colonial Change: A Nigerian Example."
                    Cahiers d'Études Africaines 18 (1/2):187–200.
Ohnuko-Tierney, Emiko
    1993   *Rice as Self: Japanese Identities through Time*. Princeton, NJ:
                    Princeton University Press.
Okri, Ben
    1991   *The Famished Road*. New York: Doubleday.
Ortner, Sherry
    1996   Is Female to Male as Nature to Culture? In *Making Gender: The
                    Politics and Erotics of Culture*. Boston: Beacon Press.
Palau Marti, Montserrat
    1973   "Le nom et la personne chez les Sabé (Dahomey)." In *La notion
                    de personne en Afrique Noire*. Paris: L'Harmattan.
Paulme, Denise
    1952   "L'Initiation des jeunes filles en pays Kissi (Haute Guinée)." *Con-
                    ferencia Internacional das Africanistas* (Lisbon, 1947) 5 (Part II):
                    303–331.
Person, Yves
    1976   *Samori: La Renaissance de l'empire mandingue*. Paris: ABC.
Phillips, Ruth B.
    1978   "Masking in Mende Sande Society Initiation Rituals." *Africa* 48
                    (3):265–277.

1980   "The Iconography of the Mende Sowei Mask." *Ethnologische Zeitschrift* (Zürich) 1:113–132.
1995   *Representing Woman: Sande Masquerades of the Mende of Sierra Leone.* Los Angeles: UCLA Fowler Museum of Cultural History.

Picton, John
1995   "Technology, Tradition and Lurex: The Art of African Textiles" In *The Art of African Textiles: Technology, Tradition and Lurex*, edited by J. Picton. London: Lund Humphries Publishers.

Picton, John and John Mack
1979   *African Textiles: Looms, Weaving and Design.* London: British Museum Publications for the Trustees of the British Museum.

Pietz, William
1985   "The Problem of the Fetish, I." *Res* 9:5–17.
1987   "The Problem of the Fetish, II." *Res* 13:23–46.
1988   "The Problem of the Fetish, IIIa." *Res* 16:105–124.
1993   "Fetishism and Materialism: The Limits of Theory in Marx." In *Fetishism as Cultural Discourse*, edited by Emily Apter and William Pietz. Ithaca, NY: Cornell University Press.

Piot, Charles D.
1993   "Secrecy, Ambiguity, and the Everyday in Kabre Culture." *American Anthropologist* 95 (2):353–370.

Pipes, Daniel
1985   "Mawlas: Free Slaves and Converts in Early Islam." In *Slaves and Slavery in Muslim Africa*, edited by John Ralph Willlis. London: Frank Cass.

Popenoe, Rebecca C.
1997   "'Girls' Work Is Stomach Work:' Female Fatness, Sexuality, and Society among the Azawagh Arabs (Moors) of Niger." Ph.D. dissertation. University of Chicago.

Porter, Philip W.
1995   "A Note on Cotton and Climate: A Colonial Conundrum." In *Cotton, Colonialism, and Social History in Sub-Saharan Africa*, edited by A. Isaacman and R. Roberts. Portsmouth, NH: Heinemann.

Potash, Betty
1978   "Some Aspects of Marital Stability in a Rural Luo Community." *Africa* 48 (4):380–397.

Pratt, Mary Louise
1992   *Imperial Eyes: Travel Writing and Transculturation.* New York: Routledge.

Price, Robert
1979   "Politics and Culture in Contemporary Ghana: The Big-Man Small-Boy Syndrome." *Journal of African Studies* 1 (2):173–204.

Prussin, Labelle
1995   *Space, Place, and Gender.* Washington, DC: Smithsonian Institution Press.

1996   "When Nomads Settle: Changing Technologies of Building and Transport and the Production of Architectural Form among the Gabra, the Rendille, and the Somali." In *African Material Culture*, edited by Mary Jo Arnoldi, Christraud M. Geary, and Kris Hardin. Bloomington: Indiana University Press.

Qur'an

1956   *The Koran.* Translated and annotated by N. J. Dawood. London: Penguin.

Radcliffe-Brown, A. R.

1950   Introduction to *African Systems of Kinship and Marriage*, edited by A. R. Radcliffe-Brown and D. Forde. London: Routledge.

1952   *Structure and Function in Primitive Society. Essays and Addresses.* New York: The New Press.

Ramphele, Mamphela

1993   *A Bed Called Home. Life in the Migrant Labour Hostels of Capetown.* Athens: Ohio University Press.

Reeck, Darrell

1976   *Deep Mende: Religious Interactions in a Changing African Rural Society.* Leiden, The Netherlands: E. J. Brill.

Renan, Ernest

1990 [1882]   "What is a Nation?," in *Nation and Narration*, edited by Homi Bhabha. London: Routledge.

Reno, William

1995   *Corruption and State Politics in Sierra Leone.* Cambridge, England: Cambridge University Press.

1997   "African Weak States and Commercial Alliances." *African Affairs* 96 (383): 165–185.

Revel, Jacques

1996   "Micro-analyse et construction du social." In *Jeux D'echelles. La micro-analyse à l'expérience*, edited by Jacques Revel. Paris: Le Seuil/Gallimard.

Richards, Audrey

1950   "Some types of Family Structure amongst the Central Bantu." In *African Systems of Kinship and Marriage*, edited by A. R. Radcliffe-Brown and D. Forde. London: Routledge.

Richards, Paul

1986   *Coping with Hunger: Hazard and Experiment in an African Rice-Farming System.* London: Allen and Unwin.

1995   "Rebellion in Liberia and Sierra Leone: A Crisis of Youth?" In *Conflict in Africa*, edited by Oliver Furley. London: I. B. Tauris Publishers.

1996a   "Chimpanzees, Diamonds and War: The Discourses of Global Environmental Change and Local Violence on the Liberia–Sierra Leone Border." In *The Future of Anthropological Knowledge*, edited by H. Moore. London: Routledge.

1996b   *Fighting for the Rain Forest: War, Youth and Resources in Sierra Leone*. London: The International African Institute, in association with James Currey and Heinemann.

Richards, Paul and Casper Fithen
m.s.   "Post-Modern Warfare in Sierra Leone? Re-asserting the Social in Global-Local Constructions of Violence." In *Transboundary Formations: Global-Local Constructions of Authority in Africa*, edited by Thomas Callaghy, Ronald Kassimir, and Robert Latham.

Ricoeur, Paul
1970   *Freud and Philosophy: An Essay on Interpretation*. Translated by D. Savage. New Haven, CT: Yale University Press.
1975   *La Métaphore vive*. Paris: Éditions du Seuil.

Riddell, J. Barry
1970   *The Spatial Dynamics of Modernization in Sierra Leone*. Evanston, IL: Northwestern University Press.

Rodney, Walter
1970   *A History of the Upper Guinea Coast, 1545 to 1800*. Oxford, England: Clarendon Press.

Roitman, Janet
1998   The Garrison-Entrepôt. *Cahiers d'Études Africaines* 37 (2–4): 297–329.

Rosaldo, Renato
1980   *Ilongot Headhunting 1883–1974*. Stanford, CA: Stanford University Press.

Rubin, Gayle
1974   "The Traffic in Women: Notes on the 'Political Economy' of Sex." In *Towards an Anthropology of Women*, edited by Rayna R. Reiter. New York: Monthly Review Press.

Sahlins, Marshall
1963   "Poor Man, Rich Man, Big Man, Chief: Political Types in Polynesia and Melanesia." *Comparative Studies in Society and History* 5(3): 285–303.
1981   *Historical Metaphors and Mythical Realities: Structure in the Early History of the Sandwich Islands Kingdom*. Ann Arbor: University of Michigan Press.
1985   *Islands of History*. Chicago: University of Chicago Press.

Santos-Granero, Fernando
1998   "Writing History into the Landscape: Space, Myth, and Ritual in Contemporary Amazonia." *American Ethnologist* 25 (2):128–148.

Saul, Mahir
1984   "The Quranic School Farm and Child Labor in Upper Volta." *Africa* 54 (2):71–87.
1991   "Bobo 'House' and the Uses of Categories of Descent." *Africa* 61 (1):71–97.

Sawyerr, Harry and S. K. Todd
1970   "The Significance of the Numbers Three and Four among the Mende of Sierra Leone." *Sierra Leone Studies* (n.s.) 26:29–36.

Scheffler, Harold
1991   "Sexism and Naturalism in the Study of Kinship." In *Gender at
            the Crossroads of Knowledge: Feminist Anthropology in the
            Postmodern Era*, edited by Micaela di Leonardo. Berkeley: Uni-
            versity of California Press.
Scheper-Hughes, Nancy
1992   *Death Without Weeping: The Violence of Everyday Life in
            Brazil*. Berkeley: University of California Press.
Schneider, David
1984   *A Critique of the Study of Kinship*. Ann Arbor: The University of
            Michigan Press.
Schneider, Jane
1989   "Rumpelstiltskin's Bargain: Folklore and the Merchant Capital-
            ist Intensification of Linen Manufacture in Early Modern
            Europe." In *Cloth and Human Experience*, edited by A. Weiner
            and J. Schneider. Washington, DC: Smithsonian Institution
            Press.
Schor, Naomi
1987   *Reading in Detail: Aesthetics and the Feminine*. New York:
            Methuen.
Scott, D. J. R.
1960   "The Sierra Leone Election, May 1957." In *Five Elections in
            Africa*, edited by W. J. M. Mackenzie and K. Robinson. Oxford,
            England: The Clarendon Press.
Scott, James C.
1985   *Weapons of the Weak: Everyday Forms of Peasant Resistance*.
            New Haven, CT: Yale University Press.
Shack, William and Elliott Skinner, eds.
1979   *Strangers in African Societies*. Berkeley: University of California
            Press.
Shaw, Rosalind
1997   "Production of Witchcraft, Witchcraft as Production: Memory,
            Modernity, and the Slave Trade in Sierra Leone." *American Eth-
            nologist* 24 (4):856–876.
Siddle, D. J
1968   "War-Towns in Sierra Leone: A Study in Social Change." *Africa*
            38 (1): 47–56.
Siegmann, William and Judith Perani
1980   "Men's Masquerades of Sierra Leone and Liberia." *Ethnologis-
            che Zeitschrift* (Zürich) 1:25–40.
Simmel, Georg
1950 [1908] *The Sociology of Georg Simmel*. Edited and translated by K.
            Wolff. Glencoe, IL: The Free Press.
1959 [1911] "The Ruin." In *Essays on Sociology, Philosophy and Aesthetics*,
            edited by Kurt Wolff. New York: Harper Torchbooks.
1978 [1907] *The Philosophy of Money*. Translated by D. Bottomore and D.
            Frisby. Boston and London: Routledge.

Skinner, Elliott P.
1965   "Strangers in West African Societies." *Africa* 33 (4):307–320.
Smillie, Ian, Lansana Gberie, and Ralph Hazleton
2000   *The Heart of the Matter: Sierra Leone, Diamonds and Human Security.* Ottawa, Canada: Partnership Africa Canada.
Speed, Clarke K.
1991   "Swears and Swearing among Landogo of Sierra Leone: Aesthetics, Adjudication and the Philosophy of Power." Ph.D. dissertation. University of Washington.
Steiner, Christopher B.
1997   "The Invisible Face: Masks, Ethnicity, and the State in Côte d'Ivoire." In *Perspectives on Africa. A reader in Culture, History, and Representation*, edited by Richard Grinker and Christopher B. Steiner. Oxford, England: Blackwell Publishers.
Stenning, Derrick
1958   "Household Viability among the Pastoral Fulani." In *The Developmental Cycle in Domestic Groups*, edited by Jack Goody. Cambridge, England: Cambridge University Press.
Stewart, Kathleen C.
1996   "An Occupied Place." In *Senses of Place*, edited by Steven Feld and Keith H. Basso. Santa Fe, NM: School of American Research Advanced Seminar Series.
Stewart, Susan
1993   *On Longing: Narratives of the Miniature, the Gigantic, the Souvenir, the Collection.* Durham, NC: Duke University Press.
Stoler, Ann L.
1991   "Carnal Knowledge and Imperial Power: Gender, Race, and Morality in Colonial Asia." In *Gender at the Crossroads of Knowledge: Feminist Anthropology in the Postmodern Era*, edited by Micaela di Leonardo. Berkeley: University of California Press.
1992   "Rethinking Colonial Categories: European Communities and the Boundaries of Rule." In *Colonialism and Culture*, edited by Nicholas Dirks. Ann Arbor: University of Michigan Press.
Strathern, Marilyn
1981   "Culture in a Netbag: The Manufacture of a Subdiscipline in Anthropology." *Man* (n.s.) 16:665–688.
1988   *The Gender of the Gift: Problems with Women and Problems with Society in Melanesia.* Berkeley: University of California Press.
Taussig, Michael
1980   *The Devil and Commodity Fetishism in South America.* Chapel Hill: University of North Carolina Press.
1987   *Shamanism, Colonialism, and the Wild Man: A Study in Terror and Healing.* Chicago: University of Chicago Press.

Tostevin, Matthew
1993   "Sinking to the Depths." *BBC Focus on Africa*. 4(3):23–26.

Tsing, Anna L.
1993   *In the Realm of the Diamond Queen. Marginality in an Out-of-the-Way Place.* Princeton, NJ: Princeton University Press.

Turner, Victor
1967   *The Forest of Symbols: Aspects of Ndembu Ritual.* Ithaca, NY: Cornell University Press.
1969   *The Ritual Process: Structure and Anti-Structure.* Chicago: Aldine.

Turton, David
1980   "The Economics of Mursi Bridewealth: A Comparative Perspective." In *The Meaning of Marriage Payments*, edited by John L. Comaroff. New York: Academic Press.

Tylor, Edward Burnett
1970 [1871] *Religion in Primitive Culture.* Gloucester, MA: Peter Smith.

Uchendu, Victor
1964   "Kola Hospitality and Igbo Lineage Structure." *Man* 54:47–50.

Van Beek, Walter E. A. and Pieteke M. Banga,
1992   "The Dogon and Their Trees." In *Bush Base: Forest Farm. Culture, Environment and Development.* London: Routledge.

Veblen, Thorstein
1967 [1899] *The Theory of the Leisure Class.* Harmondsworth, UK: Penguin Books.

Wahlman, Maud and Enyinna Chuta
1979   "Sierra Leone Resist-Dyed Textiles." In *The Fabrics of Culture: The Anthropology of Clothing and Adornment*, edited by Justine M. Cordwell and Ronald A. Schwarz. The Hague: Mouton.

Wallis, C. Braithwaite
1903   *The Advance of Our West African Empire.* London: T. Fisher Unwin.

Wass, Betty M.
1979   "Yoruba Dress in Five Generations of a Lagos Family." In *The Fabrics of Culture: The Anthropology of Clothing and Adornment*, edited by Justine M. Cordwell and Ronald A. Schwarz. The Hague: Mouton.

Watts, Michael
1992   "The Shock of Modernity: Petroleum, Protest, and Fast Capitalism in an Industrializing Society." In *Reworking Modernity: Capitalisms and Symbolic Discontent*, by Allan Pred and Michael J. Watts. New Brunswick, NJ: Rutgers University Press.

Weber, Max
1978 [1956] *Economy and Society.* Vol. 2. Edited by G. Roth and C. Wittich. Berkeley: University of California Press.

Weiner, Annette B.
1974   *Women of Value, Men of Renown: New Perspectives in Trobriand Exchange.* Austin: University of Texas Press.

Weiss, Brad
  1996   *The Making and Unmaking of the Haya Lived World: Consump-
              tion, Commoditization and Everyday Practice.* Durham, NC:
              Duke University Press.
West Africa
  1990   "Sierra Leone." August: 2290.
White, Louise
  1990   *The Comforts of Home: Prostitution in Colonial Nairobi.*
              Chicago: University of Chicago Press.
Willis, Ralph
  1985a   Preface to Slaves and Slavery in Muslim Africa. Vol 1. *Islam and
              the Ideology of Enslavement*, edited by John Ralph Willis. Lon-
              don: Frank Cass.
  1985b   "Jihad and the Ideology of Enslavement." In Slaves and Slavery
              in Muslim Africa. Vol. 1. *Islam and the Ideology of Enslavement*,
              edited by John Ralph. London: Frank Cass.
Wilson, Monica Hunter
  1950   "Nyakyusa Kinship." In *African Systems of Kinship and Mar-
              riage*, edited by A. R. Radcliffe-Brown and Daryll Forde. Oxford,
              England: Oxford University Press.
Yanagisako, Sylvia J.
  1979   "Family and Household: The Analysis of Domestic Groups."
              Annual Reviews in Anthropology 8:161–205.
Yanagisako, Sylvia, J. and Jane F. Collier
  1987   "Toward a Unified Analysis of Gender and Kinship," In *Gender
              and Kinship: Essays Toward a Unified Analysis*, edited by J. F.
              Collier and S. J. Yanagisako. Stanford, CA: Stanford University
              Press.
Zack-Williams, A. B.
  1989   "Sierra Leone 1968–85: The Decline of Politics and the Politics of
              Decline." *International Journal of Sierra Leone Studies* 1:122–30.
Zempléni, András
  1976   "Du secret." *Nouvelle Revue de Psychanalyse* 14:313–324.
  1996   "Savoir taire: Du secret et de l'intrusion ethnologique dans la vie
              des autres." *Gradhiva* 20:23–41.

Index

Compositor:	Michael Bass & Associates
Text:	10/13 Sabon
Display:	Sabon
Printer:	Data Reproduction Corp.
Binder:	Data Reproduction Corp.